annuals,
perennials & bulbs
FOR YOUR HOME

annuals, perennials & bulbs

FOR YOUR HOME

CREATIVE HOMEOWNER®, Upper Saddle River, New Jersey

COPYRIGHT © 2001, 2013

CRE**A**TIVE
HOMEOWNER®

A Division of Federal Marketing Corp.
Upper Saddle River, NJ

ANNUALS, PERENNIALS & BULBS FOR YOUR HOME

WRITER	Anne Halpin
SUPERVISING EDITOR	Timothy O. Bakke
INTERIOR DESIGN CONCEPT	Glee Barre
COVER DESIGN CONCEPT	Kathy Wityk
LAYOUT AND PRODUCTION	Scott Kraft
PRINCIPAL ILLUSTRATOR	Mavis Torke
SUPPLEMENTAL ILLUSTRATION	Vincent Alessi (page 187)
FRONT COVER PHOTOGRAPHS	Dreamstime (main); John Glover (TR), David Cavagnaro (BR)
BACK COVER PHOTOGRAPHS	David Cavagnaro (T), Charles Mann (C), John Glover (B)

Manufactured in the United States of America

Current Printing (last digit)
10 9 8 7 6 5 4 3 2 1

Annuals, Perennials & Bulbs For Your Home
Originally published as *Annuals, Perennials & Bulbs*
Library of Congress Control Number: 2012931477
ISBN-10: 1-58011-562-4
ISBN-13: 978-1-58011-562-9

CREATIVE HOMEOWNER®
A Division of Federal Marketing Corp.
24 Park Way
Upper Saddle River, NJ 07458
www.creativehomeowner.com

Health and Safety Considerations

All projects and procedures in this book have been reviewed for safety; still it is not possible to overstate the importance of working carefully. What follows are reminders for plant care and project safety. Always use common sense.

▍ Always consider nontoxic and least toxic methods of ad-dressing unwanted plants, plant pests, and plant diseases before resorting to toxic methods. Follow package application and safety instructions carefully.

▍ Always substitute rock phosphate and gypsum for bonemeal when amending soil. Authorities suggest that there's a hazard in using bovine-based products such as bonemeal, blood meal, and cow manure because they could harbor the virus that causes Mad Cow disease in cattle and humans.

▍ Always read labels on chemicals, solvents, and other products; provide ventilation; heed warnings.

▍ Always wear eye protection when using chemicals, sawing wood, pruning trees and shrubs, using power tools, and striking metal onto metal or concrete.

▍ Always wear a hard hat when working in situations with potential for injury from falling tree limbs.

▍ Always wear appropriate gloves in situations in which your hands could be injured by rough surfaces, sharp edges, thorns, or poisonous plants.

▍ Always wear a disposable face mask or a special filtering respirator when creating sawdust or working with gardening dusts and powders.

▍ Always protect yourself against ticks, which can carry Lyme disease. Wear light-colored, long-sleeved shirts and pants. Inspect yourself for ticks after every session in the garden.

▍ Always determine locations of underground utility lines before you dig, and then avoid them by a safe distance. Buried lines may be for gas, electricity, communications, or water. Contact local utility companies which will help you map their lines.

▍ Always read and heed tool manufacturer instructions.

▍ Always ensure that the electrical setup is safe; be sure that no circuit is overloaded and that all power tools and electrical outlets are properly grounded and protected by a ground-fault circuit interrupter (GCFI). Do not use power tools in wet locations.

▍ Always keep your hands and other body parts away from the business end of blades, cutters, and bits.

▍ Never employ herbicides, pesticides, or toxic chemicals unless you have determined with certainty that they were developed for the specific problem you hope to remedy.

▍ Never allow bystanders to approach work areas where they might by injured by workers or work site hazards.

▍ Never work with power tools when you are tired or under the influence of alcohol or drugs.

▍ Never carry sharp or pointed tools, such as knives or saws, in your pocket.

Metric Equivalents

All measurements in this book are given in U.S. Customary units. If you wish to find metric equivalents, use the following tables and conversion factors.

Inches to Millimeters and Centimeters

1 in = 25.4 mm = 2.54 cm

in	mm	cm
1/16	1.5875	0.1588
1/8	3.1750	0.3175
1/4	6.3500	0.6350
3/8	9.5250	0.9525
1/2	12.7000	1.2700
5/8	15.8750	1.5875
3/4	19.0500	1.9050
7/8	22.2250	2.2225
1	25.4000	2.5400

Inches to Centimeters and Meters

1 in = 2.54 cm = 0.0254 m

in	cm	m
1	2.54	0.0254
2	5.08	0.0508
3	7.62	0.0762
4	10.16	0.1016
5	12.70	0.1270
6	15.24	0.1524
7	17.78	0.1778
8	20.32	0.2032
9	22.86	0.2286
10	25.40	0.2540
11	27.94	0.2794
12	30.48	0.3048

Feet to Meters

1 ft = 0.3048 m

ft	m
1	0.3048
5	1.5240
10	3.0480
25	7.6200
50	15.2400
100	30.4800

Square Feet to Square Meters

1 ft² = 0.09290304 m²

Acres to Square Meters

1 acre = 4046.85642 m²

Cubic Yards to Cubic Meters

1 yd³ = 0.764555 m³

Ounces and Pounds (Avoirdupois) to Grams

1 oz = 28.349523 g

1 lb = 453.5924 g

Pounds to Kilograms

1 lb = 0.45359237 kg.

Ounces and Quarts to Liters

1 oz = 0.02957353 L

1 qt = 0.9463 L

Gallons to Liters

1 gal = 3.785411784 L

Fahrenheit to Celsius (Centigrade)

$°C = °F - 32 \times \frac{5}{9}$

°F	°C
-30	-34.45
-20	-28.89
-10	-23.34
-5	-20.56
0	-17.78
10	-12.22
20	-6.67
30	-1.11
32 (freezing)	0.00
40	4.44
50	10.00
60	15.56
70	21.11
80	26.67
90	32.22
100	37.78
212 (boiling)	100

Contents

Part I: Annuals 12

Part II: Perennials 68

Part III: Bulbs 138

Appendix 178

Introducing Annuals, Perennials & Bulbs

lowers are like nature's jewelry, with their gemlike colors adorning the landscape at various times during the growing season. Although the length of the growing season varies depending upon climate, gardeners everywhere can design beds and borders to show off their flowery finery from the time winter eases its grip in the early months of the year until it closes in again after the autumn leaves have fallen.

While it's possible to design a garden that's colorful throughout much of the season by growing only perennials, annuals, or bulbs, it's easier to do so by growing all three together. Annuals, perennials, and bulbs naturally work in concert to fill your garden with flowers from earliest spring until well into autumn.

This book will show you how to plant and care for all three types of flowering plants, and it profiles the particular needs of over 126 individual ones. To begin, think about where to put your garden (if you don't already have one) and how to lay it out. Design is always the first step in making a flower garden.

This lovely garden (left) is based on blue combines annuals and perennials, including petunias, campanulas, delphiniums, and salvia, with white baby's breath, silver-leaved artemisia, and dashes of yellow and white.

This cool-colored border (below) mixes bulbous alliums (front) and irises with a variety of perennials.

In late spring, these elegant pale blue Dutch irises (right) bloom amid a froth of annual white sweet alyssum.

Hardiness Zone Map

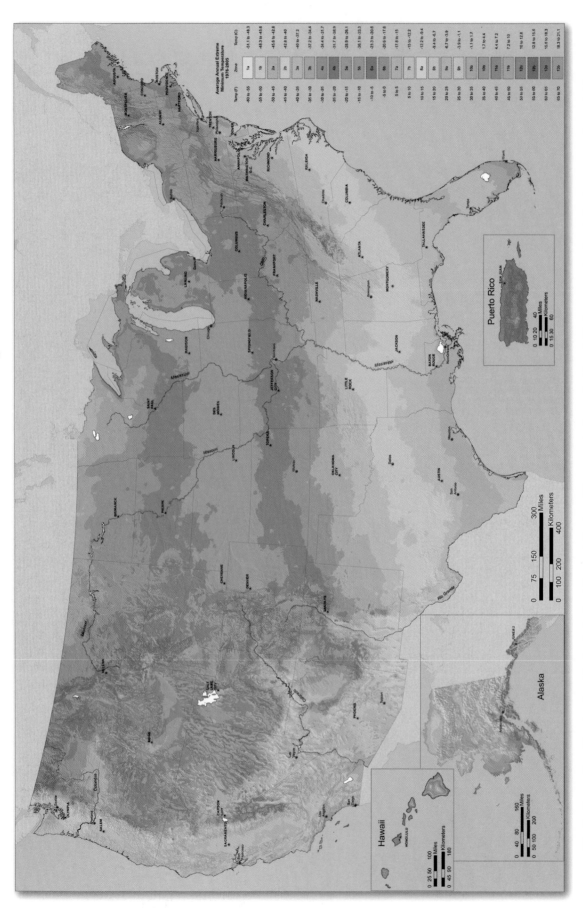

The Hardiness-Zone Map developed by the Agricultural Research Service of the USDA divides the country into 13 zones according to average minimum winter temperatures. Hardiness zones are used to identify regions to which plants are suited based on their cold tolerance, which is what "hardiness" means. Many factors, such as elevation and moisture level, come into play when determining whether a plant is suitable for your region. Local climates may vary from what is shown on this map. Contact your local Cooperative Extension Service for recommendations for your area. Or go to www.planthardiness.ars.usda.gov to find your hardiness zone based on your zip code. Mapping by the PRISM Climate Group, Oregon State University.

Temp (F)	Zone	Temp (C)
-40 to -50	1a	-51.1 to -48.3
-35 to -50	1b	-48.3 to -45.6
-50 to -45	2a	-45.6 to -42.8
-45 to -40	2b	-42.8 to -40
-40 to -35	3a	-40 to -37.2
-30 to -25	3b	-37.2 to -34.4
-30 to -25	4a	-34.4 to -31.7
-25 to -20	4b	-31.7 to -28.9
-20 to -15	5a	-28.9 to -26.1
-15 to -10	5b	-26.1 to -23.3
-10 to -5	6a	-23.3 to -20.6
-5 to 0	6b	-20.6 to -17.8
0 to 5	7a	-17.8 to -15
5 to 10	7b	-15 to -12.2
10 to 15	8a	-12.2 to -9.4
15 to 20	8b	-9.4 to -6.7
20 to 25	9a	-6.7 to -3.9
25 to 30	9b	-3.9 to -1.1
30 to 35	10a	-1.1 to 1.7
35 to 40	10b	1.7 to 4.4
40 to 45	11a	4.4 to 7.2
45 to 50	11b	7.2 to 10
50 to 55	12a	10 to 12.8
55 to 60	12b	12.8 to 15.6
60 to 65	13a	15.6 to 18.3
65 to 70	13b	18.3 to 21.1

Average Annual Extreme Minimum Temperature 1976-2005

AHS Heat-Zone Map

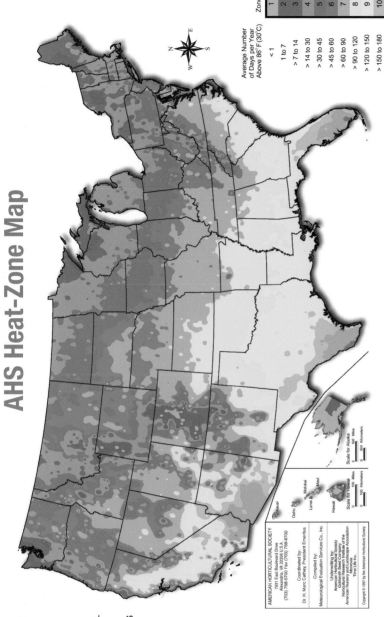

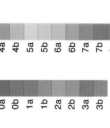

Zone
1
2
3
4
5
6
7
8
9
10
11
12

Average Number
of Days per Year
Above 86°F (30°C)

| <1 |
| 1 to 7 |
| >7 to 14 |
| >14 to 30 |
| >30 to 45 |
| >45 to 60 |
| >60 to 90 |
| >90 to 120 |
| >120 to 150 |
| >150 to 180 |
| >180 to 210 |
| >210 |

The American Horticultural Society Heat-Zone Map divides the United States into 12 zones based on the average annual number of days a region's temperatures climb above 86°F (30°C), the temperature at which the cellular proteins of plants begin to experience injury. Introduced in 1998, the AHS Heat-Zone Map holds significance, especially for gardeners in southern and transitional zones. Nurseries, growers, and other plant sources will gradually begin listing both cold hardiness and heat tolerance zones for plants, including grass plants. Using the USDA Plant Hardiness map, which can help determine a plant's cold tolerance, and the AHS Heat-Zone Map, gardeners will be able to safely choose plants that tolerate their region's lowest and highest temperatures.

Canada's Plant Hardiness Zone Map

Canada's Plant Hardiness Zone Map outlines the different zones in Canada where various types of trees, shrubs, and flowers will most likely survive. It is based on the average climatic conditions of each area. The hardiness map is divided into nine major zones: the harshest is 0 and the mildest is 8. Relatively few plants are suited to zone 0. Subzones (e.g., 4a or 4b, 5a or 5b) are also noted in the map legend. These subzones are most familiar to Canadian gardeners. Some significant local factors, such as micro-topography, amount of shelter, and subtle local variations in snow cover, are too small to be captured on the map. Year-to-year variations in weather and gardening techniques can also have a significant impact on plant survival in any particular location.

Plant Hardiness Zones: 0a 0b 1a 1b 2a 2b 3a 3b 4a 4b 5a 5b 6a 6b 7a 7b 8a

AMERICAN HORTICULTURAL SOCIETY
7931 East Boulevard Drive
Alexandria, VA 22308 U.S.A.
(703) 768-5700 Fax (703) 768-8700

Coordinated by:
Dr. H. Marc Cathey, President Emeritus

Compiled by:
Meteorological Evaluation Services Co., Inc.

Underwritten by:
American Horticultural Society
Goldsmith Seed Company
Horticultural Research Institute of the
American Nursery and Landscape Association
Monrovia
Time Life Inc.

Copyright © 1997 by the American Horticulture Society

PART 1

About Annuals

Annuals are wonderfully versatile plants. While some gardeners don't consider annuals "serious" garden plants, most think they are indispensable. A far greater variety of annuals is available in garden centers and seed catalogs than ever before—every year, you find a wider choice of colors, forms, cultivars, and even species.

Annuals are indispensable for filling the garden with color. Perennial flowers come and go, but many annuals bloom all summer long.

WHAT IS AN ANNUAL?

To botanists, an annual is a plant that completes its entire life cycle in a single growing season. But to gardeners, the category may also include biennial plants that will bloom from seed in one season if given an early start indoors as well as tender perennials that are killed by frost and thus treated as annuals in all but frost-free climates.

When used intelligently, annuals can serve a host of functions. No longer the poor relations in a flower garden, they are planted in beds and borders, either by themselves or mixed with perennials. They burst into lavish bloom early and continue to provide color as perennials come and go throughout the season. Annuals make excellent companions to spring bulbs, and their leaves and flowers eventually hide the yellowing bulb foliage. They can be used to fill gaps between shrubs and foundation plantings or can be grown around tree trunks, where their massed colors can brighten the shade.

Many annuals are classic container and window box plants; they bring instant color to patios, decks, porches, and rooftops. They can intermingle with vegetables and herbs to dress up the food garden or soften the harsh look of a front sidewalk and extend a welcome to your visitors.

Annuals are a convenient and easy way to grow flowers in a whole spectrum of colors; you can find an annual to fit into any color scheme. Many make excellent cut flowers, providing armloads of blossoms for lavish and inexpensive bouquets. Some can be potted up in autumn and brought indoors to continue flowering well into winter.

DURABLE ANNUALS

Annuals growing near driveways, streets, and sidewalks are subjected to stress from dust, fumes, and traffic. Choose tough plants like those listed below for these difficult locations.

- Cosmos (*Cosmos* species)
- Sunflower (*Helianthus annuus*)
- Blackfoot daisy (*Leucanthemum paludosum*)
- Zonal geranium (*Pelargonium × hortorum*)
- Petunia (*Petunia × hybrida*)
- Rose moss (*Portulaca grandiflora*)
- Marigold (*Tagetes* species)

Fill a corner with color by combining hanging baskets and pots of annuals with plants below. Here, sweet alyssum and lobelia freshen a warm mix of petunias and nasturtiums.

The annual palette contains all the colors of the rainbow. This garden contrasts golden marguerites and perennial tansy with purple heliotrope and verbena.

Annual Hardiness

Annuals are categorized as hardy, tender, or half-hardy according to their tolerance to cool temperatures.

Hardy annuals such as bachelor's button, calendula, and larkspur grow best in cool temperatures and can withstand some frost and freezing. They are often started from seeds sown directly in the garden. In Zones 7 and colder, gardeners can sow hardy annuals outdoors as soon as the soil can be worked in spring. Some annuals can even be sown the previous fall. In Zones 8 and warmer, gardeners more often sow hardy annuals in fall for flowers in winter or early spring.

Tender annuals such as impatiens, cockscomb, and zinnia are sensitive to cold. In most areas, they are started indoors and transplanted outdoors after the frost-free date, when the soil is warm. An indoor start is particularly important in areas with the coolest climates and a short frost-free growing season.

A third category of plants—half-hardy annuals—is accepted by some horticulturists but not by others. Half-hardy annuals are generally considered to be in between the other two types in terms of hardiness and include marguerite, lobelia, and petunia. Half-hardy plants like cool weather and tolerate a bit of light frost but are damaged by repeated exposure to frost and freezing. Gardeners in all but the warmest climates (Zones 8 to 11) tend to start them early indoors and plant them out when frost danger is past

ANNUALS BY HARDINESS

Hardy Annuals
Grow best in cool weather; tolerate a reasonable degree of frost

Rocket larkspurs

Bachelor's button (*Centaurea cyanus*)
China pink (*Dianthus chinensis*)
Flowering cabbage and kale (*Brassica oleracea*)
Pansy (*Viola* × *wittrockiana*)
Pot marigold (*Calendula officinalis*)
Rocket larkspur (*Consolida ambigua*)
Snapdragon (*Antirrhinum majus*)
Sunflower (*Helianthus annuus*)
Sweet alyssum (*Lobularia maritima*)

Half-Hardy
Prefer cool weather but are damaged by repeated exposure to frost

Blackfoot daisy, Melampodium (*Leucanthemum paludosum, Melampodium leucanthum*)
Dahlberg daisy (*Thymophylla tenuiloba*)

Petunias

Dwarf morning-glory (*Convolvulus tricolor*)
Edging lobelia (*Lobelia erinus*)
Flowering tobacco (*Nicotiana* × *sanderae*)
Licorice plant (*Helichrysum petiolare*)
Marguerite (*Argyranthemum frutescens*)
Marigold (*Tagetes species*)
Mealycup sage (*Salvia farinacea*)
Petunia (*Petunia* × *hybrida*)
Scarlet sage (*Salvia splendens*)
Spider flower (*Cleome hassleriana*)
Strawflower (*Helichrysum bracteatum*)
Yellow sage (*Lantana camara*)

Tender
Need warm weather; can't tolerate any frost

Cardinal climber, Cypress vine (*Ipomoea* × *multifida, I. quamoclit*)
China aster (*Callistephus chinensis*)
Cockscomb (*Celosia argentea*)
Coleus (*Solenostemon scutellarioides*)
Cosmos (*Cosmos bipinnatus, C. sulphureus*)
Dusty miller (*Senecio cineraria*)

Fanflower (*Scaevola aemula*)
Flossflower (*Ageratum houstonianum*)
Fuchsia (*Fuchsia* hybrids)
Globe amaranth (*Gomphrena globosa*)
Heliotrope (*Heliotropium arborescens*)
Impatiens, New Guinea impatiens (*Impatiens* species)
Love-lies-bleeding, Joseph's coat (*Amaranthus* species)
Madagascar periwinkle (*Catharanthus roseus*)
Mexican sunflower (*Tithonia rotundifolia*)
Morning glory, moonflower (*Ipomoea* species)
Nasturtium (*Tropaeolum* species)
Nemesia (*Nemesia strumosa*)
Rose moss (*Portulaca grandiflora*)
Sapphire flower (*Browallia speciosa*)
Sweet potato vine (*Ipomoea batatas*)
Wax begonia (*Begonia* Semperflorens-Cultorum hybrids)
Wishbone flower (*Torenia fournieri*)
Zinnia (*Zinnia* species)
Zonal geranium, ivy geranium (*Pelargonium* species)

Zinnias

Planting Annuals

Most gardeners buy at least some annuals from local garden centers and nurseries. They're usually sold in plastic cell packs (sometimes called "six-packs"). It's important to know how to handle seedlings when you bring them home and how to transplant them from cell packs—whether into the garden or a container.

Resist the temptation to buy seedlings already in bloom, as are these celosias. Even though blooming plants provide an "instant" garden, younger seedlings not only transplant more easily but they are also healthier in the long run. Whenever possible, purchase seedlings that are still "green," or not yet in full bud or bloom.

SELF SOWERS

Some annuals plant themselves. If you don't deadhead, or remove the faded flowers, their seeds drop on the ground and produce a new generation of plants the next year. If you like serendipity, let a few plants go to seed and allow the volunteer seedlings to grow where they will. If you want more control, transplant the volunteers in spring. And if you don't want to have volunteers, deadhead before plants have a chance to form seeds.

Many self-sown seedlings don't produce plants identical to the parents. The flowers are often smaller and the colors different. Petunias, for example, tend to revert to the magenta-purple color of the original species form of the plant. Such variation can wreak havoc with a carefully planned color scheme, but it can be fun to see what you get from one year to the next.

The following annuals are likely to self-sow in your garden:
Bachelor's button (*Centaurea cyanus*)
Candytuft, annual (*Iberis umbellata*)
Cosmos (*Cosmos bipinnatus, C. sulphureus*)
French marigold (*Tagetes patula*)
Impatiens, bedding (*Impatiens walleriana*)
Nasturtium (*Tropaeolum* species)
Petunia (*Petunia* × *hybrida*)
Poppy, annual (*Papaver* species)
Pot marigold (*Calendula officinalis*)
Rocket larkspur (*Consolida ambigua*)
Rose moss (*Portulaca grandiflora*)
Sapphire flower (*Browallia speciosa*)
Snapdragon (*Antirrhinum majus*)
Spider flower (*Cleome hassleriana*)
Sweet alyssum (*Lobularia maritima*)
Johnny-jump-up (*Viola tricolor*)

Calendula volunteers

Marigold volunteers

SMART SHOPPING

The following tips will help you choose the best plants from the sea of annuals available at your local garden center:
• Choose smaller rather than bigger plants. Plants already in bloom have a harder time making transitions, especially in hot, dry weather. Smaller plants adjust more readily and get growing more quickly.
• Avoid tiny, very young seedlings—they're delicate and can be difficult to transplant without injury.
• Look for stocky, sturdy-looking plants with good green color, leaves spaced closely together on the stem, and healthy new growth.
• Check the plants carefully for signs of pests or diseases. Insects often collect in leaf axils (where leaves meet stems), on new growth, and on leaf undersides. Fine webs and cottony or foamy blobs also indicate pest insects. Pale, yellowed, or otherwise discolored leaves, soft rotting tissues, mold or mildew, leaf spots, and dry brown leaf edges may indicate disease.
• Avoid buying plants with roots coming from the drainage holes in their containers. These are potbound, and their growth may have been stunted by spending too much time at the nursery.
• Don't buy plants with tall, lanky, or floppy stems and large gaps of bare stem between leaves. These plants haven't gotten enough light, or they've been overfertilized and grew too quickly.

ANNUALS

Planting from a Cell Pack

When planting annuals in beds and borders, mark out the planting area and dig the holes, either one at a time or several at once. If the soil is dry, fill each hole with water and let it drain before setting in the plants. Push gently on the bottom of the cell to dislodge a plant; slide the plant out of its compartment without touching the stem; and set it in the ground. If the plant is at all pot-bound, gently tease apart some of the roots, or encourage new root growth by cutting partway into the bottom of the root-ball and pulling it apart a bit. Touching only the root-ball and if necessary, the bottom leaves—not the stem—set the plant into the hole; firm the soil around it; and water well.

Planting a Hanging Basket

Begin by filling the basket with potting soil to 2 inches below the rim. Set one or more plants in the center of the basket.

HANGING-BASKET PLANTS

Cascading petunia cultivars (*Petunia × hybrida*)
Edging lobelia (*Lobelia erinus*)
Fuchsia (*Fuchsia* hybrids)
Impatiens (*Impatiens* hybrids)
Ivy geranium (*Pelargonium peltatum*)
Nasturtium, trailing cultivars (*Tropaeolum majus*)
Rose moss (*Portulaca grandiflora*)
Sapphire flower (*Browallia speciosa*)
Variegated vinca (*Vinca major* 'Variegata')
Wax begonia (*Begonia* Semperflorens-Cultorum hybrids)
Wishbone flower (*Torenia fournieri*)

POTTING SOILS

When planting in containers, it's best to use a light, porous potting mix. You can use a packaged pre-blended potting soil, as long as it contains a lightening agent such as perlite or vermiculite and is not 100 percent soil. Or you can mix 3 parts potting soil or topsoil with 2 parts crumbled compost or leaf mold and 1 part perlite or vermiculite. If you prefer a soilless potting mix, buy one or make it by mixing equal parts of peat moss, perlite, and vermiculite.

Then plant several more around the edges so they will cascade over the sides and disguise the pot.

For a fuller look, use a hanging basket made of wire. Line the inside of the basket with sheets of moistened sphagnum moss that you butt up against one another at their edges. Fill the basket one-third of the way with potting soil. Then insert some small plants around the sides, pulling aside or cutting through the moss so that the plant tops are outside the basket but their roots are planted in the soil. Add more soil mix to fill the basket two-thirds of the way, and add more plants. Then fill the basket the rest of the way, and plant the top as usual, with one plant in the center and three to five plants near the edge of the basket.

Baskets need to be watered daily in hot weather. To check whether a basket needs water without taking it down from its hanger, place your hand on the bottom and lift up so the pot rests on your hand. If it feels very light, the soil is too dry. When the pot has some weight to it, the soil is moist, and you don't have to water.

how to **Carefully Transplant**   DIFFICULTY LEVEL: EASY

Tools and Materials: Seedlings, trowel, prepared garden area

1 Water first; then gently push the bottom of the cell pack to loosen the root-ball. Rest the stem of the plant against your hand, but do not injure it by pressing on it.

2 Holding only the root-ball, carefully lower the seedling into the planting hole. Fill in and press down gently to put the roots in contact with the soil. Water well.

A cascade of color in a hanging basket (left) combines blue lobelia with yellow tuberous begonias, golden bidens, and red and pink petunias.

A romantic window box overflowing with cascading petunias softens a brick facade (below). Red and white flowering tobacco add height to the planting.

ANNUALS FOR WINDOW BOXES

China aster (*Callistephus chinensis*)
China pinks (*Dianthus chinensis*)
Coleus (*Solenostemon scutellarioides*)
Edging lobelia (*Lobelia erinus*)
Flowering tobacco (*Nicotiana* × *sanderae*)
Geranium (*Pelargonium* species)
Globe amaranth (*Gomophrena globosa*)
Heliotrope (*Heliotropium arborescens*)
Impatiens (*Impatiens* hybrids)
Madagascar periwinkle (*Catharanthus roseus*)
Marguerite (*Argyranthemum frutescens*)
Marigold (*Tagetes* species)
Nasturtium (*Tropaeolum* species)
Nemesia (*Nemesia strumosa*)
Pansy (*Viola* x *wittrockiana*)
Petunia (*Petunia* × *hybrida*)
Plume-type celosia (*Celosia argentea*)
Pot marigold (*Calendula officinalis*)
Rose moss (*Portulaca grandiflora*)
Salvia (*Salvia* species)
Sapphire flower (*Browallia speciosa*)
Snapdragon (*Antirrhinum majus*)
Stock (*Matthiola incana*)
Sweet alyssum (*Lobularia maritima*)
Variegated vinca (*Vinca major* 'Variegata')
Wax begonia (*Begonia* Semperflorens-Cultorum hybrids)
Wishbone flower (*Torenia fournieri*)
Yellow cosmos (*Cosmos sulphureus*)
Zinnia (*Zinnia* species)

Planting a Window Box

Window boxes are a delightful addition to your home. They add instant charm to a country cottage and beautifully soften the severe facade of a city brownstone. Annuals are the plants of choice for window boxes, offering practically limitless combinations of color, form, and texture.

Plan your window boxes before you buy the plants. You'll want some taller and some shorter plants, plus some trailers. (See the plant list above for some possibilities.) You'll also want to choose colors that harmonize or contrast attractively with the colors of your home.

There are three ways to plant a window box: directly in the box, in a molded plastic liner that sits inside the box, or in individual pots that you place inside the box.

Plastic liners are the most convenient way to go, especially if you want to change the plants for different seasons. You simply pop the planted liner into the box. Liners are also easy to remove when the window box or the plants need maintenance.

If you plant directly in a wooden window box, be aware that constant contact with moist soil causes wood to deteriorate quickly. You can prolong its life by painting the inside of the box with polyurethene.

Planting in individual pots allows you to change plants during the season, but makes it harder to create a natural, gardeny sort of look. If you do keep the plants in pots, cover their tops with a layer of unmilled sphagnum moss.

No matter what kind of container you use, it's important to provide drainage. Purchase metal boxes with predrilled holes, or drill holes in the bottom of wooden boxes or plastic liners. Use screening or row-cover material to cover the holes.

Caring for window boxes. Because they contain such a small volume of soil, window boxes, like hanging plants, need frequent watering. You'll need to water at least once a day in hot weather. Aim to keep the soil evenly moist but not soggy or waterlogged.

You'll need to fertilize plants in a window box regularly, too. Water-soluble liquids, granular blends, and time-released pellets are the easiest and most convenient fertilizers. Follow the fertilizer-package directions for quantities and timing. Fast-growing annual plants will probably need fertilizing at least every two weeks or so, unless you use a time-released fertilizer.

how to

Plant a Window Box

DIFFICULTY LEVEL: EASY

Tools and Materials: Window box, potting soil, bleach, brush, trowel, plants

1 Clean used boxes thoroughly with a brush and then a 10-percent bleach solution.

2 Plant the tallest plants to the rear, the shortest in the front, and midsize plants between.

3 Water well, and fill in any low spots with extra potting soil. Shade until plants are established.

4 Keep plants watered, deadheaded, and trimmed to promote season-long blooming.

how to

Plant a Large Container

DIFFICULTY LEVEL: EASY

Tools and Materials: Container, screening, potting soil, trowel, plants

1 Plant the tallest plants (here, sunflowers) at the rear or in the center, depending on how the pot will be viewed.

2 Next, place the midsize plants (here, cannas) in front of the tallest ones or surrounding them.

3 Place smaller plants (here, caladiums) either in front of or surounding the midsize ones.

4 Plant trailers (here, cascading petunias and sweet potato vines) at the edges of the pot to cascade over the sides.

Planting Large Containers

When you plant a half-barrel or other large container with several kinds of plants, choose the plants carefully. Plan for a gradation of heights, like a miniature version of a garden bed or border, to create a sense of depth and a more interesting display.

For a full barrel, plan on buying three tall plants, four to six medium-height plants, and eight to twelve small or trailing edging plants. The barrel may look a bit sparse when you first plant it, but it will quickly fill in. If you stuff a container too full of young plants, either the larger ones will soon engulf the smaller ones, or all of them will languish after a month or so for lack of space. If you plant so densely that you have an instantly overflowing container, plan to fertilize frequently throughout the growing season.

Before planting, place the container where you want it. Unless you put it on wheels, it will be too heavy to move once you have planted it. Make sure the drainage is adequate: drill holes in wooden containers, and cover them with landscape fabric or fine screening. Fill the pot to within 3 inches of the rim.

By early summer, the petunias will be in full bloom, and the caladium, sweet potato vine, sunflower, and canna foliage will be lush and full.

By late summer, the sunflowers and cannas will be in bloom, and the caladium, sweet potato vine, and petunias will still be thriving.

Caring for Annuals

Annuals are easy to grow and care for as long as you pay attention to the basics. Make certain that the soil is well prepared in the beginning of the season and that the environment—light, temperature, and soil qualities—suits the plants you're growing. Aside from these considerations, your major tasks will be to provide these fast-growing plants with plenty of water and fertilizer. Depending on the plant, you must also remove faded flowers and cut back foliage aafter the first blooms are spent.

Watering

Whether growing in the ground or in containers, newly transplanted annuals need constant, even moisture for the first couple of weeks while they establish themselves. Thereafter, water according to the plants' needs. Some, such as rose moss, prefer drier conditions than do moisture lovers

Potting-mix ingredients for annuals include soil; lightening agents such as peat moss, perlite, and vermiculite; and organic or synthetic fertilizers to supply nutrients.

such as floss flower. (See "Portraits of Favorite Annuals," pages 24–67 for moisture needs.)

Soaker hoses are a convenient and efficient way to water annuals in beds and borders—they allow water to trickle out slowly so it can be easily absorbed into the soil. For hanging baskets and other containers, a hose with a watering wand lets you water without a lot of stretching or bending.

Fertilizing Annuals

Annuals need regular fertilization to fuel their rapid growth. (Remember, annuals go through their entire life cycle in a single growing season.) Healthy soil that contains plenty of organic matter will sustain the growth of many annuals, but sometimes your plants will need an extra nutrient boost.

If you choose organic fertilizers, bear in mind that many of these take time to break down in the soil and release their nutrients. You'll have to apply granular and powdered formulas ahead of time. Fortunately, there are two easy organic options that provide instant nutrition to plants: liquid seaweed and fish emulsion. Either is good for annuals, but using both provides complete nutrition. Dilute according to label directions before applying with a watering can, or for fast results, spray a half-strength dilution on leaves in low-light conditions (before sunrise or on a cloudy day).

smart tip

DRIP SYSTEM

Setting up drip systems with spaghetti tubes and individual emitters is easy if you follow the manufacturer's directions.

These systems can be arranged to water pots as well as in-ground plants in the same area, as long as the plants' water needs are similar.

When dead-heading, clip off spent flower stems back to the next set of leaves to avoid leaving bare stems.

For flowering annuals, an all-purpose fertilizer, such as a 5-10-5 or a 15-30-15 (or, if organic, 3-4-3 or 4-5-4) formula works best. Foliage plants will thrive with a fertilizer high in nitrogen (indicated by the first number in the series). Use a granular, timed-release, or compost-based fertilizer for annuals in beds and borders; water-soluble fertilizers are best for container plants. Follow the package directions for application rates and frequency.

Deadheading

An annual plant's mission is to bloom, produce seeds, and then die. To keep plants blooming, prevent them from setting seeds. Deadheading—removing faded flowers before seeds develop—frustrates a plant's attempt to complete its life cycle and encourages it to keep producing flowers.

When deadheading, don't just snip off the flower and leave the bare stem. Instead, cut off the stem right above the next lower set of leaves. One exception to this rule is flowering tobacco. If you cut off a faded flower just under its base, new flowers will form on the stem right below the site of the old blossom.

Some plants with lots of small flowers, particularly lobelia and sweet alyssum, are hard to deadhead. To renew

these plants if flowering slows, shear back the plants rather than snipping stems. (See "Portraits of Favorite Annuals," page 24–67.)

When Not to Deadhead. Many popular annuals self-sow if you let them. If you want particular plants to self-sow or if you want to collect and save seeds for next year's garden, don't deadhead all the plants. Choose the healthiest, best-looking specimens of the types you want to save, and let them form seeds in the latter part of their seasons.

Biennials that self-sow come up the same year and winter-over as small plants. Self-sown seedlings of true annuals won't appear until the following spring. To prevent overcrowding, you usually have to thin them or transplant to new spots. To avoid weeding them out when they first appear, pay attention to the appearance of both their seed leaves and first true leaves.

End-of-Season Care

As the outdoor growing season winds down in fall, pull up all your spent annuals and toss them on the compost pile. (Throw out all China asters and any diseased plants with the trash.) If you plan to sow seeds of hardy annuals in fall for winter or spring bloom, prepare their planting areas. Spread a layer of compost and, if using them, organic fertilizers. Work this material into the soil; then rake it smooth. Sow hardy annuals at the correct time for your area. (If you are unsure about when to plant, ask a gardening friend or call your local Cooperative Extension Service for advice.)

Remove annuals from window boxes and other containers, and dump the potting soil in your garden (as long as the plants weren't afflicted with a disease). Scrub out the containers, and store them for the winter.

Deadheading is the key to keeping annuals in bloom all season. Snipping off spent blossoms prevents plants from setting seeds, so they produce more flowers.

Collecting and Saving Seeds

One of the great pleasures of growing annuals is the ease with which you can save their seeds. It's fun to save seeds from your favorite plants. You can sow them the following year, share them with friends, or give them to the birds. (They'll appreciate seeds of sunflowers, marigolds, calendulas, and zinnias, among others). If you grow heirloom varieties and save their seeds, you'll help to keep these treasured plants from disappearing forever. (To learn more about growing endangered seeds, contact the Seed Savers Exchange, 3094 North Winn Rd., Decorah, IA 52101; seedsavers.org). You can even try your hand at plant breeding after a few years of practice: selecting for qualities you most want in your plants and cross-pollinating to create your own hybrids.

If you want the seeds you save to produce plants like the mother plant, collect seeds only from nonhybrid varieties or cultivars. While you can save seeds from hybrids, the plants they produce won't look exactly like the mother plant when they germinate; they may be smaller, bloom later, or have flowers in a different color.

Procedures

After the flowers from which you want to collect seeds finish blooming, don't deadhead them. Instead, leave the plants alone so that the seeds can mature. When the seed capsules or pods seem to be dry, break or cut them off.

It's important to be certain that the seeds are dry before storing; moist seeds easily rot. Ensure this by picking the pods and placing them in paper bags (each kind in its own

ANNUALS FOR SEED-SAVING
Ageratum (*Ageratum houstonianum*)
Bachelor's button (*Centaurea cyanus*)
Bells of Ireland (*Moluccella laevis*)
Browallia (*Browallia speciosa*)
Cosmos (*Cosmos* species)
Flowering tobacco (*Nicotiana alata*)
Marigold (*Tagetes* species)
Petunia (*Petunia* cultivars)
Rocket larkspur (*Consolida ambigua*)
Rose moss (*Portulaca grandiflora*)
Salvia (*Salvia* species)
Snapdragon (*Antirrhinum majus*)
Spider flower (*Cleome hassleriana*)
Sunflower (*Helianthus annuus*)
Sweet alyssum (*Lobularia maritima*)
Zinnia (*Zinnia* species)

bag, labeled). Hang the bags in a warm, dry place to air-dry for two or three weeks. Shake the bags periodically to make the seeds fall out of their pods.

When the seeds are dry, separate them from their pods and any stray bits of chaff, as shown opposite. Store them in small envelopes or paper bags. Label each bag or envelope with the name of the plant, the flower color or other defining characteristic, and the date you harvested the seeds.

Store the seeds in a cool, dry place. If you're not sure your storage place is dry, store them in screw-top glass jars. Add a desiccant such as powdered milk or silica gel to the jar for an extra measure of protection.

how to

Collect Seeds

DIFFICULTY LEVEL: MODERATE

Tools and Materials: Dried seedheads, large smooth bowl, storage containers

1 Cut or pick dried seedheads after the seeds have turned brown but before they drop to the ground.

2 After the seeds are complely dry, gently separate them from the seedhead with your fingers.

3 Pick out as many of the the seed coats and other large pieces of chaff as you can by hand.

4 Softly blow the remaining chaff away before storing the seeds in labeled bags or glass jars in a dry, cool area.

ANNUALS

Pots full of annuals along the front steps create a welcoming entry and can change from season to season according to your taste and their blooming times.

Ageratum

Ageratum houstonianum
FLOSSFLOWER

These mostly low-growing plants form compact mounds of dark green leaves nearly covered with clusters of small, fluffy purple-blue, pink, or white flowers. Although the short varieties are the most widely grown, there are some taller cultivars too.

Hardiness: Tender.

Blooming Time: Early summer until frost.

Height: 6 inches to 2½ feet.

Spacing: 6 to 10 inches.

Light: Full sun to light shade; afternoon shade in Zones 7 and warmer.

Soil: Average to fertile, well-drained soil.

Moisture: Even, abundant moisture; does not tolerate dryness.

Garden Uses: Dwarf cultivars are favorites for edging flower beds, using in designs where a low element is needed, and in containers and window boxes.

Grow the taller cultivars in the middle of beds and borders or grow them in a cutting garden. The taller cultivars, especially, make good cut flowers.

Cut flowers when about half the blossoms on the stem are open. The best times to cut are in the morning or early evening. Condition the flowers before you arrange them by standing the stems in warm water almost to the base of the flowers. Leave them in the water for several hours. Remove all leaves that would be below the water level in the vase.

In bouquets and arrangements, the puffy little clusters of flossflower blossoms make good fillers to place between larger, more dramatic flowers. They last about a week in the vase.

Comments: Sow seeds indoors about 10 weeks be-

'Royal Hawaii'

fore the last expected frost. The plants can't tolerate frost, so do not plant them out until the weather has settled in spring.

Flossflower seeds

Deadhead regularly to keep plants looking neat and to encourage continued heavy blooming throughout the season. If some plants exhaust themselves in midsummer, remove and replace them. A good layer of mulch will help the plants withstand hot, dry conditions.

Flossflowers are prone to fungus disease problems. To decrease the chance of infection, water plants at ground level rather than with overhead hoses or sprinklers. If you do use an overhead watering system, water in the morning, or early enough in the evening so that plants have time to dry off before dark.

Recommended Cultivars: Good cultivars for cutting include 'Blue Horizon', 2 to 2½ feet, medium blue flowers, good heat tolerance; 'Red Top', 2 to 2½ feet, purple-red flowers; and 'White Bouquet', 2 to 2½ feet, white flowers. Smaller cultivars suitable for edging beds and borders and using in containers include 'Blue Mink', 10 inches to 1½ feet, powder blue flowers; 'Blue Lagoon', 8 inches, light blue flowers; 'Bavaria', 1 foot, blue-and-white bicolored flowers; Hawaii hybrids, 8 inches, medium blue, rosy purple, and white flowers.

smart tip

DEADHEADING

Deadhead flowers as soon as they begin to brown to promote continuous blooming. Snip off the faded flower at the base of its stalk, just above the leaves. With diligent deadheading, flossflowers will bloom all season long.

Amaranthus

Amaranthus caudatus
LOVE-LIES-BLEEDING
Amaranthus tricolor,
JOSEPH'S-COAT

Both of these amaranths have long, drooping, deep red flower spikes that look rather like chenille ropes. Joseph's-coat boasts colorful leaves of red, yellow, orange, bronze, and/or brown. All Amaranthus species are bushy and branched with oval leaves.

Hardiness: Tender.

Blooming Time: Summer.

Height: 1 to 4 feet.

Spacing: 1½ to 2 feet.

Light: Full sun.

Soil: Well-drained, average to poor fertility. Leaves of Joseph's-coat are less colorful in rich, fertile soils.

Moisture: Average; tolerates some dryness.

Garden Uses: These plants work best in the middle ground of a garden of large plants or in the back of a small garden of smaller plants. They also grow well in containers. The cultivars of *A. caudatus* and *A. hypochondriacus* listed below under "Recommended Cultivars" are both good for cutting.

Comments: Amaranths are easy to grow, but transplant best as young seedlings. Sow seeds indoors eight to ten weeks before the last expected frost, or direct-sow when frost danger is past. Both of these *Amaranthus* species grow best in warm weather.

'Illumination'

smart tip

SUPPORTING

Tomato cages make excellent supports for bushy, many-stalked species such as these love-lies-bleeding plants. Set cages in place before the plants begin to lean.

Recommended Cultivars: *A. tricolor:* 'Illumination', 4 feet, bright, rosy red leaves topped with yellow; 'Summer Poinsettia Mix', 3 feet, deep red leaves topped with bright red; 'Aurora', green leaves topped with chartreuse and yellow; 'Joseph's Coat', 3 feet, scarlet, cream and green leaves.

A. caudatus: 'Green Thumb', 2 to 2 feet, green leaves and vivid green flowers. A similar species, *A. hypochondriacus*, or prince's feather, has flower spikes that stand upright rather than drooping. A useful cultivar is 'Pygmy Torch', 1 to 2 feet, upright wine red flower spikes.

Joseph's-coat

A group of snapdragons in pastel hues softens the appearance of these steps and stone wall.

Rocket hybrids

Antirrhinum

Antirrhinum majus
SNAPDRAGON

The colorful spikes of snapdragons are a fine addition to any garden. They add a colorful vertical accent, are wonderful for cutting, and have been favorites of generations of children. The plants may be either annual or perennial, but they are usually grown as annuals.

Hardiness: Half-hardy.

Blooming Time: Early summer; in warm climates, winter or early spring.

Height: 9 inches to 3 feet, depending on cultivar.

Spacing: 6 inches to 1 foot, depending on cultivar.

Seed leaves

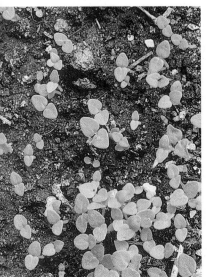

Light: Full sun to partial shade; prefers some afternoon shade in warm climates.

Soil: Well-drained, moderately rich.

Moisture: Evenly moist.

Garden Uses: Grow snapdragons in beds, borders, or cutting gardens.

Comments: Snapdragons grow best in cool weather. In Zones 3 to 6, start seeds indoors 8 to 12 weeks before the last expected spring frost and set out seedlings as soon as the soil can be worked. In Zones 9 and warmer, sow in fall. Seeds need light to germinate; do not cover them. To extend the blooming period, sow seeds in batches several weeks apart. Deadheading faded flower spikes helps prolong bloom. If you cut off entire spikes when the flowers fade, plants may rebloom in fall.

Recommended Cultivars: 'Bright Butterflies', 2½ feet, open unpouched flowers in shades of red, pink, bronze, yellow, and white; 'Sonnet Mix', 1½ feet, red, orange, pink, bronze, yellow, and white flowers; 'Floral Showers Mix', 6 to 8 inches, red, pink, purple, orange, yellow, white, and lavender-and-white bicolored flowers, blooms early in season; 'Floral Carpet Mixed', 8 inches, red, pink, yellow, and white flowers; Rocket hybrids, 2½ to 3 feet, various shades of red, pink, bronze, yellow, and white flowers.

Snapdragons make excellent garden companions for pansies

Argyranthemum

Argyranthemum frutescens
(Chrysanthemum frutescens)
MARGUERITE

Marguerites have dainty, daisylike flowers a couple of inches across. The centers are golden but the petals may be white, yellow, or pink. Some cultivars have densely packed, small upright petals around the center that can completely obscure the true disk flowers. The plants are branched and bushy, with finely divided, rather lacy-looking leaves.

Hardiness: Tender.

Blooming Time: All summer if deadheaded regularly.

Height: 1 to 3 feet.

Spacing: 1 to 1½ feet.

Light: Full sun.

Soil: Well-drained, average fertility.

Moisture: Average; water when soil is dry.

Garden Uses: Marguerites are durable plants for container gardens and window boxes as well as garden beds and borders. They perform beautifully as long as they receive regular deadheading throughout the season.

Comments: Marguerites were formerly grouped under *Chrysanthemum* but have been reclassified by botanists as *Argyranthemum frutescens*. But since some suppliers are still listing them as *Chrysanthemum*, shop for them under that name too if you can't find them as *Argyranthemum*.

Recommended Cultivars: 'Butterfly', 1½ feet, yellow flowers; 'Vancouver', 1½ to 2 feet, double pink flowers with dense "anemone" centers surrounded by narrow, widely spaced rays.

Single marguerites

'Pink Lady'

'Silver Lady'

smart tip

DEADHEADING MARGUERITE

Deadhead flowers as soon as they begin to fade. With regular deadheading, most marguerites will continue to bloom all summer.

Begonia

Begonia Semperflorens-Cultorum hybrids
WAX BEGONIA

Wax begonias have glossy, rounded leaves 2 to 4 inches long in varying shades of green and bronze. As a rule, green-leaved cultivars can tolerate more shade than bronze-leaved types. The inch-wide flowers can be either single or double (depending on the cultivar) and can come in shades of pink and red as well as white.

Hardiness: Tender.

Blooming Time: All summer into fall.

Height: 6 inches to 1 foot.

Spacing: 6 inches to 1 foot.

Light: Best in light shade; tolerates full sun in cooler climates. Plants will grow in medium to full shade, but will produce fewer flowers.

Soil: Well-drained, fertile, rich in organic matter.

Moisture: Evenly moist.

Garden Uses: Wax begonias are excellent bedding plants and work beautifully in window boxes and containers. They make good houseplants, too. In autumn, before the first frost, you can dig up plants or take cuttings to root and pot up for winter bloom indoors.

Comments: To start wax begonias from seed, sow seeds indoors in January or February. Seeds are very fine; scatter them as evenly as you can over the surface of a fine-textured potting medium and press them in gently. Keep the soil moist, with lots of light and temperatures between 65° and 80°F. Transplant to the garden after the frost-free date.

Because wax begonia plants are so slow to reach blooming size from seed, many gardeners find it easier to purchase plants at local garden centers.

Bronze-leaved cultivars tolerate more sun than green-leaved and variegated ones and are better choices for sunny locations and gardens in Zones 7 and warmer.

Recommended Cultivars: Ambassador hybrids, 8 inches, green leaves, red, pink, white, and red-and-white bicolored flowers, early blooming; Cocktail hybrids, 6 inches, bronze leaves, scarlet, pink, and white flowers; Lotto hybrids, 8 inches, green leaves, large red and pink flowers. Senator

Wax begonias in mixed colors

series, early blooming, bronze-leaved plants 8 inches high, flowers in two shades of rose, pink, white, and scarlet; Super Olympia series replaces the older Olympia hybrids, early blooming, green leaves, flowers in red, coral, pink, white, and a rose-and-white bicolor; Varsity series are early blooming and good in the Northeast, to 9 inches, green leaves, flowers in shades of scarlet, rose, pink, and white, as well as a rose-and-white bicolor.

smart tip

ROOTING CUTTINGS

Take cuttings from established plants in late summer to root for winter houseplants. You can also take cuttings in late winter, root them, and set them out once the spring weather has settled.

Browallia

Browallia speciosa
SAPPHIRE FLOWER

Sapphire flower plants bear star-shaped, violet-blue blooms about 2 inches across on branching stems with small, bright green, lance-shaped leaves. The compact plants have a bushy form.

Hardiness: Tender.

Blooming Time: Summer

Height: 8 inches to 1 foot.

Spacing: 10 inches to 1 foot.

Light: Partial to light shade; full sun in cool climates.

Soil: Well-drained; average fertility, but not too rich.

Moisture: Needs abundant moisture.

Garden Uses: An underused plant, sapphire flower is delightful for edging beds and borders, or for growing in pots, window boxes, and hanging baskets.

Comments: Grows best in fairly warm weather. Sow seeds indoors six to eight weeks before the last expected frost. Do not cover seeds. Overfertilization results in fewer blooms.

Recommended Cultivars: 'Blue Bells', 8 inches to 1 foot, blue; 'Jingle Bells', to 1 foot, mixed colors; 'Silver Bells', 8 inches to 1 foot, white flowers.

how to

Propagate

DIFFICULTY LEVEL: EASY

Tools and Materials: Established plant, rooting hormone, flat, soil mix

Browallia cuttings root faster when the end of the cutting is dipped in rooting hormone powder before planting. To avoid contaminating the hormone with a disease organism, shake some powder into another container and discard the excess after you use it.

ANNUALS

Browallia

smart tip

WINTER FLOWERS

Sapphire flowers make excellent winter houseplants. Take cuttings from established plants in late summer and root for winter houseplants.

Calendula

Calendula officinalis
POT MARIGOLD

Calendula produces golden yellow, orange, or cream-colored daisylike flowers on bushy, branching plants with narrow, oblong, somewhat coarse-textured green leaves. Some cultivars have full, double-petaled flowers.

Hardiness: Hardy.

Blooming Time: Early summer to fall, winter in warm climates.

Height: 1 to 2 feet.

Spacing: 10 inches to 1 foot.

Light: Full sun.

Soil: Well-drained, average fertility.

Moisture: Average; water during dry spells.

Garden Uses: Plant these sunny flowers near the front or middle of a bed or in containers. They also make good cut flowers.

Comments: Pot marigolds grow best in cool weather and can tolerate some frost; plant in early spring as soon as they become available from garden centers. Start seeds indoors eight weeks before the last expected frost and transplant a

Pot Marigolds

week or two before the frost-free date. Or sow seeds outdoors as soon as you can work the soil. In warm climates, plant seeds in fall for winter flowers.

Pot marigolds are easy to grow and have herbal as well as decorative uses. The edible flower petals can be used fresh as a garnish or salad ingredient or they can be dried and used as a substitute for saffron, to add color to rice dishes, or as a skin-soothing addition to homemade soaps or salves.

Recommended Cultivars: 'Bon Bon', 1 foot, orange and yellow flowers; 'Fiesta', 1 foot, yellow, orange, and bicolored flowers; 'Pacific Beauty', 1½ feet, yellow, gold, apricot, orange, and red-orange flowers.

---

how to

Cut Back for Regrowth

DIFFICULTY LEVEL: EASY

Tools and Materials: Pruning shears

1 When spring-planted pot marigolds begin to fatigue in midsummer, it's time for a rejuvenation treatment.

2 Cut back the plants to leave at least one set of leaves and stems a few inches high. Use pruning clippers or flower shears.

3 The cut-back plants will send out new growth and a fresh crop of flowers in late summer and fall.

Callistephus

Callistephus chinensis
CHINA ASTER

These popular cutting flowers are native to China and Japan. Many cultivars of China asters are available, giving a choice of heights and bloom times. Flowers can be white, purple, blue-violet, and various shades of pink and rosy red.

Hardiness: Tender.

Blooming Time: Summer into fall.

Height: 9 inches to 2 feet.

Spacing: 1 to 1½ feet.

Light: Full sun.

Soil: Average to rich, well-drained.

Moisture: Average; water during dry spells.

Garden Uses: Grow in the front to middle of beds and borders, cutting gardens, or in containers.

Comments: To avoid building up populations of the diseases that strike asters, do not grow them in the same area of the garden where they grew during the previous two or three years. For an instant bouquet, cut the whole plant; though the color will be uniform, the branch arrangement will be graceful.

Where the growing season is short, start seeds indoors about six weeks before the last expected spring frost. Elsewhere, sow outdoors after all danger of frost has passed.

'Milady Blue'

Recommended Cultivars: 'Dwarf Queen', 8 inches, double flowers of red, scarlet, rose pink, blue, and white; 'Mini Lady', 10 inches, large double flowers of scarlet, rose, blue, and white, early blooming; 'Milady Mixed', 10 inches to 1 foot, scarlet, rose, pink, blue, and white flowers; 'Massagno Mixed', 1½ feet, spider-type blossoms with long, thin petals in shades of red, pink, purple, and white; 'Galaxy Mix', 2 feet, yellow centers with pink, purple, and white spoon-shaped petals; 'Mixed Powder-puffs', 3 feet, white, crimson, rose, pink, peach, and blue flowers.

'Ostrich Plume'

Mixed China asters

Recutting Stems

When using China asters as cut flowers, recut their stems underwater before arranging them in a vase. Recut every two days to keep them fresh.

Catharanthus

Catharanthus roseus
MADAGASCAR PERIWINKLE, VINCA

Madagascar periwinkles are known for their white or rosy pink five-petaled flowers, some with a deep pink eye. The flowers are set off by glossy, dark green leaves.

Hardiness: Hardy.

Blooming Time: All summer into fall.

Height: 6 inches to 2 feet.

Spacing: 8 inches to 1 foot.

Light: Full sun.

Soil: Well-drained, average fertility.

Moisture: Evenly moist.

Garden Uses: A good plant for containers or the front to middle of beds and borders.

Comments: Purchase Madagascar periwinkle plants from garden centers because they are difficult to grow from seed. If you do try to start them, keep the medium at 80° to 85°F and cover the flat; the seeds need darkness to germinate. These plants love heat and humidity. Do not transplant until the soil has warmed in spring. They cannot tolerate cool temperatures. Vinca doesn't perform well where summers are cool; the leaves can turn yellow if the plant is exposed to cold temperatures. Cultivars in the Cooler series perform better in cooler conditions than other types do. Newer cultivars are tolerant of high winds and heavy rain. They are also *self-cleaning*, meaning that old blossoms drop off by themselves; you do not need to deadhead these plants. Madagascar periwinkle is perennial in Zones 9 and warmer.

'Parasol'

Recommended Cultivars: Cooler series, slightly over 1 foot, white, pink, orchid, and rose flowers, some with a contrasting eye; Pacifica series, 1 foot, large flowers of white, pink, apricot-pink, lilac, and red, most with a contrasting eye; 'Parasol', 15 inches, largest flowers of any cultivar, white with a red eye; Tropicana series, early- blooming, rose, pink, or white flowers with a contrasting eye.

how to

Take Cuttings — DIFFICULTY LEVEL: EASY

Tools and Materials: Mature plants, rooting hormone, pruning shears, planting flat, soil mix

After taking cuttings from established plants, remove the flowers and strip the bottom leaves so that you can bury at least two nodes in the soil mix.

Madagascar periwinkle in mixed colors

Celosia

Celosia argentea
WOOLFLOWER, COCKSCOMB

A varied species, *Celosia* offers flowerheads in feathery plumes, loose spires, or a variety of bizarre curled, crested, and fan shapes, some resembling twisted corals, brains, or deformed rooster's combs. Traditionally, the flowers have bloomed in bright, hot colors—red, magenta, scarlet, rose, pink, orange, and yellow—but now there are cultivars in softer shades of gold, yellow, apricot, and cream, particularly among the plume group (often sold as *Celosia plumosa*). All species are upright with a branching to bushy form and oval leaves.

Hardiness: Tender.

Blooming Time: All summer.

Height: 6 inches to 3 feet.

Spacing: 1 to 2 feet, depending on type. Smaller-growing cultivars can be planted at the closer spacing; larger ones farther apart.

Light: Full sun; afternoon shade in warm climates..

Soil: Any good garden soil.

Moisture: Average to damp.

Garden Uses: The traditional brilliant colors of cockscombs are difficult to mix with other flowers and are best surrounded with white flowers, silver-gray foliage (like that of artemisias or dusty millers) or lots of green leaves. The newer cultivars with softer colors are easier to work with and can be quite pretty with other warm-toned blooms. Use smaller cultivars in the front of the garden, taller types in the middle ground, or grow in containers. The flowers are good for cutting and drying.

Comments: The plants can't tolerate cold, so don't plant them out in the garden until the soil has warmed in spring. Sow indoors a month before the last expected frost.

Plume type

Recommended Cultivars: Plumosa group: 'Apricot Brandy', 1 to 1½ feet, apricot-orange flowers; Castle series, 1 foot, rosy pink, scarlet, and yellow flowers; Century series, 2 feet, red, rose, yellow, and cream flowers.

Cristata (cockscomb) group: 'Big Chief Mixed', slightly over 3 feet, red, scarlet, and yellow flowers; 'Jewel Box Improved', 6 inches, red, pink, orange, salmon, white, and bicolored flowers; 'Prestige Scarlet', 1 to 1½ feet, scarlet flowers.

C. spicata (known as wheat celosia): 'Flamingo Feather', 2 to 2½ feet, feathery pink flower spikes that show white as they open.

'Flamingo Feather'

smart tip

STAKING

Heavy flowerheads of cockscomb show to their best advantage when the plants are staked. Staking also keeps stems straight, an advantage if you cut them.

Centaurea

Centaurea cyanus
BACHELOR'S BUTTON, CORNFLOWER

Bachelor's buttons are tall, slender plants with charming, old-fashioned-looking flowers. The sparse leaves and open habit can make the plants look weedy late in the season. Spiky, pointed petals are various shades of deep sky blue, light blue, pink, purple, red, deep maroon, and white.

Hardiness: Hardy.

Blooming Time: Summer.

Height: 1 to 3 feet.

Spacing: 6 inches to 1 foot.

Light: Full sun.

Soil: Well-drained.

Moisture: Average.

Garden Uses: Bachelor's buttons make delightful additions to cottage gardens, meadow gardens, and the middle of informal beds and borders. Cut blooms when they are almost fully open. If you recut stems every second day, they hold well for up to a week.

Comments: Deadhead regularly to prolong blooming. Plants often rebloom if cut back severely after the first bloom. But to guarantee flowers all season, plant several

Deadhead flowers as soon as they begin to brown to promote continuous blooming.

successive sowings two to three weeks apart. Direct-seed in the garden as soon as soil can be worked in the spring in cool climates, but in the fall in mild ones. Bachelor's buttons grow best in cooler weather.

Recommended Cultivars: 'Dwarf Midget Mix', 1 foot, blue, pink, mauve, red, and white flowers; 'Garnet', 2 feet, burgundy flowers; 'Polka Dot Mixed', 1½ feet, blue, red, maroon, rosy pink, lavender, and white flowers.

how to

Save Bachelor's Button Seed   DIFFICULTY LEVEL: EASY

Tools and Materials: Dried seedheads, mallet, bowl, colander

1 Crush the seedheads with a heavy mallet to release the seeds.

2 Rub the seeds and chaff between your hands to further loosen the seeds.

3 Use a colander to separate the seeds from large pieces of chaff.

'Frosted Mix'

Cleome

Cleome hassleriana
SPIDER FLOWER

Spider flower

This amazing-looking plant is among the tallest of annuals, growing up to 6 feet high in a single summer. Its distinctive flowers, with their long, waving stamens (which resemble the legs of the spiders children call "daddy longlegs") are gathered into loose, round clusters at the tops of the tall, upright stems.

Flowers come in shades of rose, pink, and purple, as well as white. The medium green leaves are deeply lobed and palm-shaped.

Hardiness: Half-hardy.

Blooming Time: All summer.

Height: 3 to 6 feet; not as tall when grown in containers or in less-than-optimal conditions.

Spacing: 1 to 2 feet.

Light: Full sun to partial shade.

Soil: Average, well-drained.

Moisture: Average; tolerates dry soil, but not prolonged drought.

Garden Uses: These tall plants are striking massed in the back of the garden, where they provide a strong vertical line. Or try spider flowers in the center or back of a tub garden of mixed flowers. The flowers of *Cleome* are good for cutting.

Comments: Transplant spider flowers with care; they don't transplant very well. Or direct seed outdoors in spring, after the weather begins to warm but before all danger of frost is past.

The plants may self-sow, but self-sown plants will not grow as large as their parents. In warm climates, they can become invasive if left to go to seed. The tall stems may need staking, especially if your garden is in a windy location.

Recommended Cultivars: 'Helen Campbell', 3 feet, white flowers; Queen series, 3 feet, pink, rosy pink, and lilac-purple flowers; 'Color Fountain Mixed', 3 to 3½ feet, pink, rose, purple, lilac, and white flowers.

ANNUALS

how to

Start Seeds Indoors
DIFFICULTY LEVEL: EASY

Tools and Materials: Seeds, sand, flat, soil mix, water mister

1 Add sand to the seed packet to make seeds easier to plant.

2 Tap out the seeds and sand mixture into furrows in the medium.

3 Use a spray mister to moisten the flat without disturbing seed placement.

Volunteer plants

Coleus

Solenostemon scutellarioides
Coleus hybrids

These branched, bushy plants are grown for their oval to lance-shaped leaves that come in various combinations of colors: green, chartreuse, red, maroon, white, pink, apricot, brown, and yellow. The leaves have toothed, scalloped, or frilled edges and a somewhat quilted texture. In summer the plants send up small spikes of little white or purple flowers; these detract from the plants' appearance and are best removed.

Hardiness: Tender.

Blooming Time: Mid- to late-summer.

Height: 8 inches to 2 feet.

Spacing: 8 inches to 1 foot, depending on cultivar; set smaller-growing plants at the closer spacing.

Light: Partial to light shade; tolerates full sun. In full shade, plants will be smaller and less full; in full sun, the colors won't be as rich.

Soil: Average to fertile, rich in organic matter; tolerates a range of soil conditions.

Moisture: Needs even moisture, especially in dry weather.

Garden Uses: Coleus is a good source of color and mass in the front of a shady garden or in the middle ground of a bed of small plants. It also grows well in pots.

Comments: The plants are tender, so don't plant them in

smart tip

REMOVING FLOWER STALKS

Flower stalks on coleus plants are often considered unattractive. Remove them to keep the plants looking tidy and neat.

the garden until all danger of frost is past. Pinch back the tips of young stems to encourage bushier plants. Pinch off flowers when they form to keep plants growing vigorously.

You can take stem cuttings at the end of summer and root them in water, then pot them up to grow as houseplants in winter. Coleus plants are perennial in Zones 10 and 11.

Recommended Cultivars: 'Wizard Mixed', 10 inches, large assortment of colors and combinations; 'Rainbow Blend', 1½ feet, vigorous plants in a variety of colors and combinations; Fiji series, serrated or deeply cut leaves in 11 different colors and combinations; Old Lace series, 1½ feet, ruffled, serrated, or deeply cut leaves in a range of colors and combinations; Poncho series, cascading plants for hanging baskets.

how to

Root Stem Cuttings   DIFFICULTY LEVEL: EASY

Tools and Materials: Established plant, scissors, water in a container, pots, soil mix

1 Clip off healthy, 4- to 6-inch long stem tips for your cuttings.

2 Remove the lower leaves from each stem before inserting it into the water.

3 Plant the rooted cuttings in 4- to 6-inch pots in moist, porous potting soil.

Coleus

Consolida

C. ambigua (Consolida ajacis)
ROCKET LARKSPUR

Tall spikes of single or double flowers in violet, purple, blue, pink, and white grace these hardy plants. The flowering stems may be up to 4 feet tall.

Hardiness: Hardy.

Blooming Time: Late spring to early summer.

Height: 1½ to 4 feet.

Spacing: 10 inches to 1 foot.

Light: Full sun to partial shade.

Soil: Rich, fertile, well-drained.

Moisture: Evenly moist.

Larkspur

Garden Uses: These tall, graceful plants mix beautifully with peren-nials. Plant them in the middle or back of a bed or border, in a cottage garden, or wherever you need a strong vertical line. They make lovely cut flowers and also dry well.

Comments: Larkspur grows best in cool weather. Plant seeds directly in the garden. Plant in the fall in warm climates; where the ground freezes in winter, plant as soon as the soil can be worked in spring. You can also sow seeds indoors in individual peat pots (seeds need darkness to germinate). Transplant outdoors, with care, when the soil is workable. Larkspur does not transplant well, so move them before they become pot-bound. Plants often self-sow if not deadheaded. Tall cultivars may need staking.

Recommended Cultivars: 'Earlibird Mixed', 1½ to 2 feet, early blooming, double, rose, lilac, blue, and white flowers; 'Kaleidoscope Mix', 1½ to 2 feet, single to double, violet-blue, lavender, rose, pink, and white flowers; 'King Size Mix', 1½ to 2 feet, double, rose, shades of pink, salmon, carmine, lilac, blue, and white flowers.

smart tip

COLLECTING SEEDPODS

Wait to collect the seedpods until they have turned brown and have begun to dry. If you are concerned that the seeds will drop before you get them, twist-tie a paper bag around them before they are completely dry.

Larkspurs give an excellent vertical accent at the back of a border.

Convolvulus

Convolvulus tricolor
DWARF MORNING-GLORY

Dwarf morning-glories are bushy and sprawl instead of climbing. The flowers look like smaller, fancier versions of the familiar vining morning-glories. The center of each blossom is yellow, a white zone surrounds it, and the remaining half of each petal is blue, purple, red, or pink.

Hardiness: Half-hardy.

Blooming Time: Late spring to late summer.

Height: to 2 feet and spreading.

Spacing: 10 inches to 1 foot.

Light: Full sun.

Soil: Average, well-drained.

Moisture: Evenly moist.

Garden Uses: Plant dwarf morning-glory in a hanging basket; let it ramble about the front of a bed or border; or plant it where it will tumble over the edge of a raised bed or retaining wall.

Comments: Abrade the hard seed coat with sandpaper, or soak the seeds overnight before planting. After danger of frost has passed, direct-seed outside. Or sow seeds early indoors in peat pots and carefully transplant outdoors when the danger of frost is past.

Recommended Cultivars: Ensign series, 1 to 2 foot spread, red, blue, rose, or white flowers with a yellow eye and white throat; 'Dwarf Picotee Mixed', 1 foot, variegated leaves, red, pink, salmon, and blue flowers edged in white.

'Royal Ensign'

Dwarf morning-glory

Seed leaves

smart tip

Planting

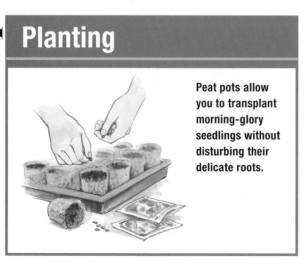

Peat pots allow you to transplant morning-glory seedlings without disturbing their delicate roots.

Cosmos

Cosmos species

The gold-centered daisylike flowers of crimson, rose, pink, and white (*Cosmos bipinnatus*) or scarlet, orange, gold, and yellow (*C. sulphureus*) are extraordinarily appealing in summer beds and borders. Cosmos foliage is finely divided and has a feathery appearance. The branching plants have a light, open texture. They sometimes look a bit weedy late in the season.

Hardiness: Tender.

Blooming Time: Midsummer until frost.

Height: 2 to 5 feet, depending on variety and growing conditions.

Spacing: 1 foot.

Light: Full sun is best; also grows reasonably well in partial shade.

Soil: Average fertility, tolerates poor soil; good drainage is essential.

Moisture: Tolerates some drought.

Garden Uses: Cosmos are wonderful, exuberant plants for the middle to the back of the garden, depending on the mature height of the cultivar. The flower colors combine beautifully with many other flowers. Cosmos hold up well in hot weather. The flowers are excellent for cutting.

Comments: In most climates, it's best to direct-seed. Where the frost-free season is short, start seeds early indoors in peat pots. Transplant to the garden after all danger of frost is past in spring, taking care not to disturb the roots.

Bright Lights Mix

Cultivars of *C. bipinnatus* bloom in groups of three flowers. When deadheading the first blooms, cut them off immediately below the flowerhead; two new buds will then form below the cut. After these flowers fade, deadhead by clipping off the stems at the next pair of leaves. Flowers of the yellow and orange species appear singly on long stems; cut back to the next pair of leaves when deadheading.

Recommended Cultivars: *C. bipinnatus:* 'Gazebo', 4 feet, crimson, lavender-pink, and white flowers; 'Early Wonder', 4½ feet, crimson, rose, pink, and white flowers; 'Sonata', 1½ to 2 feet, red, rose, pink, and white flowers; 'Versailles', 1½ to 2 feet, flowers are red, white, and shades of pink; 'Seashells', 3 to 3½ feet, tubular petals of red, rose, pink, and cream; 'Bright Lights', 3 feet, early, semidouble, scarlet, orange, gold, and yellow flowers.

C. sulphureus: 'Lady-bird' series, 1 foot, red, yellow, and orange flowers; 'Polidor Mix', 3 feet, semidouble, red, gold, and orange flowers.

'Seashells'

smart tip

DEADHEADING COSMOS

Deadhead flowers as soon as the petals fade or begin to dry to encourage plants to bloom all summer. If you want the plants to self-seed, leave only a few faded flowers on the plant late in the summer.

Dianthus

Dianthus chinensis
CHINA PINKS

China pinks are biennials or short-lived perennials that are usually grown as annuals. Their clove-scented flowers come in shades of red, pink, white, and many bicolors, generally with a central, darker eye. The petals are fringed. The upright mounded plants have narrow bluish green leaves.

Hardiness: Hardy.

Blooming Time: Late spring to midsummer.

Height: 1 to 1½ feet.

Spacing: 6 inches to 1 foot.

Light: Full sun; some afternoon shade is helpful where summers are hot.

Soil: Average fertility; light, well-drained, sandy soil with a neutral to slightly alkaline pH.

Moisture: Average.

Garden Uses: Position China pinks in the front of the garden or grow them in containers. They're charming in a cottage garden or rock garden as well.

Comments: Sow directly outdoors when frost danger is past or start them indoors about 10 weeks before the last frost. Set plants with the crowns right at the soil surface; don't plant too deep.

smart tip

CUTTING BACK

Cut back the stems after plants have finished their first bloom. They will regrow and reward you with a second bloom later in the season.

Recommended Cultivars: Parfait series, 6 inches, flowers are small and weather-resistant and single or bicolored in shades of pale pink or light red, usually with a red eye; Carpet series, 6 inches, single red, rose, white, and bicolored flowers; Magic Charms series, 6 inches, red, coral, pink, white, and bicolored flowers; Princess series, 6 inches, red, scarlet, salmon, pink, purple, and white flowers; 'Black & White Minstrels', 6 to 10 inches, a deep purplish black-and-white bicolored bloom; 'Color Magician', to 10 inches, small, single flowers that change from white to pink to rose-pink as they age.

smart tip

Siting

Place China pinks where they will get some afternoon shade if you live in an area with hot summers. This is particularly important for plants growing in containers because they are so exposed when growing alone.

China pinks

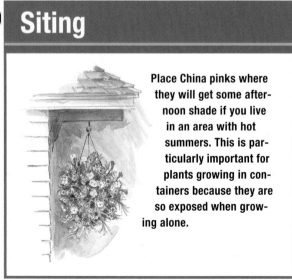

'Raspberry Parfait'

Fuchsia

Fuchsia hybrids

Fuchsias' dangling flowers look like ornate earrings. They are usually tubular and pendent, often with a corolla and sepals of one color and petals of another. The flowers have a waxy texture and may be single, with 4 petals, semidouble, with five to seven petals, or double, with eight or more petals. Flowers bloom in shades of red, purple, pink, or white. The plants have long cascading stems with small, glossy, oval leaves.

Hardiness: Tender.

Blooming Time: All summer.

Height: Trailing roughly 1½ to 2 feet long.

Spacing: If using as bedding plants, about 1 foot apart.

Light: Partial shade to shade.

Soil: Well-drained, average fertility.

Moisture: Even, regular.

Garden Uses: Although shrubby in warm climates, trailing types of fuchsias are ideal for hanging baskets in cool

Fucshia cascades from a window box in a showy display.

climates. The long stems, carrying the pendent flowers, arc gracefully over the sides of the container.

Comments: In frost-free climates, fuchsias may be grown outdoors all year. In cooler climates, gardeners can start seeds indoors in January. Young plants are widely available at garden centers. Don't take plants outside until all danger of frost has passed.

Recommended Cultivars: 'Chimes Mixed', 1 foot, mix of upright and trailing types, mixed colors; 'Florabelle', trailing, to slightly over a foot, purple-and-red flowers.

'Kathy Louise'

smart tip

TRAINING FUCHSIA

Fuchsia plants can be trained as tree-like "standards," meaning that a central stem takes the place of a trunk.

'Tom Thumb'

Gomphrena

Gomphrena globosa
GLOBE AMARANTH

Rounded flowerheads resembling clover blossoms grace globe amaranth plants. The oval leaves grow on stiff, branching stems. Flower colors include red-violet, red, pink purple, lavender, and white. The related *G. haageana* expands the color range to orange shades.

Hardiness: Tender.

Blooming Time: Summer into fall.

Height: 8 inches to 2 feet.

Spacing: 10 inches to 1½ feet.

Light: Full sun; tolerates partial shade.

Soil: Well-drained, average to poor fertility.

Moisture: Average, tolerates drought.

Garden Uses: Grow globe amaranth in containers or in the front of beds and borders. The flowers dry beautifully; cut them while the flower heads are still round, before they open fully.

Hang the flowers upside down in bunches in a dry, airy location to air-dry. The stems become rather brittle when dried and will hold up better in arrangements if you first wrap them with green florist's wire to brace them. You can hide the wire with green florist's tape if necessary.

To use globe amaranth as a fresh-cut flower, remove the lower leaves and place the stems in a container of water almost up to the base of the flowers for several hours before arranging them.

Globe amaranth seeds

Comments: Direct-seed in the garden when frost danger is past, or start seeds indoors about six weeks before the last frost. Soak seeds overnight or for a day or two before you sow them. Globe amaranth holds up well in hot, dry summer weather.

Recommended Cultivars: 'Bicolor Rose', 2 feet, rosy lilac flowers with white centers; 'Dwarf Buddy', 6 inches, purple flowers; 'Lavender Lady', 2 feet, lavender flowers; 'Woodcreek Mixed', 1½ feet, red, rose, pink, orange, lilac, purple, and white flowers; 'Strawberry Fields', 2½ feet, brilliant red flowers to 2 inches long; 'Dwarf White', 6 inches, long-lasting white flowers.

Globe amaranth

smart tip

CUTTING *GOMPHRENA* FOR DRYING

Cut globe amaranth flowers for drying while the petals are still tight. Hang upside down in bunches to air-dry in an airy, sheltered location.

Helianthus

Helianthus annuus
SUNFLOWER

These tall golden flowers are easy to grow and long-blooming. The most common sunflowers are golden yellow, but lately the palette has expanded. Particular cultivars may also bloom in shades of orange, mahogany, maroon, and cream. Some have large brown centers. This species includes the giant sunflower that provides seeds for birds and human snackers; its flowers can easily grow to 1 foot across. Most cultivars are tall, upright, branched plants with large, coarse leaves.

Hardiness: Hardy.

Blooming Time: Mid- to late-summer.

Height: 2½ to 7 feet (10 or even 12 feet is common for the giant sunflower).

Spacing: 1 to 2 feet.

Light: Full sun to partial shade.

Soil: Well-drained, average fertility.

Moisture: Evenly moist; tolerates some dryness.

'Music Box'

Garden Uses: Sunflowers are cheerful, lively plants that are most at home in informal gardens; most are too coarse for formal beds and borders. Dwarf cultivars are the most versatile; all but the smallest sunflowers belong in the back of the garden. Giant sunflowers can be planted in a row; their tall, straight stems will form a border or light screen.

Comments: Sunflowers grow best in warm weather, but they are reasonably hardy when established. Direct-seed when all danger of frost is past in the spring.

Recommended Cultivars: 'Mammoth Russian', 12 feet, golden yellow flowers with yellow centers; 'Valentine', 5 feet, pale lemon yellow flowers with dark centers; 'Sonja', 3½ feet, deep orange flowers; 'Italian White', 5 to 7 feet, cream to very pale yellow flowers with dark centers; 'Music Box', 2½ to 3 feet, mixed flower colors—yellow shades to red; 'Sunspot', 2½ feet, 10-inch flowers; 'Teddy Bear', 3 feet, very double fuzzy-looking yellow flowers without visible centers.

ANNUALS

how to

Save Sunflower Seeds

DIFFICULTY LEVEL: EASY

Tools and Materials: Flowers, paper bag, scissors, stapler

1 Sunflower pollen is large and quite visible when it is ready to fertilize the seeds. Both wind and insects pollinate sunflowers.

2 After the pollen has dropped and the seeds have been fertilized, the seeds begin to develop. They become larger as the days go by.

3 Prepare a paper bag for covering the seed head by cutting off one corner so that any rainwater that gets into it can also drip out.

4 The bag prevents birds from eating the seeds. Staple it around the stem with the cut corner positioned at the lowest point.

Helichrysum

Helichrysum bracteatum
STRAWFLOWER
Helichrysum petiolare
LICORICE PLANT

Strawflowers (*H. bracteatum*) produce papery-petaled blossoms in warm shades of red, orange, yellow, pink, and creamy white. The branching plants have narrow, oblong leaves. Some references now list these plants as *Bracteantha bracteatum*.

Licorice plant (*H. petiolare*) is a low sprawling plant with small, rounded, fuzzy, silvery gray-green leaves with a mild licorice scent. These plants are perennial in Zones 10 and 11.

Hardiness: Half-hardy.

Blooming Time: Summer into autumn.

Height: Strawflower, 1½ to 3 feet; licorice plant, 1½ feet.

Spacing: 8 to 14 inches.

Light: Full sun.

Soil: Well-drained, average.

Moisture: Average, let soil dry between waterings; tolerates dry conditions.

Garden Uses: Strawflowers are excellent for drying and can be used in fresh arrangements, too. Plant them in the cutting garden or in the middle to the back of beds and borders.

Licorice plant blends with most flower colors. It is delightful cascading over the edge of a mixed container or hanging basket and also works well in the front of a bed or mixed border.

Comments: Direct-seed when all danger of frost is past in spring and the soil is warm. Or start indoors about six weeks before the last expected frost. Seeds need light to germinate; press into the soil surface.

Cut strawflowers for drying before they are fully open. Strawflower stems are brittle and break easily; avoid problems by replacing them with florist wire. Immediately after you cut the flowers, poke a length of florist wire through the center of each, make a small hook in the end of the wire that you pushed through the flower, and then draw it back down into the center of the blossom so that it is invisible. Dry the flowers by sticking the wires into a block of styrofoam in a dark place with good air circulation. The wire will allow you to arrange the flowers once they are dry.

Recommended Cultivars: *H. bracteatum:* 'Bright Bikini Mix', slightly over a foot tall, red, rose, pink, yellow, and white flowers; 'Fiery Mix', red, orange, yellow, and white flowers; 'Victorian Pastels', to 4 feet, rose, pink, salmon, and white flowers; 'Monstrosum', 2½ feet, red, rose, orange, purple, and white flowers.

H. petiolare: 'Limelight', chartreuse leaves; 'Variegatum', variegated with creamy white markings.

Strawflowers

CUTTING STRAWFLOWERS FOR DRYING

Cut flowers for drying right below the calyx because the stems are too brittle to retain.

Licorice plant

Heliotropium

Heliotropium arborescens
HELIOTROPE

These shrubby plants are loved for their rounded clusters of tiny, fragrant, dark purple flowers. Though tender perennials, they are usually grown as an annuals. The scent of their flowers is reminiscent of vanilla, or to some noses, cherry pie. The oval, deep green leaves are heavily veined and textured.

Hardiness: Tender.

Blooming Time: Summer to frost.

Height: 8 inches to 3 feet.

Spacing: 1 to 1½ feet.

Light: Full sun; needs some afternoon shade in warm climates.

Soil: Well-drained, fertile.

Moisture: Even, regular.

Garden Uses: Grow heliotrope in pots, use it as a bedding plant, or plant it in an old-fashioned cottage or fragrance garden. Heliotrope also makes a wonderfully fragrant cut flower. Cut stems when about half the flowers in the clusters have opened. Make the blooms last longer by cutting a vertical slit in the bottom of the stem, quickly dipping the stem end into boiling water to seal the cuts, and then conditioning the flowers by placing the stems in a container of warm water for several hours.

Heliotrope makes an excellent companion to the magenta petunias and yellow blackfoot daisies in this garden.

Comments: Heliotrope is slow to grow from seed, so start it early indoors, 10 to 12 weeks before the last expected frost. Seeds need light to germinate; press them into the soil but do not cover. Feed them as young seedlings with a half-strength seaweed/fish emulsion dilution. Transplant to the garden with care when all danger of frost has passed; roots do not like to be disturbed. Because you must start the plants so early, many people purchase seedlings from a garden center. Pinch back stem tips of young plants for bushier growth.

To ensure sufficient nutrients for this heavy feeder, make sure the soil is well supplied with compost, or fertilize throughout the growing season with a liquid all-purpose fertilizer or a fish/seaweed product that has been diluted according to the directions on the package. You can also use a half-strength fish/seaweed dilution as a foliar feed if you spray in low-light conditions.

Recommended Cultivars: 'Dwarf Marine', slightly over a foot, royal purple flowers; 'Hybrid Marine', 1½ feet, royal purple flowers, good for cutting; Marine Lemoine strain, to 2 feet, deep purple, good for cutting; 'Mini Marine', 8 to 10 inches, deep purple flowers.

'Hybrid Marine'

ANNUALS

smart tip

DEADHEADING HELIOTROPE

Deadhead heliotrope as the flowers fade, cutting back to the next set of leaves. The plants will send up new flower stalks for much of the summer but eventually exhaust themselves.

'Fiesta Pink Ruffles' double impatiens

Impatiens

Impatiens cultivars

Bedding impatiens bloom in every imaginable shade of pink as well as red, orange, lavender, red-violet, and white. Some flowers have a contrasting eye, some are bicolored, and some are full and double. Plants are bushy and mounded with soft oval leaves.

Balsam impatiens are erect and bear their flowers close to the central stem. Many types have double flowers; some are bicolored.

The New Guinea hybrids have larger flowers, mostly in shades of red, rose, lavender, and pink. These are borne on taller plants with longer leaves that are often veined with red and shaded with yellow in the center. Some cultivars have dark red-purple leaves.

Hardiness: Tender.

Blooming Time: All summer until frost.

Height: Bedding impatiens, 4 inches to 1 foot, depending on cultivar; balsam impatiens, 1 to 2½ feet, New Guinea impatiens, 1 to 2 feet.

Spacing: 6 inches to 1 foot.

Light: Bedding and balsam impatiens, partial to full shade, tolerates sun with enough moisture; New Guinea impatiens, full sun to partial shade.

how to

Save Impatiens Seeds
DIFFICULTY LEVEL: EASY

Tools and Materials: Large bowl, mature seedpods

1 Ripe impatiens seedpods burst when touched, so grasp them firmly and hold a bowl underneath to catch the seeds.

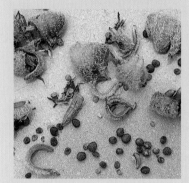

2 The ripe pods appear plump but are still green. They burst open and curl back to release the seeds.

Balsam impatiens

Soil: Well-drained, average fertility, lots of organic matter; tolerates a range of soils.

Moisture: Needs even, regular moisture.

Garden Uses: Bedding impatiens is widely grown—perhaps too widely—but is still hard to beat for massing in the front of shady beds and borders, under shrubs, or using in pots, window boxes, and hanging baskets. It is easy to grow and among the most versatile of garden plants. Balsam impatiens grows well in the middle of shady or partially shaded gardens where it can add a colorful vertical accent. New Guinea impatiens grows well in the middle of sunny to partly shady gardens. It is also particularly effective in hanging baskets and other containers.

Comments: Impatiens species can't take cold, so don't plant them out until all danger of frost is past and the weather has warmed in spring.

Impatiens don't require deadheading—old flowers will

'Accent Orange'

drop off by themselves. The double-flowered type of bedding impatiens tends to drop many of its pretty blossoms shortly after they open, so it's best to water and handle plants with extreme care.

Recommended Cultivars: Bedding types: Accent hybrids, 10 inches, 20 colors and combinations; Mosaic hybrids, 10 inches to 1 foot, lilac or rose blossoms splashed with white; Swirl hybrids, 10 inches to 1 foot, pastel pink, peach, and coral petals with a darker center and edges; 'Confection Mix', double flowers colored rose, red, orange, and pink; 'Super Elfin', 6 to 10 inches, 20 colors; 'Tempo', early blooming, 16 colors; 'Dazzler', 8 inches, 11 colors.

Balsam impatiens: 'Blackberry Ice', slightly over 2 feet, double purple flowers with white markings; Tom Thumb series, to 1 foot tall, large, double, pink, red, violet, or white flowers; Camellia-flowered series, 2½ feet, double pink or red flowers with white markings.

New Guinea hybrids: 'Tango', 1 foot, bright orange flowers; 'Spectra Mix', 10 inches to 1 foot, red, rose, coral, scarlet, pink, orchid, and white flowers.

how to

Space Plants
DIFFICULTY LEVEL: EASY

Tools and Materials: Seedlings, ruler or marked stick, prepared garden area

1 Impatiens are lovely massed under trees or shrubs. Use a ruler to plant at the correct spacing—don't crowd the plants.

2 Plants will fill in quicky to provide a mass of color. Stagger plants so they are equidistant in all directions for best coverage.

'Light Salmon' New Guinea impatiens

Ipomoea

Ipomoea tricolor, I. purpurea, I. nil, MORNING-GLORY
I. alba, MOONFLOWER
I. batatas, SWEET POTATO VINE

These relatives of potatoes and tomatoes are fast-growing twining vines with a multiplicity of uses. The funnel-shaped morning-glory flowers bloom in shades of red, pink, purple, and white, sometimes flushed or striped with a contrasting color. Moonflower vines have large, fragrant white flowers that open in the late afternoon or evening and close with the dawn. The blooms of both moon flowers and morning-glories often have a sheen when they first open. Both plants have large, heart-shaped leaves.

Sweet potato vines have heart-shaped or lobed leaves in attractive colors. The varieties described under "Recommended Cultivars" on the facing page were developed to be purely ornamental. Because the tubers they produce are so tiny, you probably couldn't make these plants do double duty as a food crop anyway; use them only as decorative elements. Cultivars used for food crops tend to have leaves that are far more coarse than those of the cultivars that are used as ornamental plants.

Cypress vine (*I. quamoclit*) has small, brilliant red funnel-shaped flowers with bright white throats. The deep green leaves are so finely divided that they often look threadlike.

Cardinal climber (*I. multifida*) has small scarlet flowers and leaves that are less finely divided. Leaves are a medium green color.

Hardiness: Tender.

Blooming Time: Summer until frost.

Height: Morning-glories, 15 to 20 feet tall; moonflower, 10 to 20 feet tall (or more in warm climates); sweet potato vine, cascading, 5 to 10 feet long; cypress vine, 6 to 12 feet; cardinal climber, 3 to 6 feet.

'Blackie' sweet potato vine

Cypress vine

Morning glories in mixed colors

Spacing: 8 inches to 1 foot.

Light: Full sun for the flowering species; sweet potato vines tolerate partial shade.

Soil: Well-drained, average fertility.

Moisture: Moderate to even.

Garden Uses: Morning-glories and moonflowers are lovely on trellises, tripods, obelisks, and fences. Their large leaves make them ideal for camouflage, screening, or training on arbors. Or train them up a lamppost or around a mailbox. Moonflowers are heavenly trained around a porch or trellised near a patio or deck where you can sit outdoors on warm summer evenings and enjoy their delightful fragrance. Sweet potato vines are excellent trailing over the edges of containers or hanging baskets. You can also allow them to ramble about the feet of flowers growing in a bed or border, especially in a lush, tropical-looking garden. Try them with colorful coleus and bold cannas and caladiums, along with some hot-colored impatiens, for an exuberant tropical effect.

The smaller, more delicate-looking vines of cardinal climber and cypress vine are charming scrambling over shrubs or decorating net trellises or wire mesh fences. They attract hummingbirds, so place them where you can see them from inside the house or a porch.

Comments: Seeds of these plants, especially moonflowers, have hard seed coats. Rub them on sandpaper or nick them with a file before sowing, and/or soak in warm water several hours or overnight before planting. direct-seed outdoors after all danger of frost is past and the soil is warm. The plants thrive on heat and do not grow well in chilly soil or cool weather. Flowering is also affected by temperature; in cool summers your plants won't flower well.

Ornamental sweet potato vines are widely available in garden centers; it's easiest to purchase plants instead of starting your own.

Recommended Cultivars: Morningglories: 'Heavenly Blue', 8 feet, large sky blue flowers; 'Early Call Mix', 8 to 10 feet, rose, pink, lavender, purple, and white flowers; 'Flying Saucers', to 10 feet, white flowers streaked with purple; 'Milky Way', to 15 feet, white flowers streaked with carmine; 'Pearly Gates', 8 to 10 feet, white flowers; 'Scarlett O'Hara, 8 feet, crimson flowers; 'Star of Yelta', to 6 feet, deep velvety purple flowers with a rose-pink splash in the center and a white throat. *I. × imperialis* 'Tie Dye', to 8 feet, large lavender flowers streaked with darker purple, lobed leaves splashed with grayish white.

Moonflower: 'Giant White', to 15 feet, 6-inch wide, fragrant white flowers.

Sweet potato vine: 'Blackie', deep purple-black leaves with angular, pointed lobes; 'Margarita', heart-shaped leaves of luminous yellow-green.

Cypress vine and Cardinal climber: cultivars of these species are not available; just look for the species name on packets, in catalogs and at nurseries.

how to

Prepare *Ipomoea* Seeds — DIFFICULTY LEVEL: EASY

Tools and Materials: Seeds, sandpaper, bowl of water

1 Prepare the hard-coated seeds of this family for planting by scratching them gently against a piece of fine sandpaper.

2 After sanding the seedcoats, soften them further by soaking them in a bowl of lukewarm water for 8 to 24 hours.

ANNUALS

Moonflower   Cardinal climber

Lantana

Lantana camara
YELLOW SAGE

Lantana has wide, domed flower clusters up to 2 inches across. The small individual flowers can be white, yellow, pinkish lavender or a yellow-red-rusty brown combination. Flowers of some cultivars change colors as the blooms age: cream changes to pink, pink to lavender, and yellow to orange. In color-changing cultivars, flower clusters may contain three colors at once. The plants are upright, branched, and bushy with toothed, oval leaves. In Zones 10 and 11, where they are perennial, the plants are shrubby.

Hardiness: Half-hardy.

Blooming Time: All summer.

Height: 4 feet when perennial, 2 feet when annual.

Spacing: 1 to 1½ feet.

Light: Full sun.

Soil: Well-drained, average fertility.

Moisture: Average; tolerates some dryness.

Garden Uses: *Lantana* is an interesting plant for a large container as well as the center or back of the garden. Children find the color-changing flowers magical. *Lantana* is

Lantana

salt tolerant and useful in seashore gardens. Its flowers are attractive to butterflies.

Comments: Plants grow best in warm weather. All parts of the plants are poisonous.

Recommended Cultivars: Mixed hybrids, 1½ to 2 feet, red-and-yellow, pink-and-yellow, and lilac-and-white flowers; 'Patriot Rainbow', 1 foot, red-and-yellow flowers. Cultivars of *L. montevidensis* are trailing and grow well in hanging baskets; look for 'White Lightnin' and 'Lavender Swirl'.

how to

Propagate Yellow Sage

DIFFICULTY LEVEL: EASY

Tools and Materials: Mature plants, sharp scissors, softwood rooting hormone, flat, soil mix

1 Take cuttings from established plants in late summer. Choose stems with at least four nodes. Trim off the blooms and the leaves from the bottom two nodes.

2 Dip each cutting in softwood rooting hormone, and shake off the excess. To avoid contaminating your supply, put the hormone powder in an old bottle or another container.

3 Poke a hole in the planting medium before placing the stem bottom in it. Gently firm the soil so that it is in contact with the stem bottom.

Leucanthemum

Leucanthemum paludosum
(Melampodium paludosum)
BLACKFOOT DAISY, BUTTER DAISY

These bushy, low-growing plants with light green oval leaves are covered with small, yellow or yellowish white daisylike blooms with bright yellow centers. Blackfoot daisies are durable, tough plants.

Hardiness: Half-hardy.

Blooming Time: All summer until frost, sporadically in winter in frost-free climates.

Height: 8 inches to 1½ feet.

Spacing: 1 foot.

Light: Full sun.

Soil: Well-drained, average to poor fertility.

Moisture: Average; tolerates drought.

Garden Uses: Plant in the front of the garden or in containers. Blackfoot daisies make the most effective displays when they are planted in masses rather than in small groups. They are excellent companions for annual fountain grass (*Pennisetum* species), especially the purple-leaved cultivars, and other hot-colored annual flowers, such as scarlet salvia or celosia. In a large mixed container, try them with ornamental sweet potato vines 'Blackie' or 'Margarita', or with spiky dracaena for contrast.

'Showstar'

Comments: This plant stands up to hot, humid conditions as well as drought. Start seeds indoors six to eight weeks before the last expected frost, and transplant after the danger of frost is past and the soil has warmed. Or direct-seed when the soil is warm. If grown in fertile soils, especially soils rich in nitrogen, the plants will not produce as many flowers. Plants may self-sow.

Blackfoot daisy is easy to maintain. Plants will grow bushy even if you don't pinch them back when young. Best of all, they are self-cleaning and need no deadheading to keep blooming all summer.

Recommended Cultivars: 'Million Gold', 8 to 10 inches, golden yellow flowers; 'Showstar', 10 inches, yellow flowers.

ANNUALS

Blackfoot daisy with ornamental grass

Blackfoot daisy seeds

Lobelia

Lobelia

Lobelia

Lobelia erinus
EDGING LOBELIA

Dainty, lipped flowers in clear shades of deep blue, sky blue, red, maroon, pink, and white liberally cover these compact or cascading plants. Leaves are small, elliptical, and dark green. The colored flowers often have a white eye, which adds to their impact.

Hardiness: Half-hardy.

Blooming Time: All summer.

Height: 4 to 6 inches.

Spacing: 6 inches.

Light: Full sun to partial shade; appreciates afternoon shade where summers are hot.

Soil: Well-drained, fertile, rich in organic matter.

Moisture: Needs even moisture all summer, but soil must not be soggy.

Garden Uses: These small, delicate-looking plants are lovely in the front of a window box or container where they will spill over the sides. Or use them as edging in a partly shaded garden. The flowers of the blue cultivars positively glow in the shade.

Comments: Lobelia may stop blooming in hot, humid weather, and plants may die back. If flowering slows, shear back the plants—they grow back and resume flowering later in the summer, when nighttime temperatures begin to cool off.

Recommended Cultivars: 'Crystal Palace', 5 inches, dark blue flowers, bronze leaves; 'Mrs. Clibran', 5 inches, dark blue flowers with a white eye; 'Cambridge Blue', 5 inches, light green leaves, light blue flowers; 'Rosamond', 5 inches, wine red flowers with a white eye; 'White Lady', 5 inches, white flowers; Riviera series, 4 inches, early blooming, deep blue, light blue, blue with a white eye, blue-and-white bicolor, and white flowers; 'Cascade Mix', 8 inches, cascading, blue, lavender, red, rose, white, and blue flowers with a white eye.

smart tip

PROMOTING A SECOND BLOOM

Cut back lobelia plants if bloom slows in summer or the plants become rangy. Once the weather begins to cool, they will rebloom with vigor.

Lobularia

Lobularia maritima
SWEET ALYSSUM

Clusters of tiny flowers in shades of white, lavender, pink, or purple liberally cover these low, sprawling plants with little green leaves. The sweet honey fragrance that carries a short distance adds to this plant's charm.

Hardiness: Hardy.

Blooming Time: Late spring into autumn.

Height: 4 to 6 inches, older types to 1 foot.

Spacing: 6 inches.

Light: Full sun to partial shade.

Soil: Well-drained, average fertility.

Moisture: Average to evenly moist.

Garden Uses: Sweet alyssum is a low-growing, light-textured favorite for edging and tumbling over the front of containers or window boxes. It is also quite nice rambling among the stones in a rock garden. For a different look, plant sweet alyssum in clumps or drifts among other plants in the front of the garden. It makes an appealing carpet at the feet of clematis or lilies that are growing near the outside of a garden bed.

Because it starts blooming early and can take very cool temperatures, sweet alyssum also makes a good companion for pansies and spring bulbs.

Easter Basket mix

smart tip

SHEARING BACK SWEET ALYSSUM

Shear back sweet alyssum plants when flowering slows; they will regrow and bloom again.

Sweet alyssum has practical uses too. Its flowers attract small beneficial wasps (such as *Chalcid* and *Braconid* species) that prey on aphids and other pest insects in the garden. Many gardeners plant sweet alyssum in the vegetable garden as well as the flower garden, to help keep it free of pests.

Comments: Plants grow best in cool weather; they can go into the garden as soon as the danger of heavy frost is past in spring. Start seeds indoors four to six weeks before you plan to transplant them; don't cover seeds in starting containers.

If bloom slows in midsummer and the plants partially die back, shear back the stems to a few inches above the soil surface; in only a few weeks they will rebloom with new energy.

Sweet alyssum is easy to grow. Plants may self-sow or return, although with less vigor, in subsequent years. Plan on starting with fresh plants every year.

Recommended Cultivars: 'Carpet of Snow', 4 inches, white flowers; 'Snow Crystals', 4 inches, white flowers; 'Rosie O-Day', 4 inches, rosy pink flowers; Easter Basket series, compact, 4 to 6 inches, mix of violet, lavender, deep rose, deep pink, and white flowers; 'Navy Blue', 4 inches, deep purple; 'Easter Bonnet', 4 inches, a mix of rose, pink, lavender, and violet flowers.

Nicotiana

Nicotiana × *sanderae*
FLOWERING TOBACCO

The star-shaped white, red, rose, pink, lavender, and light green flowers have long, tubular throats. They bloom on branched, bushy plants with rather large, narrow to oblong leaves of medium green. Plants have an open, rather than a dense, form. The leaves are covered with soft hairs and feel rather sticky to the touch. The flowers of the species form are fragrant at night, but most of the commonly available hybrids have only a faint scent after sundown.

Hardiness: Half-hardy.

Blooming Time: All summer.

Height: 1 to 3 feet; the species form grows to 5 feet.

Spacing: 9 inches to 1 foot.

Light: Full sun to partial shade.

Soil: Well-drained, average fertility.

Moisture: Moist; water during spells of hot, dry weather.

Garden Uses: Easy to grow and a prolific bloomer, flowering tobacco is a charming plant to add mass and color in the front or middle ground of a bed or border. It flowers happily in containers too. Place the species form and larger hybrids in the back of the garden.

smart tip

VOLUNTEER PLANTS

Flowering tobacco self-seeds easily. Thin or transplant the volunteer seedlings as soon as they have their first true leaves.

smart tip

SAVING *NICOTIANA* SEEDS

Cut whole seed stalks after the pods turn brown. Don't wait until they are completely dry, or they will drop their seeds on the ground in the first stiff breeze to come along.

Comments: A most versatile plant, flowering tobacco performs well in hot sun if given enough water; it also blooms nicely in partial to light shade. Sow indoors six to eight weeks before the last expected frost. Do not cover seeds; they require light to germinate. Transplant to the garden after all danger of frost is past. The leaves and flowers are delicate and easily damaged; handle the plants carefully during transplanting.

If you deadhead regularly, the plants will bloom all summer. When deadheading, cut off the old flower right below its base; new buds will develop on the stem immediately below the old blossom.

Japanese beetles love these plants, so take appropriate measures if these bugs are a problem in your garden.

Recommended Cultivars: Domino series, 1 foot, crimson, red, pink, rose-pink, salmon-pink, purple, white, and lime green flowers; 'Heaven Scent Mix', 2 to 3 feet, fragrant at night, red, rose shades, purple, and blush white flowers; Merlin series, to 1 foot, crimson, purple, peach, white, and lime green flowers; Nicki series, 1½ to 2 feet, red, pink, white, and pale green flowers.

'Lime Green'

Pelargonium

Pelargonium × hortorum
ZONAL GERANIUM
Pelargonium peltatum
IVY GERANIUM

Zonal geraniums have round, medium green leaves with scalloped edges, sometimes marked with dark bands (or zones). Large, round clusters of flowers that grow on straight stems bloom in shades of red, pink, red-violet, orange, salmon, and white.

Ivy geraniums have lobed leaves reminiscent of English ivy. The smaller clusters of flowers are airy and graceful and come in shades of red, pink, lavender, and white. The plants have a sprawling or cascading habit no matter where they grow.

‘L’ Elegance’, an ivy geranium

‘Kim’, a zonal geranium

Hardiness: Tender.

Blooming Time: All summer until frost.

Height: Zonal, 1 to 3 feet; ivy, trailing 2 to 3 feet.

Spacing: 8 inches to slightly over a foot.

Light: Full sun to partial shade.

Soil: Average to fertile, well-drained.

Moisture: Moderate.

Garden Uses: Zonal geraniums are excellent for bedding, tubs or pots, and the back of a window box. Ivy geraniums are ideal for hanging baskets or window boxes.

‘Mr. Henry Cox’, a zonal geranium

Comments: In cool climates, start seeds of zonal geraniums indoors ten to twelve weeks before the last expected frost; transplant out after all danger of frost is past. Take cuttings in late summer to root for indoor bloom in winter. In Zones 10 and 11, zonal geraniums will grow outdoors all year.

Ivy geraniums are usually propagated from cuttings. Take your own in late summer and overwinter indoors or purchase plants in spring.

Recommended Cultivars: Zonals: Elite series, 10 inches, early blooming, zoned leaves, flowers are rose-pink, salmon-orange, red shades, or white; Multibloom series, 8 to 10 inches, red, scarlet, rose, pink, salmon, lavender, and white flowers; Orbit series, 1 foot, zoned leaves, compact plants, red shades, scarlet, pink shades, lavender-pink, violet, and salmon flowers.

Ivy geraniums: ‘Summer Showers Mixed’, 2 to 3 feet, red, burgundy, pink, rose, lavender, and white flowers; Tornado series, 2 to 3 feet, two-toned lilac and rose or white and pink flowers.

smart tip

PROPAGATING GERANIUMS

Take cuttings In late summer to root and grow as houseplants over the winter. In late winter, take cuttings again to grow for the summer garden.

ANNUALS

Petunia

Petunia × *hybrida*

Fragrant, funnel-shaped flowers in many shades of red, purple, pink, blue, white, and pale yellow cover petunia plants. Some are bicolored and some are striped or edged with white. Flowers are single or double, smooth or ruffled. Multiflora types bear smaller, mostly single flowers, while grandiflora types have larger, often double flowers. Wave types spread or cascade much farther than others. The leaves are soft, hairy, and somewhat sticky.

Hardiness: Half-hardy.

Blooming Time: All summer if deadheaded regularly.

Height: 8 inches to slightly over a foot for upright types.

Spacing: 10 inches to 1 foot.

Light: Full sun to partial shade.

Soil: Average, well-drained; tolerates a range of soils.

Moisture: Average to moist.

Garden Uses: Plant petunias in the front of beds and borders, or in pots or window boxes. Spreading types, particularly the Wave series, can be used for ground covers.

Comments: Sow indoors about 10 weeks before the last expected frost. Do not cover the seeds; they need light to germinate. Seedlings will be tiny. Transplant them to cell packs or peat pots after they have several sets of leaves. If you seeded them in a soilless mix, water with a seaweed/fish dilution to keep them healthy.

Transplant out when danger of frost is past. Petunias tend

Multiflora petunia

to look ratty by midsummer; cutting back the lanky stems encourages a neater habit and renewed bloom. Heavy rain and wind may damage plants, especially grandiflora types.

Recommended Cultivars: Multifloras: Fantasy series, 10 inches, called "milliflora" in the nursery trade, the earliest to bloom, small red, pink, blue, salmon, and white flowers cover each plant; Celebrity series, 9 inches to 1 foot, red shades, pink shades, salmon, peach, lilac, blue, and white flowers, all with white throats; Merlin series, 10 inches, early blooming, red, rose, pink, salmon, blue, white, and several picotees (white-edged); Primetime series, 11 inches, many colors and combinations; Wave series, spreading plants 4 to 6 inches high and 2 to 4 feet wide, plum, coral, and rose-pink flowers; 'Heavenly Lavender', 1 foot, deep lavender flowers; 'Polo Mixed', 10 inches, weather-resistant flowers in shades of red, pink, purple, and white, some striped or with deeper colored veins

Grandifloras: 'Blue Danube', 1 foot, lavender flowers with blue veins; Daddy series, about 1 foot, flowers are veined with dark, contrasting colors in shades of pink, orchid, and blue; 'Double Delight Mixed', 1 foot, double red, pink, purple, white, and bicolored flowers; 'Double Cascade', about 1 foot, double pink and burgundy flowers resembling carnations; Falcon series, shades of red, pink, salmon, blue, white, and plum, some with colorful veins.

Grandiflora petunia

smart tip

CUTTING BACK PETUNIAS

Cut back elongated, bare stems in midsummer, trimming to just above a node or pair of leaves. Plants will respond by developing new, more tidy, growth.

Portulaca

Portulaca grandiflora
ROSE MOSS

Silky, ruffly diaphanous blossoms, single or double, characterize rose mosses. Flowers bloom in many warm shades—red, rose, magenta, pink, salmon, gold, yellow, and white. The plants are low and creeping, with fleshy, needlelike foliage.

Hardiness: Tender.

Blooming Time: All summer into autumn.

Height: The trailing stems grow to 10 inches long, but plants are usually no more than 6 inches tall.

Spacing: 8 to 10 inches.

Light: Full sun.

Soil: Well-drained, preferably sandy; tolerates poor, dry soil.

Moisture: Prefers soil on the dry side; drought tolerant.

Garden Uses: Rose moss is an excellent small plant for hot, dry conditions. The brilliantly colored flowers are a cheerful edging along paths and pavements and in the front of sunny beds and borders. It's also a terrific plant for containers and hanging baskets. Some newer hybrids that are especially well suited to hanging baskets have smaller flowers and spoon-shaped leaves streaked with white and green. Try planting rose moss in pockets of soil in stone walls, or use them to add a bright festive touch in front of or along

Rose moss seeds next to a dime

the top of a wall. Portulacas make a wonderful carpet for an area of poor, somewhat dry soil.

Comments: Sow indoors four to six weeks before the last expected frost; transplant outdoors when all danger of frost is past. Don't fertilize because high nutrient levels suppress flowering.

The plants may self-sow; dig up unwanted volunteers and transplant them to a different spot.

Blossoms close late in the day and reopen in the morning.

Recommended Cultivars: 'Calypso Mixed', 5 inches, double, mixed warm colors; Sundial hybrids, 5 to 6 inches, large double flowers, red, scarlet, pink, gold, white, and peach flowers.

Rose moss

smart tip

Siting Rose Moss

Rose moss can thrive in areas that are adjacent to hot pavement, such as this sidewalk cutout. Because the plants don't require much moisture or nutrients, they make a good understory plant for limbed-up trees too.

Salvia

Salvia coccinea,
Salvia farinacea, MEALYCUP SAGE
Salvia splendens,
SCARLET SAGE

Annual *Salvia* species vary tremendously from one another. But even though they display a wide range of colors and flower types, all of them are easy to grow and long blooming. *Salvia coccinea* has loose spikes of tubular flowers of red, coral, or white. Mealycup sage bears spikes of tiny, tubular flowers of rich violet-blue or grayish white on straight, slender stems. Cultivars of scarlet sage have smaller spikes of somewhat larger tubular blossoms of brilliant scarlet or, less commonly, purple, pink, or creamy white. The upright, branched to bushy plants have oval to lance-shaped leaves.

Hardiness: Half-hardy.

Blooming Time: All summer to frost.

Height: 10 inches to 3 feet, depending on variety.

Spacing: 8 inches to 1½ feet; don't crowd the plants because they become bushier as they mature.

Light: Full sun to partial shade; provide some afternoon shade in hot climates.

Soil: Well-drained, average fertility.

Moisture: Average to moist; salvias don't grow well in arid climates. Scarlet sage needs more even moisture than mealycup sage.

Garden Uses: Annual *Salvia* species are rewarding; they send up new flower spikes all summer long and need deadheading much less frequently than many

Mealycup sage

other flowers. The plants provide a welcome vertical accent in the front or middle of beds and borders or in containers. The flowers can also be cut for fresh arrangements or dried.

Mealycup sage is perennial in Zones 8 and warmer. It is among the most rewarding of garden flowers—adapting to a wide range of soils and growing conditions, blooming lavishly all season, and holding its flowers for a long time. The plants branch naturally and need no pinching when they are young to make them full and bushy. The flowers are excellent for cutting. Blue cultivars dry to a lovely soft shade of blue that can add bulk and color to lavender flowers in a potpourri.

To use *Salvia* in fresh arrangements, cut flowers when the lowest blooms on the spike have opened and the higher blossoms are still closed. Place the stems in a container of warm water for several hours to condition the flowers. Before arranging them, remove any leaves that would be underwater in the vase. The narrow flower spikes add vertical interest to bouquets and arrangements.

The flowers can be air-dried, but to preserve the most color when drying salvias, lay them horizontally in a container of silica gel, and carefully sprinkle or brush more desiccant over and around the flowers until they are completely covered.

The bright red of scarlet sage can be difficult to combine with flowers in cool hues, but surrounding it with white flowers and deep green foliage makes for a very effective display. The newer, softer pink and purple shades are easier to work with. In Zones 9 and warmer, plant for spring or fall bloom.

Comments: Sow mealycup sage indoors about 10 weeks before the last expected frost and scarlet sage six to eight weeks before then. Do not cover the seeds; *Salvia* needs light to germinate. They also require warm temperatures; don't plant them outdoors until all danger of frost is past in spring. With occasional deadheading, the plants will keep blooming all summer long, right up until frost strikes them.

Recommended Cultivars: *S. coccinea* 'Lady in Red', 2 feet, bright red flowers; 'Coral Nymph', 2 feet, coral-and-white bicolored flowers; 'Snow Nymph', 2 feet, white flowers.

S. farinacea 'White Porcelain', 1½ feet, white flowers; 'Victoria', 1½ feet, violet-blue flowers, long-blooming; 'Cirrus', 1½ feet, white flowers; 'Strata', 1½ feet, blue-and-white bicolored flowers.

S. splendens 'Flare', 1½ feet, bright red flowers; 'Carabiniere', slightly over 1 foot, blood red flowers; 'Bonfire', 2 feet, later blooming, bright red flowers; 'Maestro', 8 inches, dark red flowers; Hotline series, 10 inches to 1 foot, flowers of red, burgundy, salmon, violet, and purple streaked with blue and white; Sizzler series, 1 to 1½ feet, red, burgundy, rose, pink, purple, plum, lavender, salmon, and white flowers.

Scarlet sage

Scaevola

Scaevola aemula
FANFLOWER

Fanflower is a tender perennial usually grown as an annual. The low sprawling plants sport unusual, pointed-lobed flowers shaped like little fans; they grow to form circular clusters. The flowers are blue to lavender-blue, though there is also a mauve-flowered cultivar.

Hardiness: Tender.

Blooming Time: Late spring until frost.

Height: Trailing or prostrate, to 8 inches high.

Spacing: 1 foot or slightly over.

Light: Full sun.

Soil: Well-drained; tolerates a range of soils.

Moisture: Average to regular, even moisture.

Garden Uses: Fanflower's wide, sprawling habit makes it a good choice for a hanging basket, to cascade over the edge of a mixed container, or to tumble over a wall or the side of a raised bed.

Comments: Buy plants from a garden center or nursery. Pinch back the stem tips of young plants for bushier growth. To keep the plants blooming lavishly all summer, feed them once a month with a liquid all-purpose fertilizer or seaweed/

smart tip

Pinching

Pinch off stem tips on young plants to encourage the plants to develop more branches and become bushy.

fish emulsion product, diluted according to package directions. Fertilize plants in containers every two weeks with a half-strength dilution.

Gardeners in Zones 10 and 11 can grow fanflower as a perennial; it blooms throughout much of the year. Everywhere else, you can move a plant indoors in fall to bloom as a houseplant in winter. Dig up a plant and pot it up in a loose, porous, all-purpose potting mix. Cut back the stems, and set the pot in a sunny window.

Recommended Cultivars: 'Mauve Clusters', 6 inches tall, can spread up to 5 feet, lilac-mauve flowers; 'Blue Wonder', 6 inches tall, to 5 feet wide, lilac-blue flowers.

Fanflower blooms

Fanflower makes a lovely edging plant along sidewalks and other kinds of paving.

Fanflower makes an excellent companion for many plants, including this sprawling prickly pear (*Opuntia phaeacantha*).

Senecio

Senecio cineraria
DUSTY MILLER

These upright, branched bushy plants are grown for their velvety, deeply cut, silver-white foliage. The leaves have a lacy, frilly look.

Hardiness: Tender.

Height: 8 inches to 2 feet, depending on variety.

Spacing: 10 inches to 1 foot.

Light: Full sun.

Soil: Very well drained, average fertility.

Moisture: Average to rather dry.

Garden Uses: The silver-leaved dusty millers are valuable accents for flower gardens and containers; they are especially pretty with pink and blue flowers. Their cool foliage can also be used to tone down beds of hot-colored flowers or to add shimmer to a garden of white flowers.

Comments: Start seeds indoors in late winter (February) and plant outdoors when all danger of frost has passed. Or purchase plants; they are widely available. The plants are actually tender perennials and may winter over in Zones 8 to 11. Plants may send up clusters of small, not very ornamental ivory or yellow flowers at the tips of upright stems; for appearance's sake, pinch out the flower stems if they appear.

smart tip

PINCHING SENECIO

Promote bushiness by pinching back stem tips as the plants grow.

Like most silver-leaved plants, dusty miller tolerates a fair degree of drought and suffers in soils that are continuously wet. Pinch the plants when they are young to encourage bushy, compact growth.

smart tip

REMOVING FLOWERS

Remove the flower stalks from dusty miller plants as soon as they form rather than after they bloom.

'Silverdust'

In addition to *Senecio* cultivars, some other plants are sold under the name of dusty miller. Two particularly nice ones are cultivars of *Chrysanthemum* (or *Tanacetum*) *ptarmiciflorum*: 'Silver Lace', to about 10 inches high with finely dissected, lacy-looking leaves, and 'Silver Feather', to 12 inches high, also with finely cut, feathery leaves.

Recommended Cultivars: 'Silverdust', 8 inches; 'Cirrus', 8 to 10 inches, larger, whiter leaves, good tolerance to rain and light frost.

Tagetes

Tagetes erecta,
AFRICAN OR AMERICAN MARIGOLD
Tagetes patula,
FRENCH MARIGOLD
Tagetes tenuifolia,
SIGNET MARIGOLD

Marigolds are loved for their freely blooming, sunny flowers of bright yellow or rich orange. African marigolds are upright plants with flowers that are usually 2 to 4 inches across. The so-called "white" cultivars have flowers that are really a lovely pale yellow. French marigolds are small, bushy plants with small flowers of yellow, orange, or deep, mahogany red. Signet marigolds are smaller still, with masses of diminutive flowers of yellow or orange and somewhat lemon-scented foliage; the blossoms are edible. All marigolds have divided, rather ferny leaves composed of narrow leaflets.

Hardiness: Half-hardy.

Blooming Time: All summer until frost if deadheaded regularly.

Height: African, 1 to 2½ feet; French, 6 inches to 1½ feet; signets, 6 inches to 1 foot.

Spacing: African, 1 to 2 feet; French and signet, 6 inches to 1 foot.

Light: Full sun.

Soil: Well-drained, average to good fertility.

Moisture: Average.

Garden Uses: All are good additions to beds, borders, and cottage gardens; they also grow well in pots, tubs, and window boxes. Place African marigolds in the middle of the garden and use the smaller types for edging. Taller cultivars of African and French marigolds make good cut flowers, too.

African marigold

Comments: Marigolds are tender annuals and thrive in hot weather. Start seeds indoors six to eight weeks before the last expected frost; don't plant outdoors until all danger of frost is past. In Zones 9 and warmer, direct-seed in early spring.

French marigold

Recommended Cultivars: African: Antigua series, 1 to 1½ feet, orange and yellow flowers; Discovery series, 10 inches, yellow and orange flowers; Excel series, slightly over 1 foot, flowers in yellow shades and orange; Inca series, 1 to 1½ feet, yellow, gold, and bright orange flowers; 'Jubilee', 1½ to 2 feet, flowers in yellow shades and orange; Lady series, 1½ feet, lemon yellow, gold, and orange flowers; 'Snowdrift', to 2 feet, ivory to pale yellow flowers; 'French Vanilla', 2 feet, ivory-white flowers

French: Bonanza series, 8 inches, flowers are yellow and gold bicolors with red shades; Disco series, 1 foot, single flowers in red, orange, and yellow shades; Janie series, 8 inches, flowers are orange and yellow bicolors with red; Zenith series, 1 foot, yellow, orange, and orange-and-red flowers; 'Mr Majestic', 1 foot, red-striped yellow flowers look like pinwheels.

Signet marigold

Signet: 'Starfire Mix', 1 foot or slightly over, yellow, orange, and red flowers; 'Tangerine Gem', small orange flowers; 'Lemon Gem', small yellow flowers.

smart tip

DEADHEADING MARIGOLDS

Deadhead flowers as soon as they fade, and plants will reward you with flowers through the season.

Thymophylla

Thymophylla tenuiloba
(Dyssodia tenuiloba)
DAHLBERG DAISY, GOLDEN FLEECE

These low-growing, sprawling plants are covered with small, bright yellow daisylike flowers. The plants bloom all summer without deadheading. Leaves are finely divided and needlelike. The rather delicate appearance of Dahlberg daisies belies their durability. Natives of Texas and Mexico, they withstand dry conditions and high temperatures.

Hardiness: Half-hardy.

Blooming Time: All summer. Bloom continues through fall in mild climates. In Zones 9, 10, and 11, you can plant in fall for winter or early spring bloom.

Height: to 1 foot.

Spacing: 6 inches.

Light: Full sun.

Soil: Well-drained, sandy, average fertility.

Moisture: Moderate to dry; fairly drought tolerant.

Garden Uses: Plant in the front of an informal garden for a spot of bright color throughout much of the season. Dahlberg daisies do well in sunny rock gardens and are good choices for hanging baskets or other containers. You can also grow them in pockets in a dry stone wall, or between paving stones in a path or patio.

Dahlberg daisy

Comments: Good drainage is essential for success with Dahlberg daisy—it cannot tolerate soggy soils. Although the plant is a summer annual in all but the mildest climates, it prefers cool weather. Sow directly in the garden or start seeds indoors two months before the last expected frost. They are slow to germinate and may do poorly indoors, particularly if temperatures are above 65°F. The easiest option is to purchase plants at a local nursery and transplant them out to the garden after the last

smart tip

CONTAINER-PLANTING

Deadhead flowers as soon as they fade, and plants will reward you with flowers through the season.

frost date. *Thymophylla* self-sows easily in milder climates.

The plants are time-consuming to deadhead because they produce so many flowers on their thin stems. If bloom slows, clip off as many dead flowers as you can with fine-pointed flower shears or scissors, or shear back the ends of the stems to encourage renewed flowering. In mild areas, plants can begin to look ratty over the course of the long season; pull up and discard any that do.

Recommended Cultivars: Cultivars of Dahlberg daisy are not available at this time.

smart tip

Starting Early

Start Dahlberg daisies early indoors if you can control temperatures. They germinate well at soil temperatures of 50°F to 55°F and grow well at air temperatures of 55°F to 65°F.

Tithonia

Tithonia rotundifolia
MEXICAN SUNFLOWER

These big, branching plants bear large, hot-colored, daisy-shaped blooms in shades of bright red-orange and brilliant yellow with yellow centers. The flowers look similar to zinnias or single-petaled dahlias. The large, coarse deep green leaves are oblong and feel velvety. These are tender perennials but gardeners in most locations grow them as annuals.

Hardiness: Tender.

Blooming Time: All summer until frost, peaks in late summer.

Height: 2½ to 6 feet, depending on cultivar.

Spacing: 2 to 3 feet.

Light: Full sun.

Soil: Well-drained, average to poor fertility.

Moisture: Moderate to somewhat dry; some drought tolerance.

Garden Uses: Plant Mexican sunflowers in the back of the garden or use them for screening or even a temporary hedge. The flowers attract butterflies and hummingbirds. Plants tolerate high heat, humidity, and drought. The flowers are good for cutting and are long lasting in the vase. Cut flowers when they are almost fully open and the centers are still tight. Morning or early evening is the best time to

Mexican sunflower

cut. Before arranging in a vase, pass the cut ends of the brittle, hollow stems over a candle flame or dip them briefly in boiling water to seal them. Unsealed stems will bleed and foul the water. After sealing, stand the stems in a container of warm water almost to the base of the flowers for several hours before arranging them. (See "Balloon flower," page 129 for an illustration of sealing stems.)

Comments: Direct-sow in spring, when frost danger is past, or sow indoors six to eight weeks earlier and plant out after the last frost date.

Stake plants growing in windy locations; the tall stems may snap or blow over if buffeted by strong winds on a regular basis.

Recommended Cultivars: 'Aztec Sun', 4 feet, yellow-orange flowers; 'Fiesta Del Sol', 2 feet, bright orange flowers; 'Goldfinger', 2½ feet, red-orange flowers; 'Torch', 6 feet, scarlet-orange flowers.

smart tip

SAVING MEXICAN SUNFLOWER SEEDS

Wait until the petals drop and the flower heads dry to cut for seed-saving. Allow the seeds to dry several more weeks before packing for winter storage.

smart tip

STAKING

Stake Mexican sunflower plants if you live in a windy area. Without staking, the stems are likely to topple over onto the ground, as these have.

Torenia

Torenia fournieri
WISHBONE FLOWER

Wishbone flowers get their name from paired stamens inside the throat that resemble a wishbone. The enchanting tubular flowers are two shades of violet-blue and purple, or violet and white, with a yellow splash in the throat. There are also cultivars with white or rosy to clear pink flowers. The petals are velvety like those of pansies. The small, upright, bushy plants have more or less oval leaves.

Hardiness: Tender.

Blooming Time: Midsummer to frost.

Height: 10 inches to 1 foot.

Spacing: 6 to 8 inches.

Light: Partial to light shade.

Soil: Well-drained, average to poor fertility.

Moisture: Keep evenly moist but not soggy; wishbone flowers don't tolerate dry soil.

Garden Uses: These pretty little plants deserve to be known better. They are lovely for edging shady beds and borders or massing on a shady slope or under a tree with an open, high canopy. Because this plant flowers so prolifically and is so eye-catching, it makes a large impact when massed. Wishbone flowers also grow well in pots and hanging baskets in partly shaded locations. They make a nice change from, or companion to, impatiens because they thrive in the same sort of conditions.

Wishbone flower

The flowers can also be used for fresh-cut blooms, serving as fillers or accents in arrangements. Cut stems that have several just-opened blossoms in the morning or early evening. Cut one or two vertical slits up into the cut end of each stem, then condition them by standing the stems in a container of tepid water nearly to the base of the lowest blooms. Leave them in the water for several hours before arranging the flowers. Buds will continue to open after the flowers are placed in the vase and arranged.

Comments: Don't plant wishbone flowers in the garden or set potted plants outside until all danger of frost is past in spring. Sow seeds indoors 10 to 12 weeks earlier. Press seeds lightly into moist soil, but do not cover them; they need light to germinate. The plants do not tolerate cold but thrive on heat, as long as they are not allowed to dry out.

Recommended Cultivars: 'Clown Mix', 8 to 10 inches, violet, rose-pink, and white flowers.

smart tip

TRANSPLANTING

Transplant wishbone flowers after the frost-free date.

smart tip

STARTING SEEDS

Use plastic film over the flats to keep the soil medium moist.

Tropaeolum

Tropaeolum majus, T. minus
NASTURTIUM

Wide-petaled, funnel-shaped, gently fragrant flowers with spurs characterize nasturtium plants. Various cultivars bloom in shades of red, orange, pink, mahogany, yellow, and white. The leaves are large, round, and flat with prominent veins. In newer cultivars the blossoms are carried above the foliage, but flowers of the old-fashioned types often hide in the leaves.

Hardiness: Tender.

Blooming Time: All summer into autumn.

Height: Dwarf types (*Tropaeolum minus*) grow 6 inches to 1 foot tall; climbing cultivars (*T. majus*) can grow to 10 feet long and trail along the ground if not fastened to a support.

Spacing: 1 foot for dwarfs or climbers trained on a trellis; 1½ to 2 feet for climbers that are allowed to sprawl on the ground.

Light: Full sun to partial shade.

Soil: Well-drained, average fertility.

Moisture: Average to somewhat dry; tolerates some drought.

'Whirlybird Mix'

Garden Uses: Climbing types can be attached to a trellis or screen for support or allowed to trail from hanging baskets. You can let them ramble about in the front of the garden or on a slope or bank. Plant dwarf types as edgings, in the front of the garden, or in pots.

Both the lightly fragrant flowers and the leaves are edible, with a peppery flavor similar to the related watercress.

Comments: Nasturtiums are easy to grow when established, but they don't transplant terribly well. Direct-sow when danger of frost is past or start them in peat pots three to four weeks before the last expected frost and transplant them before roots emerge from the pot.

Nasturtiums grow best in cool weather. Warm-climate gardeners can grow them as winter flowers. The plants often self-sow.

Very rich soil or too much shade causes plants to produce lots of leaves but few flowers.

Recommended Cultivars: 'Alaska Mix', 1 to 1½ feet, green and white variegated leaves, good range of colors; 'Empress of India', 1 foot, bushy, blue-green leaves, deep red flowers; 'Jewel Mix', 1 foot, good range of colors; 'Moonlight', vining to 7 feet, light yellow flowers; 'Tall Dark Foliage Mixed', 2 feet, trailing, red, orange, and gold flowers; Whirlybird series, rose, mahogany, scarlet, orange, gold, and yellow flowers held well above the foliage.

Leaves of volunteer nasturtium seedlings

how to

Start Nasturtium Seeds   DIFFICULTY LEVEL: EASY

Tools and Materials: Seeds, water, peat pots, soil mix

1 Soak nasturtium seeds before you plant them. Here, the seeds on the right have been soaked overnight.

2 Nasturtium roots are large but delicate. Plant seeds in peat pots to avoid disturbing the roots when you transplant.

Viola

Viola × wittrockiana
PANSY

A favorite for spring planting, pansies are available—with or without the distinctive clown-face markings—in an extensive range of colors, including shades of purple, blue, yellow, orange, red, pink, white, and deep blue-black. The compact plants are found in practically every garden center where bedding plants are sold in early spring and also, increasingly, in fall.

Blooming Time: Spring into summer, or autumn; winter to early spring in warm climates.

Height: 5 to 10 inches.

Spacing: 6 to 8 inches.

Light: Full sun to partial shade.

Soil: Well-drained, fertile, rich in organic matter.

Moisture: Abundant, even.

Garden Uses: Use pansies as edging, in the front of beds and borders, as companions to spring bulbs, and in pots and window boxes.

The flowers can be used in small arrangements by themselves or in arrangements with other flowers; they last up to about five days in the vase. Keeping the arrangement in a cool room will maximize the life of the flowers. Cut flowers when nearly open, in the morning or early evening. Soak the flowers, stems and all, in cold water for an hour or so to firm them up so they don't go limp; then stand the stems upright in a container of cool water nearly to the base of the flowers for several hours before arranging them.

Pansies are edible too, and make charming additions to

'Universal True Blue'

salads. You can candy them by painting the petals with beaten egg white and dusting them with superfine granulated sugar. Let the flowers dry; then store them, if necessary, between sheets of wax paper in a covered container. Use the candied blossoms to decorate baked goods and desserts.

Comments: Sow indoors 12 weeks before the last expected heavy frost. Set out plants two weeks before the

'Accord Clear Primrose'

last expected frost. Warm-climate gardeners can sow in late summer or fall for late winter flowers. Plants will overwinter in a cold frame as far north as Zone 5.

Pansies grow best in cool weather. Regular deadheading will prolong their bloom, but hot weather will shut down the plants no matter what you do. Pull them up and replant the area with hot-weather annuals.

Recommended Cultivars: 'Antique Shades', 6 inches, pastel pink, rose, apricot, yellow, and cream flowers; 'Crystal Bowl Mixed', 6 to 8 inches, scarlet, rose, orange, yellow, white, and blue shades; Swiss Giant hybrids, red, burgundy, rose, orange, bronze, yellow, blue, white, and violet flowers; 'Fall Colors', scarlet, orange, yellow, and bronze flowers; 'Jolly Joker', orange-and-purple bicolored blooms; Maxim series, 6 inches, mahogany, red, orange, pink, violet, and bicolored flowers with white, all with a contrasting blotch or "face"; 'Springtime Black', deep blue-black flowers.

smart tip

SAVING PANSY SEEDS

Collect the seeds before they drop to the ground. Try to pick the pods just before they split. If that will be impossible, tie row cover material around nearly ripe pods to catch the falling seeds.

Zinnias are ideal companions for the tansy, goldenrod, mums, asters, and nasturtiums in this arrangement.

Zinnia

Zinnia angustifolia,
NARROW-LEAVED ZINNIA
Zinnia elegans,
COMMON ZINNIA

Common garden zinnias (*Z. elegans*) come in a range of sizes. Flowers are single or double and the palette contains many shades of red, orange, pink, and yellow, along with creamy whites and an unusual light green. Narrow-leaved zinnia is a charming smaller plant with small, single flowers.

Blooming Time: Summer.

Height: Narrow-leaved, to 1 foot, sprawling; Common, 6 inches to 3 feet.

Spacing: Narrow-leaved, 6 inches to 1 foot; Common, 6 inches to slightly over 1 foot.

Zinnia elegans

Light: Full sun; tolerates a bit of shade in warm climates.

Soil: Well-drained, average fertility; common zinnias tolerate somewhat richer soils.

Moisture: Average; tolerates moderate dryness.

Garden Uses: Zinnias are dependable plants for beds and borders; plant them in the front or middle of the garden according to their size. There are tall, large-flowered common zinnias for the back of the garden, dwarf sizes for the front of the garden, and medium-size plants to use in between. Narrow-leaved zinnia is good for edging or the front of window boxes and containers. Both are delightful in cottage gardens. Garden zinnias make good cut flowers, too.

Zinnia angustifolia

Comments: Zinnias thrive in hot weather. Sow seeds outdoors after all danger of frost is past in spring. In short-season areas, start indoors six weeks before the last expected frost. Seedlings don't like root disturbance; plant in peat pots and transplant carefully.

In cool, humid conditions, zinnias are often troubled by powdery mildew and leaf spots, especially late in the season. Water early in the day so leaves dry before nightfall and pick off affected leaves. Cultivars with narrow leaves are often more resistant to these diseases than common zinnias.

Recommended Cultivars: *Z. angustifolia*: 'Crystal White', 8 inches, white flowers; 'Star Gold', 8 inches to 1 foot, yellow; 'Star Orange', 8 inches to 1 foot, orange flowers; 'Star White' (sometimes listed as 'White Star'), 8 inches to 1 foot, white flowers; Pinwheel series, 1 foot, single flowers of red, rose, pink, orange, yellow, and white.

Z. elegans: 'Big Red', 3 feet, rich red flowers; Border Beauty series, 1½ to 2 feet, red, rose, pink, orange, and yellow flowers; 'Candy Stripe', 2 feet, white flowers splashed with red and rose-pink; 'Envy', 1½ to 2 feet, lime green flowers; Peter Pan series, 1 foot, scarlet, orange, pink, gold, and cream flowers; Pulcino series, 1 to 1½ feet, red shades, rose, pink, orange, salmon, and gold flowers; Ruffles hybrids, 2½ feet, ruffled petals colored cherry red, pink, and yellow.

Cut zinnias for arrangements and deadhead excess flowers to keep plants blooming well.

PART 2

About Perennials

A perennial is a plant that lives for at least three years. The plants we think of as perennials are, for the most part, herbaceous, meaning that above-ground parts of the plant—the stems and leaves—are soft and green, not woody. In cold climates the top growth of most herbaceous perennials dies back each winter and the plants become dormant; in spring, new top growth develops. In warm climates, some perennials are evergreen, retaining their leaves and stems all year; others become dormant during summer droughts.

Using Perennials

Perennials are flower garden classics. You can grow them in beds and borders by themselves, in combination with annuals and bulbs, or with small shrubs, trees, and ground covers.

The majority of perennials are most valued for their flowers, though many produce attractive foliage. The art of garden design is partially a matter of combining plants with various blossom colors, textures, and shapes. With perennials—as opposed to annuals that bloom all season—timing also becomes an important design element. Because most perennials bloom for just a few weeks during a season, you'll need to choose plants that bloom at differing times to have garden color that lasts throughout the season.

Many perennials spend most of the growing season as a clump of stems and leaves, so good design also depends on choosing plants for their overall form, texture, and foliage. In fact, experienced garden designers treat plant form, texture, and foliage as the primary design qualities, and flower color as a secondary consideration. See pages 72–73 for examples of some of the most common plant and flower forms as well as illustrations of foliage qualities.

Choosing Plants. As you begin to choose perennials, make a list of plants that you've seen and liked in other gardens, books, and nursery catalogs. For each one, note the flower color and form, its time of bloom, the height and shape of the plant, and its foliage shape and color. This may sound like a lot of work, but it makes things much easier when you lay out your garden. To narrow down your list, weed out all of the plants that aren't suited to your growing conditions—temperatures, light, soil, and moisture.

If making this list seems daunting, rest assured that many a good garden has come into being through a process of trial and error. Don't be intimidated. After all, if you don't like a perennial in one spot, you can always dig it up and move it next year.

In this mixed border, left, perennials of different heights grow happily with roses. Shown are purple bellflowers and alliums, white China pinks, and, for foliage, lady's mantle and artemisia.

Add interest to your garden by combining plants with a variety of sizes, forms, and flower types, as well as a pleasing mix of colors.

An artful contrast of plant forms is achieved here by placing geraniums, aloe, and snakeplant in front of the yucca.

Plant Forms and Habits

Plants grow in a number of forms, or **growth habits**. Combining plants with a variety of growth habits adds interest to any planting. Choose from the following when planning your beds and borders:

1. **Mounded**—rounded and bushy, mounded plants form a cushion of foliage, usually close to the ground. Examples include bergenia (left) and lady's mantle (*Alchemilla*, right).

2. **Branching**—branching plants grow upright, with branched stems that give them an open appearance. Examples include false spirea (*Astilbe* species, left) and asters (right).

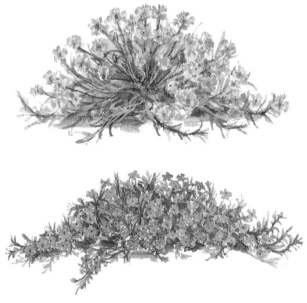

3. **Upright**—some plants are decidedly vertical with a narrow, upright form. Blazing star (*Liatris spicata*, left) and irises (right) are common upright plants.

4. **Trailing or matlike**—some plants stay low to the ground because they sprawl. Perennials that fit this category include these garden pinks (*Dianthus* species, top), and creeping phlox (*Phlox subulata*, bottom).

Seasonal Stars

Most perennials bloom for just two to three weeks a year, so if you want to have flowers blooming throughout the growing season, you'll need to combine plants with different bloom times. For a long display, interplant spring- and summer-blooming bulbs and annuals, many of which flower all summer long, with your perennials.

Orchestrating a succession of bloom from spring to fall can be a complicated job. To make it easier, first make a map of the garden-to-be. Draw in the locations of clumps of plants before you decide what they will be. After that, choose your color scheme and assign colors to the different plant clumps.

Now it's time to select plants. Choose those in the appropriate colors, being mindful to plan for a variety of blooming times, heights, plant forms, flower shapes, and textures. Use the boxes on pages 72–73 to guide you to perennials that flower at different times. (See pages 80–137 for profiles of these plants.)

Flower Forms

To make your garden more exciting, include flowers in a variety of shapes. Because many flowers are spherical, include some of the following:

Trumpet flowers, exemplified by daylilies and lilies, as illustrated above, have a narrow, tubular throat and widely flared, pointed petals.

Cup-shaped or bell-shaped flowers, such as those of tulips and this bellflower, look like upward-facing cups or dangling bells.

Spiky flowers are often clusters of small blooms growing along a vertical stem. Speedwells (*Veronica* species) and salvias, as illustrated above, are good examples of spiky flowers.

Daisylike flowers, such as tickseed and this boltonia, have round centers surrounded by lots of narrow petals. These blooms are actually composed of disc flowers, which make up the center; ray flowers, which often look like petals, circle the central disc flowers.

Tubular flowers are elongated and sometimes flare at the top. They are more narrow and slender than trumpets. Good examples are foxglove (*Digitalis* species) and this nicotiana.

PERENNIALS

BLOOMING SEASON

Spring-Blooming Perennials
Bergenia (*Bergenia* species)
Bleeding heart (*Dicentra spectabilis*)
Candytuft (*Iberis sempervirens*)
Christmas rose (*Helleborus niger*)
Cranesbill (*Geranium* species)
Columbine (*Aquilegia* species)
Foxglove (*Digitalis purpurea*)
Garden pinks (*Dianthus* species)
Goatsbeard (*Aruncus dioicus*)
Iceland poppy (*Papaver nudicaule*)
Iris (*Iris* species and cultivars)
Lady's mantle (*Alchemilla* species)
Lenten rose (*Helleborus orientalis*)
Oriental poppy (*Papaver orientale*)
Peony (*Paeonia* species)
Primrose (*Primula* species)
Red-hot poker (*Kniphofia uvaria*)
Salvia (*Salvia* species)
Sweet violet (*Viola odorata*)
Thrift (*Armeria maritima*)

Summer Perennials
Baby's breath (*Gypsophila paniculata*)
Balloon flower (*Platycodon grandiflorus*)
Beard-tongue (*Penstemon* species)
Bee balm (*Monarda didyma*)
Bellflower (*Campanula* species)
Blanket flower (*Gaillardia* × *grandiflora*)
Blazing star (*Liatris spicata*)
Butterfly weed (*Asclepias tuberosa*)
Cardinal flower (*Lobelia cardinalis*)
Catmint (*Nepeta* × *faassenii*)
Coneflower (*Rudbeckia* species)
Cranesbill (*Geranium* species)
Daylily (*Hemerocallis* cultivars)
Delphinium (*Delphinium* species)
False indigo (*Baptisia australis*)

False spirea (*Astilbe* species)
Fringed bleeding heart (*Dicentra eximia*)
Garden phlox (*Phlox paniculata*)
Garden pinks (*Dianthus* species)
Great blue lobelia (*Lobelia siphilitica*)
Lavender (*Lavandula* species)
Ligularia (*Ligularia* species)
Meadowsweet (*Filipendula* species)
Monkshood (*Aconitum* species)
Obedient plant (*Physostegia virginiana*)
Pincushion flower (*Scabiosa caucasica*)
Plantain lily (*Hosta* species)
Purple coneflower (*Echinacea purpurea*)
Red-hot poker (*Kniphofia uvaria*)
Rose mallow (*Hibiscus moscheutos*)
Russian sage (*Perovskia atriplicifolia*)
Salvia (*Salvia* species)
Showy primrose (*Oenothera speciosa*)
Speedwell (*Veronica* species)
Sundrops (*Oenothera fruticosa*)
Thrift (*Armeria maritima*)
Tickseed (*Coreopsis* species)
Tufted pansy (*Viola cornuta*)
Yarrow (*Achillea* species)

Late Summer and Fall Perennials
Aster (*Aster* species)
Autumn Joy stonecrop (*Sedum* 'Autumn Joy')
Blazing star (*Liatris* species)
Boltonia (*Boltonia asteroides*)
Bugbane (*Cimicifuga* species)
Coneflower (*Rudbeckia* species)
Garden chrysanthemum (*Chrysanthemum* × *grandiflorum*)
Goldenrod (*Solidago* cultivars)
Monkshood (*Aconitum* species)
Obedient plant (*Phystostegia virginiana*)

Blazing star

Bellflower

Bleeding heart

Tickseed

Wind flower

LONG-BLOOMING PERENNIALS

Some perennials bloom for an especially long time. They are beautiful in themselves but are also valuable because they help bridge gaps between more seasonal flowers that come and go. The following plants bloom continuously for four to six weeks, or produce flushes of bloom off and on all summer. Some plants, such as foxgloves and some delphiniums, often bloom a second time if cut back after flowering.

'Autumn Joy' stonecrop (*Sedum* 'Autumn Joy')
Balloon flower (*Platycodon grandiflorus*)
Bee balm (*Monarda didyma*)
Blanket flower (*Gaillardia* species)
Bugbane (*Cimicifuga racemosa*)
Catmint (*Nepeta* × *faassenii*)
Coneflower (*Rudbeckia fulgida* 'Goldsturm')
Daylily (*Hemerocallis* 'Stella de Oro', 'Black Eyed Stella', and 'Happy Returns')
Fringed bleeding heart (*Dicentra eximia*)
Lancaster geranium (*Geranium sanguineum* var. *striatum*)
Obedient plant (*Physostegia virginiana*)
Purple coneflower (*Echinacea purpurea*)
Speedwell (*Veronica spicata* 'Goodness Grows' and 'Sunny Border Blue')
Thrift (*Armeria maritima*)
Tickseed (*Coreopsis verticillata* 'Moonbeam')
Yarrow (*Achillea* species)

PERENNIALS

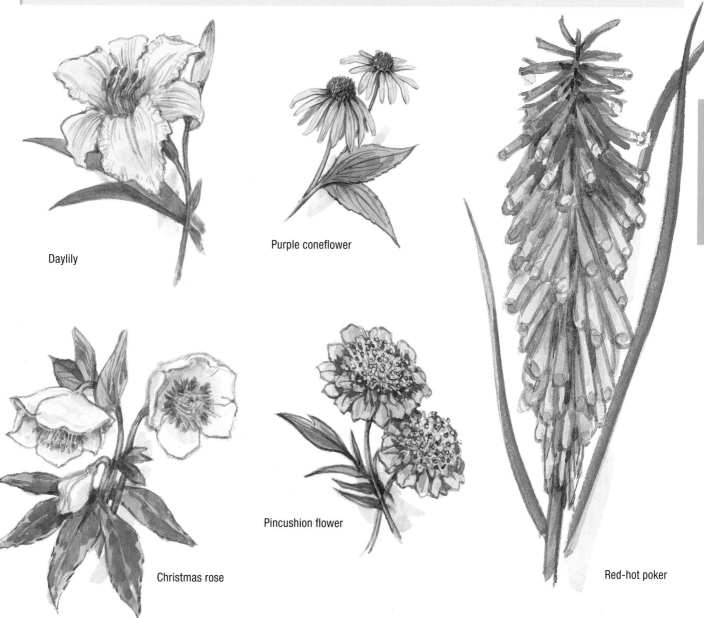

Daylily

Purple coneflower

Pincushion flower

Christmas rose

Red-hot poker

Consider the Foliage

Flowers come and go in a perennial garden, but from spring until fall the leaves are always there. One secret of great garden design is to choose plants for their foliage as well as their flowers. Here are some guidelines to get you started.

A variety of leaf sizes and textures adds interest. Big, bold leaves, such as those of bergenia or hosta, bring substance and drama to a composition. Delicate, feathery leaves, such as those of yarrows, fringed bleeding heart, and threadleaf coreopsis, look airy and light. Spiky, upright foliage, like that of irises, contributes vertical lines that add drama to a collection of low or mounded plants.

Different shades of green add complexity to a bed or border. Combine blue-green, gray-green, yellow-green, deep forest green, and light spring green for more appeal. Lighter greens can bring an area forward visually or light up a shady spot while darker greens can make areas recede. Once you begin to notice foliage colors, you'll appreciate their subtleties.

Colored foliage can add excitement or help soften bright colors. Chartreuse and golden leaves such as those of some hostas can light up a dim corner of the garden. Purple-red leaves, such as those of 'Husker Red' penstemon (*P. digitalis*), are dramatic. Silver foliage, such as that of artemisias, helps blend strong colors (especially in sunny gardens) and softens harsh contrasts; it imparts a feeling of misty softness to a more subdued garden of blue and pink flowers.

Variegated leaves, patterned with two or more colors, can add dimension. They may be edged, streaked, striped, splashed, spotted, flushed, or mottled with two, three, or even more colors. Use a light hand when adding variegated plants—too many make plantings look busy and chaotic and can actually detract from the flowers.

Growing Perennials

Growing perennials successfully is easy and straight-forward. You'll have to plant them well and then take care of them by fertilizing, pinching and pruning as necessary, preparing them for winter, and dividing them when they get crowded.

When you order plants from a nursery catalog, you may receive them planted in a pot. Or they may be dormant and in "bare-root" form, with their roots surrounded by a moist packing material and then wrapped in plastic or other material. Planting techniques are different for each type of plant.

A symphony of color from easy-to-grow plants, this garden includes Shasta daisies, columbines, campanula, and delphiniums.

Planting Bare-Root Perennials

DIFFICULTY LEVEL: EASY

how to

PERENNIALS

Tools and Materials: Bucket, hose or watering can, spade or shovel, mulch

1 Transplant bare-root plants in early spring, while they are still dormant. When the plants arrive, unpack them right away and examine them. The roots and crowns should be firm, with no mold or soft spots. Shoots should be woody and only a couple of inches long—new green growth means the plant is no longer dormant, and thus more susceptible to damage from cold weather or frost.

2 Set the plants in a bucket, and soak the roots overnight or for several hours. Dig the planting holes before you remove the plants from the bucket. Fill the holes with water, and let them drain. Follow the nursery's directions for planting depth—it's important for the plants' long-term health. Most plants thrive if the crown is level with the soil surface, but there are exceptions.

3 Make a mound of soil in the bottom of the hole, and set the plant on top, gently spreading the roots out over the mound. If the roots are too few or too short to cover a mound, just spread them out in the bottom of the hole. Work soil around and between the roots with your fingers. When the hole is half filled with soil, water again. When the water drains away, fill the hole the rest of the way with soil.

4 Firm the soil around the base of the plant, and then water again. If necessary, add more soil to level the surface. Water as necessary to keep the soil consistently moist for a few weeks as the plants settle in. If you're planting in the spring, make a berm around the planting hole to retain irrigation water. If you're planting in the fall, mulch the plant once the top inch of the ground is frozen.

Give plants enough space to develop to their full mature size. Crowded plants don't grow as well or flower as profusely and are more prone to disease.

This plant is pot-bound from being in the nursery container for too long.

Planting Container Plants

When choosing plants at a local garden center or nursery, look for sturdy, stocky plants with good color. Young, compact plants will be less likely to suffer transplant shock than older, bigger plants that are already in bloom. Avoid plants that look spindly, lanky, or pale; also avoid those with torn or broken leaves, signs of insect or disease damage, or moss growing on the soil.

When you buy perennials in pots at a local outlet, ask the staff whether the plants were field-grown or container-grown. If the plants were grown in the field and just potted up for sale, treat them like bare-root plants, and get them into the ground as soon as you can. With container-grown plants, you have a few more options.

Timing. Container-grown plants can be transplanted whenever the weather is not too stressful. It's best to plant when you can count on rain and moderate temperatures for a few weeks, so spring is a good planting time in most climates. Fall is also favorable except in Zones 5 and cooler. Where the heat is not too intense and the weather is not too dry, you can also plant in summer.

If you can't transplant right away, water and set your plants in a shady spot as soon as you get them home. When you're ready to plant, first decide exactly where they will go.

smart tip

Pinching Plants

To encourage a bushier, fuller form in perennials with a branched habit of growth, pinch off the growing tips of the young plants. Pinch off the tip of each stem to the next set of leaves. A new shoot will grow in each leaf axil, giving you two branches in the place of one. To make the plant even bushier, pinch the tips of these secondary shoots after they develop.

smart tip

Disbudding

Chrysanthemums are one of the plants that most benefit from pinching; a well-branched plant will produce many blooms. But if you want to grow exhibition-size mums, you want the plant to produce fewer, larger flowers. To get larger flowers, pinch off, or *disbud*, all but the side shoots from the main stems, and when flower buds form, remove all but one or two from each stem.

smart tip

Handling Pot-Bound Plants

If you find roots at the bottom of the root-ball that are tightly coiled around and around in the shape of the pot, you've unwittingly purchased a pot-bound plant. Simply putting the plant in the ground may not solve the problem—the roots may continue to grow in a circle, even in the garden (a condition known as "container habit"). A plant with container habit won't send new roots out into the soil. It can survive only as long as you give it regular doses of water and fertilizer, and only if the soil does not freeze to the depth of the root-ball in winter.

Here are some ways to help a pot-bound plant:

With a heavy-duty screwdriver, pry loose some of the largest, toughest roots in the center of the root mass. Pull them out and cut them off.

Gently untangle and spread out some of the roots.

If the plant has a taproot, straighten it out as much as you can without breaking it.

With a sharp knife, make 2 or 3 vertical cuts up into the root-ball from the bottom. Gently spread the roots when you set the plant in the hole.

Cut off any roots growing on top of the soil or wrapped around the plant's stem.

PERENNIALS

Set the pots out on top of the soil surface to refine your arrangement. Once you're satisfied with the design, dig the planting holes before proceeding.

Remove the plant from the pot. Place your fingers around the stem, and hold the edges of the pot or soil with one hand while you turn over the pot with your other hand. Let the plant slide out of its pot. If the plant sticks, tap the bottom of the pot with a trowel handle or slide a knife blade vertically around the inside of the pot to separate the root-ball from it. Once the plant is out of the pot, *gently* squeeze and pull apart the root-ball a bit to loosen and separate the roots; then set the plant in its hole, keeping the root-ball as intact as you can.

Set the plant at the same depth it was growing in its pot. Fill the hole, working the soil in around the root-ball with your fingers. Water well; then add more soil if necessary to fill the hole to the top.

Maintaining Perennials

Although perennials remain in the garden year after year once planted, they do need some regular maintenance in order to continue looking their best. Most perennials benefit from watering during dry spells and periodic fertilizing. Some plants benefit from having their stems pinched back when they are young—to encourage bushier growth. Many bloom longer if you deadhead them. Most perennials need to be dug up and their root clumps divided periodically to keep them vigorous. It's also a good idea to cut back the stems of perennials as they die back for the winter. Not only does this give you a neat looking garden all winter, it also removes some hiding places for pests and plant diseases. Finally, in climates where the ground freezes in winter, a good mulch can protect perennial roots from suffering damage during the cold months.

Fertilizing Perennials. All perennial garden areas benefit from a topdressing of compost or aged manure in early spring to maintain the soil's organic matter content and make better use of any fertilizers you apply, whether synthetic or organic.

If you use organic fertilizers, add them to the soil when you first prepare it or when you set out new plants. You can also topdress with compost two or three times during the growing season or apply liquid fertilizers such as seaweed products and fish emulsion as foliar feeds, spraying them onto the leaves as plants grow. Follow package directions for dilution and application rates, and spray only before the sun is up or on cloudy (but not rainy) days.

If you use synthetic fertilizers, apply them when you set out new plants or when established plants begin to show new growth in spring. Thereafter, in sandy, poor to moder-

Cut back perennials at the end of the growing season. These Siberian irises are ready for cutting back in fall, when the leaves begin to yellow.

ately fertile soils, fertilize every four to six weeks at half the rate recommended on the label. In heavier soils with marginal fertility, fertilize every six to eight weeks. In good soil, fertilize every two months or so at half-strength if it is sandy, but every eight to ten weeks if it is heavy. No matter what your soil type, stop fertilizing six weeks before the average date of the first fall frost in your area.

Fall Cleanup. At the end of the growing season, it's time to clean up the garden and prepare it for winter. In cold climates, cut back all the herbaceous plants in fall, to 3 to 4 inches from the ground. Wait until early spring to cut back shrubby plants such as lavender; fall pruning could induce these plants to send out new growth that would in all likelihood be damaged by winter cold. In warm climates, cut back spring and summer bloomers in autumn, but wait until they finish flowering to trim later bloomers. No matter where you live, fall is a good time to remove stakes and clean up any weeds or debris that have found their way into the garden.

Winter mulches. After the soil freezes at least an inch deep, spread a winter mulch of evergreen boughs or a 6- to 8-inch layer of loose straw or shredded leaves throughout the garden. This mulch protects the dormant roots because it prevents winter sunlight from warming the underlying soil, keeping it more consistently frozen. When the soil experiences repeated cycles of freezing, thawing, and refreezing over the course of the winter, it can warp and buckle. This action can tear roots or heave (push) them right out of the ground. Thus exposed, the roots can be damaged or killed by cold temperatures and drying winter winds.

Fertilize new plants after you transplant them. Spread the fertilizer around the plants, and scratch it into the soil.

Dividing Perennials

As perennials grow year after year, most of them expand, forming ever-larger clumps of roots. After a number of years, as the clump of roots becomes crowded and the older central portions grow woody, the plants tend to grow less vigorously and flower less lavishly. You may even notice that the stems appear to grow in a ring, with none growing up from the central part of the crown. When this happens, it's time to give the plants a new lease on life by dividing them. Division is also a great way to increase your stock of plants, because what was one plant becomes two, three, or even five new ones. How often plants need to be divided varies widely; chrysanthemums need to be divided every year or two, while peonies can remain in place for decades without needing division.

If you live where autumn weather is cool and frost comes early, it's best to divide your perennial plants in spring. But in Zones 6 and warmer, you can divide in early- to mid-fall. (In unseasonably warm years, Zone 5 gardeners can divide fast-growing plants in fall.) Transplant the divisions early enough so that the divided plants have several weeks to send out new roots and establish themselves in the soil before it freezes.

how to

Dividing Perennials

DIFFICULTY LEVEL: MODERATE

PERENNIALS

Tools and Materials: Spade or shovel, pruning shears, bucket, knife

1 To minimize plant stress, try to divide and transplant on a cloudy day. Unless it has rained recently, water the plants well two or three days beforehand. Cut back stems by about one-third to make plants easier to handle. Because this decreases water loss from the leaves, it eases transplant shock.

2 On moving day, first dig holes for the new transplants. Then loosen the roots by digging around the outside of the clump to be divided with a spade or shovel. Dig straight down until you are below the root-ball; then angle the shovel beneath the plant. Push back and forth to loosen the plant; then lift it out of the soil.

3 Shake off loose soil; then divide the clump into sections that have both roots and growth buds. Pull apart loose clumps with your fingers, but use a sharp knife to cut apart dense clumps. If the clump is large and tough, get an assistant to help you push two garden forks back to back into the middle of it and pry apart.

4 When dividing a number of plants, keep a pail of water or a wet towel handy to soak or wrap up divisions until you get them replanted. Discard the old, woody central parts of the clump; replant only the firm, young, outer portions. Before replanting, check the roots and prune any broken or straggly ones.

5 Water the planting hole, set the division, and gently fill in around the roots with soil. Plant the divisions at the same depth they were growing before or with their crowns even with the soil surface. Water well, but do not fertilize for a few weeks. In dry weather, water as necessary to keep the soil evenly moist.

6 Label the new transplants in the garden and on your garden map so you'll know what you planted where next spring. Make notes about any special care the plant will need in the following year. If you live where the ground freezes, wait until the top inch or so is frosty before mulching to protect the plant over winter.

Achillea

Achillea species
YARROW

These perennials are grown for their flat-topped, tight clusters of tiny white, pink, yellow, red, cream, and burnt-orange flowers. Most species of yarrow grow tall. Their foliage is fernlike—toothed or divided. In some species it's very finely divided and feathery- looking. The leaves are aromatic when crushed, and some yarrows are grown in herb gardens for their healing properties.

Hardiness: Zones 3 to 10.

Blooming Time: Midsummer; until fall for some cultivars if deadheaded regularly.

Height: 1½ to 4 feet, depending on species.

Spacing: 1½ feet.

Light: Full sun.

Soil: Well-drained, average fertility.

Moisture: Average; tolerates some drought.

Garden Uses: Grow yarrow in the middle to the back of beds and borders. The golden yellow cultivars are lovely with blue and violet flowers, and the pale yellow 'Moonshine' is especially versatile. Yarrows are good cut flowers and can also be dried.

Comments: Yarrows tolerate hot, dry conditions and do well in dry, exposed locations.

'Summer Pastels'

smart tip

DRYING YARROW

Yarrow air-dries beautifully. Gather cut stems in bunches with rubber bands, and hang upside down in a dry, airy place.

Recommended Cultivars: 'Coronation Gold', to 3 feet, deep golden yellow.

A. filipendulina 'Gold Plate', to 4 feet, golden yellow.

A. millefolium, to 3 feet, 'Cerise Queen', rose pink; 'Lilac Beauty', lilac; 'Red Beauty', crimson.

A. 'Moonshine', to 2 feet, light lemon yellow.

A. ptarmica 'The Pearl', 1½ to 2 feet, double round white flower heads.

Galaxy Series, hybrids of *A.* 'Taygetea' and *A. millefolium*, salmon, pink and yellow.

smart tip

CUTTING YARROW FOR THE VASE

For cut flowers, gather yarrow stems when about half the florets in the cluster have opened and before any pollen is evident. The foliage is also attractive in arrangements.

'Arendsii'

Aconitum

Aconitum species
MONKSHOOD

The deep blue flowers of monkshoods are evocatively named—they resemble little helmets or a monk's cowl. They are borne on erect spikes rising on tall stems above glossy, dark green, lobed or deeply cut leaves.

Hardiness: Zones 3 to 7.

Blooming Time: Mid- to late-summer, sometimes into early fall.

Height: 3 to 4 feet, depending on cultivar.

Spacing: 2 feet.

Light: Full sun to partial shade; some shade needed in warmer climates.

Soil: Fertile, humusy.

Moisture: Even.

Garden Uses: Handsome plants for the middle to the back of beds and borders, monkshoods are also lovely additions to woodland gardens and shady beds and borders where the overhead tree canopy is not too dense. Monkshoods are especially valuable for their late-season bloom that adds color to the garden when many perennials are winding down. Their deep blue-violet color combines especially well with soft pink or white Japanese anemones or with golden flowers such as goldenrod and rudbeckia.

Comments: All parts of the plants are extremely poisonous when ingested; don't plant in locations where small

children, unsuspecting guests, and pets can reach it. Even coming in contact with the foliage can cause skin irritation in sensitive individuals. If deer are a problem in your garden, however, monkshood can be a good choice—deer will not usually eat these plants.

The helmet-shaped flowers of monkshood

Plant bare-root plants in fall, except in the coldest climates. Or purchase container-grown specimens, and plant them in spring. Mulch in summer to help keep the roots cool. The plants don't like heat and generally grow best in cooler climates. Divide every three to four years but only if absolutely necessary because they are overcrowded. Handle the roots carefully—they don't like to be disturbed.

Recommended Cultivars: *A. × cammarum:* 'Bicolor', 3 feet, white flowers edged with blue; 'Bressingham Spire', 3 feet, violet-blue, long blooming; 'Eleonara', 3 feet, white.

A. carmichaelii, Azure monkshood: 4 feet, purplish blue. 'Arendsii' is late blooming, to 4 feet, and has rich blue flowers.

A. napellus: 3 feet, violet-blue; 'Carneum', 3 to 4 feet, pink; 'Newry Blue', 3 feet, clear blue.

Monkshood grows well in partially shaded beds or borders.

0016 Aconitum Monkshood Newry Blue

"WARNING - Keep out of reach of children. Seeds may be harmful or fatal if swallowed." Antidote: Induce vomiting and call physician immediately

Label warning

PERENNIALS

Alchemilla

Alchemilla mollis
(formerly *A. vulgaris*)
LADY'S MANTLE

These low, mounded plants are grown primarily for their rounded, lobed, grayish green leaves. The combination of plant habit and color make lady's mantles decorative all through the season. In late spring they produce airy clusters of small chartreuse flowers on slender, branched stems.

Hardiness: Zones 3 to 9.

Blooming Time: Late spring to early summer.

Height: 10 inches to 1½ feet.

Spacing: 1 to 1½ feet.

Light: Full sun in cool climates, partial shade elsewhere.

Soil: Well-drained, average fertility.

Moisture: Average to even.

Garden Uses: Grow lady's mantle as an edging or in the front of a bed or border. They look good with almost every color and make a good filler plant, both in the garden and in the vase.

Comments: These small plants have a charming ability to hold glistening drops of rain or dew on their leaves. They form low, spreading clumps and may self-sow. Lady's mantle grows best where summers are not too terribly hot.

Recommended Cultivars: No cultivars are commonly available.

Lady's mantle leaves after a rain

smart tip

VOLUNTEER LADY'S MANTLE PLANTS

Lady's mantle self-seeds easily, as evidenced by the volunteer plants growing in the crevices on the steps. Deadhead the blooms before they set seed to avoid volunteer plants.

The spring blooms of lady's mantle look like a lovely chartreuse green froth rising above the leaves.

Aquilegia

Aquilegia species
COLUMBINE

Columbines are native to the mountainous regions of the world. Their gracefully spurred blooms are a highlight of many spring flower gardens. A number of species are native to North America, and a host of hybrid cultivars is available in a lovely range of colors. The flowers are carried at the top of slender stalks rising from a low mound of distinctively scalloped leaves. The handsome leaves in combination with the graceful plant habit make columbines attractive all through the season.

Hardiness: Zones 3 to 10, varies with species.

Blooming Time: Spring to early summer.

Height: 1 to 3 feet.

Spacing: 1 to 1½ feet.

Light: Full sun in cooler climates, partial shade elsewhere.

Soil: Well-drained, average fertility.

Moisture: Average.

Garden Uses: Grow columbines in the front to middle ground of beds and borders, in rock gardens, and in cottage gardens.

Comments: Columbines self-sow readily in many gardens and cross freely with one another. For best results, divide or replace with new plants every three or four years. If leaf miners attack, remove and destroy affected leaves at the first sign of tunneling.

McKana Giant hybrid columbines

Recommended Cultivars: 'Blue Butterflies', slightly over a foot tall, blue with white edges.

A. caerulea: Rocky Mountain columbine, to 2½ feet, white petals with lavender to blue spurs.

A. flabellata: 'Alba', Japanese fan columbine, 1 to 1½ feet, white.

Biedermeier Group, 1½ feet, white-tipped petals, many colors.

'Hensol Harebell', 2½ to 3 feet, deep violet-blue, blooms longer — until midsummer in most areas.

McKana Giant hybrids, to 2½ feet, light and dark pink, bi-colors of red, yellow, and blue.

Music hybrids, 1½ feet, yellow and cream, red-and-white, pink-and-white, blue-and-white, pink-and-yellow, red-and-yellow.

Music strain

smart tip

SAVING COLUMBINE SEEDS

When seedpods are dry and seeds rattle inside them, clip the stems and sprinkle the seeds over the garden where you want new columbines next year.

Thrift

Armeria

Armeria maritima
THRIFT, SEA PINK

These low-growing plants bear 1-inch round, pom-pom shaped clusters of small flowers on tall slender stems. The mounded plants form tufts of grassy, evergreen leaves. The plants remain attractive all through the season and can double as a ground cover on slopes or in other hard-to-mow locations. They tolerate both salty and dry soils, too.

Hardiness: Zones 3 to 10.

Blooming Time: Late spring to early summer.

Height: 6 inches to slightly over a foot.

Spacing: 8 inches to 1 foot.

Light: Full sun.

Soil: Well-drained, sandy to loamy, average fertility.

Moisture: Average to slightly dry.

Garden Uses: Grow thrift in the front of beds and borders, in seashore gardens, in rock gardens, on slopes, or as edging plants.

Taller varieties are good for cutting, and cut flowers last up to a week in the vase. Cut the flowers when they have just begun to open, and condition them before arranging by standing them in fresh water nearly up to the base of the flower heads for several hours. The small, round flowerheads make good fillers in arrangements of larger daisylike and spiky flowers.

Comments: Deadhead to encourage reblooming. Thrift flowers cut well and add nice form and color to arrangements. Divide plants every few years.

Recommended Cultivars: 'Alba', 6 inches, white; 'Ornament', 1 foot, rose pink, white, and deep salmon.

The combination of thrift and catmint is particularly effective with this pebble mulch. Both plants fare well in less-than-ideal soils, making this a good combination for areas with dry or thin soils.

how to

Plant Armeria Seeds   DIFFICULTY LEVEL: EASY

Tools and Materials: Seeds, soil mix, flat, plastic wrap, newspaper

1 Sow the seeds indoors in a container of moist, porous potting medium. Cover with plastic film to retain soil moisture and humidity. Seeds will germinate in approximately 10 days.

2 Thrift seeds need darkness to germinate. Cover the flat with layers of newspaper to block light.

'Powis Castle'

'Silver King'

Southernwood

Artemisia

Artemisia species
ARTEMISIA

Artemisia is a large genus of aromatic plants grown primarily for their foliage. The varied plant habits, leaf forms, and foliage colors make them extremely useful in flower gardens. Artemisias may be low and mounded or tall and upright; the foliage can be cut or lobed or finely dissected and lacy-looking. Colors range from green through gray-green and silvery white. The plants produce tiny clusters of yellow or white flowers, but most gardeners remove them because the flowers themselves are not particularly attractive and also because they can distract from the overall appearance of the plant.

Hardiness: Zones 4 to 10, depending on species.

Height: 1 to 5 feet, depending on species.

Spacing: 1 to 2 feet.

Light: Full sun.

Soil: Well-drained, sandy, average to poor fertility.

Moisture: Average to occasionally dry.

Garden Uses: An asset in beds and borders, the muted foliage is a good blender for bright-colored flowers and brings a soft, misty feeling to a garden of pink and blue flowers. Plant artemisias in the front, middle, or back of the garden, depending on their height.

Comments: Artemisias are easy to grow. If plants start to look straggly in hot, humid weather, cut them back to stimulate new growth. Artemisias are also easy to dry for use in winter wreaths and arrangements. Dry them by hanging in a dark, airy location. If you plan to use them for a wreath, tie the stems onto a circular form while they are still green and let them dry that way.

Recommended Cultivars: *A. abrotanum:* southernwood, to 4 feet; *A. schmidtiana:* 'Silver Mound', 1 foot; A. 'Powis Castle', 2 to 3 feet, feathery, finely dissected leaves; *A. ludoviciana* var. *albula*, 'Silver King', to 3 feet, silvery white toothed leaves.

smart tip

PRUNING ARTEMISIA FLOWER STALKS

Blooms on this 'Silver Mound' artemisia rise above the silvery gray foliage, giving a ragged look to what was a tidy mound of delicate leaves. It's easy to prune them off to retain the plant's good looks.

Aruncus

Aruncus dioicus
GOATSBEARD

Goatsbeard

Goatsbeards are bushy, shrubby plants with toothed, compound, rough-textured leaves. Their feathery clusters of tiny white flowers are similar to those of astilbe. Goatsbeard is an American native, hailing from eastern North America.

Goatsbeard plants are either male or female. Both kinds bloom, but the flowers of female plants are more drooping and a slightly greenish white color. Flowers of male plants are creamy white with prominent stamens.

Hardiness: Zones 3 to 9.

Blooming Time: Late spring to early summer.

Height: 4 to 6 feet.

Spacing: 3 feet.

Light: Full sun to partial shade; in warmer climates, provide some shade, especially in the afternoon.

Soil: Fertile, humusy.

Moisture: Even to abundant.

Garden Uses: Goatsbeard makes a good background or screening plant; it can take the place of a shrub in summer borders. It is also a great plant for a woodland garden.

Goatsbeard flowers are good for cutting, too, and can be dried as well. Cut the flowers when they are just beginning to open, early in the morning if possible. Condition them before arranging by immediately placing them in a container of water filled to just below the base of the flower heads. Leave the stems in the deep water for several hours. Then strip off all the leaves that would be underwater in the vase, and recut the stems when you arrange the flowers in a vase.

If you wish to dry goatsbeard, use silica gel rather than air-drying the flowers. The flowers dry quickly, so check them frequently after the first few days to prevent them from becoming brittle.

Comments: After several years, if flowering declines and plants look less vigorous, divide them in early spring while still dormant.

Recommended Cultivars: 'Kneiffii' grows only to 3 feet.

---

how to — Divide Goatsbeard Plants
DIFFICULTY LEVEL: EASY

Tools and Materials: Spade or shovel, pruning shears

1 When goatsbeard plants become crowded, dig the clumps and divide them. Grasp near the base of the stem, and pull or cut the root clump into sections.

2 Make certain that each section contains both roots and stems. Cut back the stems for easier handling, before or after digging. Replant the divisions, and water them well.

Butterfly weed

Asclepias

Asclepias tuberosa
BUTTERFLY WEED

Like other milkweeds, butterfly weeds grow in clumps of sturdy upright stems lined with narrow oblong leaves. Butterfly weeds are smaller than many milkweeds. In summer they produce many dense clusters of bright orange, yellow-orange, or red-orange flowers that attract butterflies.

Hardiness: Zones 3 to 10.

Blooming Time: Mid- to late-summer.

Height: 1½ to 2½ feet.

Spacing: 6 inches to 1 foot.

Light: Full sun.

Soil: Well-drained, sandy or coarse-textured, average fertility.

Moisture: Average to low; tolerates drought when established.

Garden Uses: Plant butterfly weed near the front of an informal garden, especially one designed to attract butterflies.

Comments: Butterfly weed must have good drainage; it will not thrive or even survive long in wet conditions. Start new plants from seed; the tuberous roots do not like to be disturbed. Mulch roots over the winter in Zones 3 to 6 to protect them from heaving.

Recommended Cultivars: Gay Butterflies mixture is a mix of red, orange, and yellow shades.

Butterfly on butterfly weed

smart tip

SAVING BUTTERFLY WEED SEEDS

Asclepias seeds blow away in the slightest wind when they are mature. To keep them, use a rubber band to tie a paper bag over the seed stalks when they begin to turn brown. When the pods split, the seeds will fall into the bag.

PERENNIALS

Aster

Aster species
MICHAELMAS DAISY

The best perennial asters for gardens belong to three different species: *A × frikartii*, Frikart's aster; *A. novae-angliae*, New England aster; and *A. novi-belgii*, New York aster. All produce daisylike flowers with many narrow petals or ray flowers around a central disk. Plants bloom in shades of purple, blue, pink, and red, as well as white. Asters are upright and branching, and their somewhat sparse foliage can sometimes make them a bit weedy looking.

Hardiness: Zones 4 to 8, depending on cultivar.

Blooming Time: Late summer into autumn.

Height: 1 to 4 feet.

Spacing: 1 to 2 feet.

Light: Full sun.

Soil: Well-drained, average fertility.

Moisture: Evenly moist.

Garden Uses: Plant asters in the middle or back of beds and borders, depending on height.

Comments: For best bloom, divide asters every two or three years in the early spring. Discard the old, woody central parts of the crowns, and replant the vigorous outer sections. Stake plants as they grow. Pinch back the stems to keep them more compact and encourage flowering.

New England aster

Recommended Cultivars: *A. × frikartii* 'Wonder of Staffa', to 2½ feet, lavender-blue; 'Mönch', 2 to 2½ feet, light lilac-blue.

A. novae-angliae 'Alma Pötschke', 3 feet, rose pink; 'Harrington's Pink', 4 feet, clear pink; 'September Ruby', 3½ feet, deep crimson.

A. novi-belgii 'Audrey', 15 inches, lavender-blue; 'Boningale White', 3½ feet, white, double; 'Crimson Brocade', 3 feet, crimson; 'Patricia Ballard', 2 feet, deep pink; 'Professor Kippenburg', 1 foot, light blue. 'Coombe Violet', 2 feet, blue-purple.

'Mönch'   'Coombe Violet'

smart tip

ATTRACTING BUTTERFLIES

Butterflies need late season food sources as much as they need the early- and mid-season bloomers. Asters, particularly in combination with goldenrod, make a pretty display while also providing an excellent source of nectar.

Astilbe

Astilbe species
FALSE SPIREA

These lovely, feathery perennial garden favorites, sometimes (incorrectly) called spireas, are native to China and Japan. *Astilbe* plants are noted for their tall, airy panicles of tiny fluffy flowers that arise from a mass of glossy green, toothed foliage.

Hardiness: Zones 4 to 8.

Blooming Time: Early- to mid-summer.

Height: 1 to 4 feet.

Spacing: 10 inches to 2 feet.

Light: Partial shade; full sun may burn the foliage and bleach out the flower colors.

Soil: Fertile, rich in organic matter.

Moisture: Abundant.

Garden Uses: Use *Astilbe* plants in the perennial border or massed in damp, shady spots. Place the dwarf cultivars in the front of beds and borders or use them as an edging. *Astilbe* plants make good cut flowers and can be dried for winter bouquets. For fresh arrangements, cut flower heads when they are just beginning to open. If possible, cut in the morning or early evening. As soon as you cut them, plunge the stems into a container of cool water up to the base of the flowers. Let the flowers stand in the water for several hours; then remove the leaves; recut and split the stem ends; and immediately arrange the flowers.

Dry *Astilbe* blossoms in silica gel—they usually shrink and lose their form when air-dried.

'Purple Lance'

Comments: Propagate *Astilbe* by division in spring or fall. In Zone 7 and warmer, the plants may not live long. You can often prolong their lifespan as well as keep them healthier if you provide them with at least 1½ inches of water (3 gallons per square foot of root area) each week.

Recommended Cultivars: The many hybrids of *A. × arendsii* bloom in early summer in shades of pink, rose, red, and white.

A. chinensis: 'Fanal', 1 to 1½ feet, light pink, blooms in midsummer; 'Pumila', to 1 foot, raspberry pink, mid- to late-summer.

A. chinensis var. *taquetii*, 3 to 4 feet, dense, upright panicles, 'Superba', rosy purple; 'Purple Lance', deep rosy purple.

A. simplicifolia: 'Sprite', to 1 foot, pink.

PERENNIALS

how to

Divide *Astilbe* Plants

DIFFICULTY LEVEL: EASY

Tools and Materials: Spade or shovel, pruning shears

1 *Astilbe* responds well to division. Dig crowded clumps in spring or fall. Cut clumps into sections with a sharp shovel.

2 Drive the shovel blade completely through the root clump. Then prune out the old woody parts, and replant the younger divisions.

'Fanal'

Baptisia

Baptisia australis
BLUE FALSE INDIGO

This perennial grows into a clump of stems that looks something like a bush. Given its height and width, it can pinch-hit for a narrow shrub in the summer garden. It bears attractive oval, gray-green, three-part leaves on its upright stems. The spikes of striking violet-blue flowers resemble those of lupines or peas, and the individual flowers are formed like those of peas and beans. Flowers are followed by pealike pods that rattle when dry.

Hardiness: Zones 3 to 9.

Blooming Time: Early summer.

Height: 3 to 5 feet.

Spacing: 2 to 3 feet.

Light: Full sun to partial shade; some shade is beneficial in warm climates.

Soil: Well-drained, mildly acid.

Moisture: Average; tolerates some drought but does not tolerate wet soil.

Garden Uses: Grow blue false indigo in place of a small shrub in a mixed bed or border, in the back of the perennial garden, or in a row to make a summertime hedge. Both the flowers and seedpods are good for cutting; the seedpods make a lovely addition to fall and winter bouquets.

Comments: Attractive when in bloom and pleasantly green the rest of the season, false indigo is easy to grow as long as you can give it well-drained soil. Don't deadhead if you want to use the seedpods in dried arrangements or retain them for late-season interest in the fall garden.

Recommended Cultivars: No cultivars are commonly available, although there are two white-flowered *Baptisia* species—*B. alba* and *B. lactea.* The flowers of *B. alba* hang down, and the blooms of both species may be marked with blue streaks.

Blue false indigo

smart tip

CUTTING BAPTISIA PODS

Baptisia **seedpods are decorative in fresh or dried flower arrangements. Cut stems containing a group of pods.**

Pealike *Baptisia* flowers

Bergenia

Bergenia cordifolia
HEARTLEAF BERGENIA

Bergenias send up loose, rounded clusters of pink flowers at the top of upright stems that rise from clumps of thick, rounded, glossy green, cabbage-shaped leaves. The leaves turn coppery bronze to reddish in fall.

Hardiness: Zones 3 to 9.

Blooming Time: Early spring.

Height: 1 to 1½ feet

Spacing: 1 foot.

Light: Full sun to partial shade; some afternoon shade is beneficial in warm climates.

Soil: Well-drained, humusy, but tolerates a range of soils and pH.

Moisture: Average to moist.

Garden Uses: Heartleaf bergenia is attractive in the front of the garden, along a sidewalk or path, or under deep-rooted trees or shrubs.

Bergenia cordifolia 'Perfecta'

Comments: The plants are usually evergreen in mild climates and semi-evergreen elsewhere. They spread a bit to form clumps. Slugs can be a problem. Propagate by division of crowded clumps.

Recommended Cultivars: 'Perfecta', pinkish red flowers; 'Bressingham Ruby', rosy pink flowers and in winter, reddish leaves; 'Bressingham White', white flowers; 'Purpurea', deep pink flowers and leaves tinged with purple; and 'Sunningdale', carmine flowers topping red stems and reddish winter leaves.

smart tip

SITING HEARTLEAF BERGENIA PLANTS

Bergenia plants are equally at home in gardens exposed to morning sun (top) as they are in those that are partially shaded for much of the day (above). No matter where you grow them, plant in masses to get the strongest effect.

Boltonia

Boltonia asteroides
BOLTONIA

Boltonias are tall branching plants covered with blue-green to gray-green leaves that are narrow and lance-shaped and up to 5 inches long. Late in the season the plants bear thin-petaled, small daisylike flowers. They give a light, airy feeling to beds and borders when most perennials are finished blooming.

Hardiness: Zones 4 to 9.

Blooming Time: Late summer to mid-autumn.

Height: 3 to 5 feet.

Spacing: 1½ to 2 feet.

Light: Full sun; tolerates partial shade in warm climates.

Soil: Any average soil.

Moisture: Average, tolerates somewhat dry to somewhat moist conditions.

Garden Uses: Plant boltonia in the back of beds and borders in naturalistic gardens, or use it as a hedge by spacing plants close together. The species is big and rather weedy-looking; choose the tidier-growing cultivars instead.

The flowers are also good for cutting and look pretty in the vase. They are particulary good fillers in combinations with spiky blooms such as salvia or veronica, late-blooming lilies, yarrow, or bachelor's buttons, and dahlias and chrysanthemums.

'Snowbank'

Comments: Boltonia plants are practically maintenance free. Boltonia can tolerate heat and humidity when required. Divide, if necessary, in early spring. The strong stems need no staking.

Recommended Cultivars: 'Pink Beauty', 5 feet, pink flowers; 'Snowbank', 3 to 4 feet, white flowers.

'Pink Beauty'   **Boltonia** looks best in informal gardens.

how to

Transplant Bellflower Seedlings
DIFFICULTY LEVEL: EASY

Tools and Materials: Seedlings, mulch materials

1 Transplant perennial *Campanula* seedlings in either the early spring or fall. Leave enough space between the seedlings so they can grow for several years before they need dividing.

2 Mulch the transplanted plants as soon as possible, particularly if you are planting in fall. Mulches keep weeds down during the summer and protect roots from heaving during the cold months.

Campanula

Campanula species
BELLFLOWER, HAREBELL

Known for their old-fashioned cup- or bell-shaped flowers, bellflowers grow in a range of sizes and habits—from small, low growers for rock gardens to tall, upright species for the middle of beds and borders. Most are erect and branching, though not really bushy, and have narrow to oblong leaves of medium to deep green.

Hardiness: Zones 4 to 8.

Blooming Time: Early to late summer, depending on species.

Height: 6 inches to 4 feet.

Spacing: 10 inches to 1½ feet.

Light: Full sun to partial shade.

Soil: Average to fertile, well-drained, humusy.

Moisture: Average to moist.

Garden Uses: Plant low-growers as an edging, in the front of beds and borders, or in rock gardens. Use taller species in the middle ground of beds and borders. Bellflowers are delightful additions to cottage gardens.

Comments: Generally easy to grow. Some taller types need staking. Many will repeat bloom if deadheaded.

Recommended Cultivars: *C. carpatica*, Carpathian harebell: 6 to 10 inches; 'Alba', white; 'White Clips', white; 'China Doll', lavender-blue; 'Blue Clips', blue, midsummer, rebloooming till fall.

C. glomerata, Clustered bellflower: 2 feet, blue or white.

C. lactiflora, Milky bellflower: 3 to 4 feet, blue or white, arching stems with clusters of flowers near the ends; 'Loddon Anna', to 4 feet, light pink; 'Prichard's Variety', 3 to 4 feet, blue-violet.

C. persicifolia, Peach-leaved bellflower: 2 to 3 feet; 'Alba', white; 'Grandiflora Alba', white; 'Telham Beauty', lavender-blue.

Milky bellflower

Carpathian harebell, 'Alba'

Clustered bellflower

Chrysanthemum

Chrysanthemum × *grandiflorum*
GARDEN MUM

Chrysanthemums are the undisputed queens of the fall garden and a staple of both the cut-flower garden and gift plant market. Commercial greenhouses force mums into bloom year-round, but for gardeners, chrysanthemums and autumn are synonymous. Their rich, earthy colors are unbeatable in late summer and fall. There are many, many cultivars available, and a large assortment of plant heights, flower forms, and flower sizes. They are easy to overwinter but some people treat them as annuals and buy new ones each year.

Hardiness: Zones 4 to 10.

Blooming Time: Late summer to fall.

Height: 1 to 6 feet.

Spacing: 1½ feet.

Light: Full sun is crucial—even a little bit of shade will interfere with performance.

Soil: Rich, very well-drained, light and loose.

Moisture: Even.

Garden Uses: Mums are a classic for late-season beds and borders. When grown as annuals, they make good plants for containers.

Comments: Start preparing the mum's soil a couple of months or even a season before you intend to plant. Dig plenty of compost, leaf mold, or well-aged manure into the bed, and check the drainage; mums are subject to root rot in wet soils. If your soil is heavy, consider making raised beds.

'Blanche Poitevene'

'Autumn Kimberly' 'Louisa'

'Legend'

'Deanne Joy'

Individual plants bloom for three or four weeks each, but choosing cultivars with different blooming periods can give you chrysanthemum flowers from late summer well into fall, through several frosts.

A few weeks before planting in spring, fertilize the planting area with an all-purpose fertilizer and some superphosphate. If you garden organically, incorporate rock phosphate into the soil when you dig in the compost or manure, and add greensand to the top few inches when you plant.

Start your chrysanthemum bed with plants or rooted cuttings from a nursery. Hybrid cultivars won't come true from seed, and plants from the florist don't often survive in the garden. Spacing distance will vary according to the sizes of the cultivars you are growing.

During the growing season, feed the plants weekly with half-strength fish emulsion or use a commercial timed-release fertilizer twice during the season. Make sure the plants get plenty of moisture, especially during hot summer weather. Keeping plants mulched helps ensure even moisture levels.

Most chrysanthemums need to be pinched back. When the plant is at least 5 inches tall, pinch out the growing tip to force it to branch. Pinch the plant at least once more as it grows, and pinch the tips evenly all over the plant to give it a symmetrical shape. Where the growing season is short, stop pinching in midsummer so that the plants will bloom before the onset of cold weather.

In cold-climate gardens, a good winter mulch is important because the plants are not always entirely hardy. As an alternative to mulching, you can dig up the plants after they bloom and put them in a cold frame for winter.

Recommended Cultivars: The range of cultivars expands each year. Choose according to color, flower form, and plant habit.

'Coral Rynoon'

'Yellow Illusion'

'Pennine Oriel'

PERENNIALS

Cimicifuga

Cimicifuga species
BUGBANE, SNAKEROOT

Bugbanes deserve to be more widely grown. For much of the growing season, the plants form neat mounds of toothed, divided leaves similar to those of astilbes. Then, late in the season, they send up tall, slender, candlelike spires of tiny, fluffy-looking, white flowers atop long, slender, branched stems.

Hardiness: Zones 3 to 9.

Blooming Time: Midsummer to fall, depending on species.

Height: 3 to 6 feet; varies with species.

Spacing: 1½ to 3 feet; varies with species.

Light: Full sun to partial shade.

Soil: Well-drained, rich in organic matter.

Moisture: Even to abundant.

Garden Uses: Excellent for late-season interest in beds and borders, bugbanes are also at home in naturalistic gardens or in bright spots of a woodland garden. The graceful wands of white flowers can light up a partially shaded corner when little else is blooming there. The taller types, such as black snakeroot (*C. racemosa*), are especially useful at the back of the garden.

Comments: Bugbanes are native to moist, shady grassland, woodland, or scrub in north temperate areas from North America to China and Japan. These plants are easy to grow as long as they have sufficient moisture and soil with adequate levels of organic matter. Add about ½ inch of compost to their growing area each spring to maintain good soil quality. In dry conditions the leaves tend to brown and may appear burned.

The plant gets its common name, bugbane, because the flowers of some cultivars have an unpleasant odor. You're unlikely to notice this unless you

C. simplex

actually put your nose close to the flower and sniff. But if you think that you might be bothered by this characteristic, check with your supplier to learn if this is the case with the cultivar you are purchasing. If so, site the plants a few feet away from outdoor dining or lounging areas.

The tall stems of bugbane are usually able to support themselves. The plants spread to form clumps but seldom need division. If you do need to divide them or wish to propagate new plants, spring is the best time.

To start from seed, plant in flats as soon as the seeds are mature in the fall. Overwinter the flats in a cold frame; the seeds will germinate the following spring.

Recommended Cultivars: *C. racemosa:* 'Hillsided Black Beauty', 5 to 6 feet, purple foliage; *C. simplex:* 'Brunette', 5 feet, purple foliage; 'White Pearl', to 4 feet, larger wands of flowers than most bugbanes; 'Elstead' blooms later than other cultivars and is distinguished by purple-tinted buds that open to white flowers.

C. racemosa

C. racemosa —close-up of flower

Coreopsis

Coreopsis species
TICKSEED

The golden yellow, daisylike flowers of coreopsis are a mainstay of the summer flower garden. The plants are branched and bushy. The foliage varies from one species to another; the leaves of some are fine and threadlike, others have toothed, somewhat coarse leaves, and the leaves of some species are narrow and lance shaped.

Hardiness: Zones 3 to 9; varies with species.

Blooming Time: Summer.

Height: 8 inches to 3 feet.

Spacing: 8 inches to 1 foot.

Light: Full sun.

Soil: Any well-drained, average garden soil.

Moisture: Average; avoid damp to wet soil.

Garden Uses: Plant *Coreopsis* in the front to middle of beds and borders or in a cutting garden.

Comments: Deadhead regularly to prolong bloom. Divide established clumps in spring or fall. The plants hold up well in hot weather. Cut flowers can hold their quality for as much as a week.

Recommended Cultivars: *C. grandiflora*, 2 feet, yellow flowers, does well in warm climates; 'Early Sunrise', semi-double, yellow flowers, blooms all summer; 'Goldfink', 9 inches, yellow flowers; 'Sunray', 20 inches, double or semi-double yellow flowers.

    C. lanceolata, Lance-leaved coreopsis: 2 feet, yellow flowers; 'Ruth Kelchen', to 1½ feet, gold flowers with a brick red "eye."

    C. verticillata: Threadleaf coreopsis, to 3 feet, threadlike leaves; 'Moonbeam', 2 feet, pale yellow flowers, blooms all summer; 'Grandiflora', golden yellow flowers.

    C. rosea, 15 inches, pink flowers, threadlike leaves.

'Moonbeam'

Self-sown seedlings in early spring

PERENNIALS

smart tip

PROLONGING BLOOMTIME

Deadhead *Coreopsis* promptly to keep plants blooming. Pick off spent flowers by hand, or use flower shears for efficiency.

'Early Sunrise'

Delphinium

Delphinium species

Delphinium plants are highlights of the summer flower garden for two reasons—the glorious shades of blue in which their flowers bloom and the sheer size of their flower spikes, which can top out at 6 feet or even more. The vertical flowering stems soar above divided, deep green leaves.

Hardiness: Zones 3 to 7.

Blooming Time: Summer.

Height: 2 to 7 feet, depending on species or cultivar.

Spacing: 1 to 2½ feet.

Light: Full sun.

Soil: Well-drained, fertile, rich in organic matter, and loose to a depth of 2 feet.

Moisture: Constant, even.

Garden Uses: Plant smaller species and dwarf cultivars in the front to the middle of beds and borders, tall hybrids in the back of the garden. *Delphinium* plants are stately and elegant for formal gardens and perennial beds and borders. They also make good cut flowers.

Comments: *Delphinium* plants demand ideal growing conditions—rich soil is essential. They prefer cool weather but

'Fancy Diana'

Pacific Coast hybrid

in very cold climates are best treated as annuals. The tall stems need staking. The plants are prone to black spot and crown rot. Plants may produce a second, smaller batch of flowers in fall if you remove the faded flower spikes.

Recommended Cultivars: Blackmore and Langdon strain, 4 to 7 feet, blue shades, purple, white, and cream. Pacific Coast hybrids (Round Table series), to 7 feet: 'Black Knight', deep violet with a black center; 'Blue Bird', medium blue with a white center; 'King Arthur', violet with a white center; 'Galahad', white; 'Pennant Mix', 2 to 2½ foot dwarfs in shades of blue, lavender, rose, and creamy white.

D. × *belladonna*, 5 feet, light blue, deep blue, white, easier to grow than other types; 'Bellamosum', 4 feet, deep blue; 'Casa Blanca', 5 feet, white.

Save *Delphinium* Seeds
DIFFICULTY LEVEL: EASY

Tools and Materials: Pruning shears, paper bag, bowl, storage containers

1 To save seeds: cut stems when the seed heads are dry, and place them in paper bags to dry completely.

2 When the seeds are fully dry, separate the seed from the chaff. Store seeds in airtight, labeled containers in the freezer.

smart tip

STAKING *DELPHINIUM*

Delphinium flower spikes can be heavy. To prevent their blowing over and to keep the stems straight for cutting, tie them to tall stakes.

Dianthus

Dianthus species
GARDEN PINKS

The perennial pinks most often found in garden centers—allwood pinks (*Dianthus × allwoodii*), cheddar pinks (*D. gratianopolitanus*), and cottage or grass pinks (*D. plumarius*)—bear small disk-shaped flowers on slender upright stems. The petals have fringed or toothed edges. Perennial pinks come in many shades of pink, rose, red, salmon, and white; many are bicolored. The low, mat-forming plants have grassy, gray- or blue-green leaves.

The flowers of sweet William (*Dianthus barbatus*) are gathered into clusters at the top of upright, branched plants 1 to 2 feet high; they bloom in many shades of pink, rose, red, red-violet, and white, often with bands of a lighter or darker shade. The plants are biennial but sometimes behave as perennials.

Blooming Time: Late spring to midsummer.

Height: 4 inches to 2 feet.

Spacing: 6 to 12 inches.

Light: Full sun to partial shade; some afternoon shade is helpful where summers are hot.

Soil: Average fertility; light, well-drained, sandy, with neutral to slightly alkaline pH.

Moisture: Some can tolerate drought; most need average moisture.

Garden Uses: Many garden pinks have a delightful, spicy-sweet clove fragrance. Position them in the front of the garden; low forms are especially pretty spilling over the edges of a path.

Comments: Plant with the crowns right at the soil sur-

'Zing Rose'

face; do not plant too deeply. All *Dianthus* species self-seed easily. You'll notice this particularly with sweet Williams; volunteers are likely to grow many feet away from their parents. *Dianthus* flowers are edible and have a spicy clove-like flavor. They will dye sugar syrups pink if warmed in them. Strain before using.

Recommended Cultivars: *D. × allwoodii:* Allwood hybrids, 4 inches to 1 foot high, bear fragrant flowers in shades of red, rose, and pink.

D. deltoides, Maiden pink: 4 inches to 1 foot high, red, rose, or white flowers, tolerates partial shade; 'Zing Rose', deep rosy red.

D. plumarius, border pinks: 9 inches to 1½ feet high; fragrant white or pink flowers.

'Bath's Pink', 6 to 10 inches; many small, fragrant, light pink flowers; tolerates summer heat and humidity well.

PERENNIALS

smart tip

DEADHEADING *DIANTHUS*

Deadhead garden pinks to keep plants producing flowers. If you want plants to self-sow, let some flowers mature late in the blooming season. Collect ripe seedpods, or let them shatter where they grow.

'White Joy'

Dicentra

Dicentra species
BLEEDING HEART

Bleeding hearts produce distinctive heart-shaped pink flowers that dangle from their slender arching stems like a string of lockets. The flowering stems arise from a mound of attractive divided leaves. Old-fashioned bleeding heart (*Dicentra spectabilis*) dies back after blooming; fringed bleeding heart (*D. eximia*) blooms later, lasts longer, and has finely divided, ferny leaves.

Hardiness: Zones 3 to 9.

Blooming Time: Old-fashioned bleeding heart, mid- to late-spring; fringed bleeding heart, late spring to late summer.

Height: 10 inches to 2½ feet, depending on species.

Spacing: 1½ to 2 feet.

Light: Partial to light shade; can tolerate full sun in moist, cool climates.

Soil: Humusy, fertile.

Moisture: Evenly.

Garden Uses: Bleeding heart is a nice addition to the middle of an informal bed or border, a shady cottage garden, or a woodland garden with filtered light.

Flower stems make a charming linear element in fresh arrangements. Cut the stems when a few of the lowest flowers have opened. The best time to cut is in the early morning or evening when the flowers and stems are full of moisture. Take a bucket of water to the garden with you, and place the stems in water as soon as you cut them. Condition the flowers and foliage by placing the stems in a container of cool water up to the lowest flowers for several hours before arranging them. Unlike the leaves of some cut flowers, those of bleeding heart can be left on the stems when the flowers are placed in the vase. You can also dry individual flowers

'Alba'

of bleeding heart in silica gel. They won't last more than six months or so, but they are nice additions to potpourri.

Comments: Plant spreading or vining annuals, ferns, or hostas with old-fashioned bleeding hearts to fill the space left when the plants die back. Bleeding hearts do not grow well in hot, arid climates.

Each spring, spread a generous handful of fully finished compost or aged manure around each plant.

The plants often self-sow when growing in a congenial spot, but the new seedlings will not appear until the following spring.

Recommended Cultivars: *D. spectabilis* 'Alba' has white flowers.

D. eximia 'Snowdrift', white flowers all summer, 10 inches to slightly over a foot.

D. 'Luxuriant', hybrid with red-pink flowers all summer, 1 foot.

D. 'Langtrees', pink-tinted white flowers.

how to

Divide *Dicentra*	DIFFICULTY LEVEL: EASY

Tools and Materials: 2 spading forks

Divide *Dicentra* in early fall when the plant looks crowded, usually in 3 to 4 years.

'Luxuriant'

Digitalis

Digitalis purpurea
FOXGLOVE

Foxgloves are excellent in partially shaded areas.

Foxgloves' tall spikes of tubular flowers appear above low clumps of oblong leaves. They come in shades of pink, rose, purple, and white, with spotted throats. In ideal conditions, they self-sow readily, forming large colorful patches.

Hardiness: Zones 4 to 8.

Blooming Time: Late spring to early summer.

'Glittering Prizes'

Height: 2 to 5 feet.

Spacing: 1 to 2 feet.

Light: Partial shade to full sun.

Soil: Well-drained, humusy, fertile.

Moisture: Average to moist.

Garden Uses: Foxgloves make a good vertical accent for the middle or back of beds and borders. They're also good in cottage gardens. Because they thrive in partial shade, use them to brighten areas under trees or by a wall.

Comments: Foxgloves are biennials that often self-sow. In rural areas, you'll often see a group of foxgloves that have seeded themselves from plants in a nearby garden. They're likely to grow in a mass on the margins of fields or the edges of woods. If you cut back the plants after their first flowering, they may rebloom in late summer. All parts of the plant are poisonous if eaten.

Recommended Cultivars: 'Alba', 4 feet, white flowers; 'Glittering Prizes', 4 feet, white, pink, rose; 'Foxy', 3 feet, shades of cream, yellow, rose (the only cultivar that blooms the first year from seed); *D.* × *mertonensis*, 3 feet, rich strawberry-red blooms.

A related species, *D. grandiflora*, is a perennial growing to 30 inches with light yellow flowers.

PERENNIALS

how to

Save Foxglove Seeds

DIFFICULTY LEVEL: EASY

Tools and Materials: Pruning shears or scissors, paper bag, bowl, storage containers

1 Cut the seed stalks when the pods are completely dry but before they have opened.

2 Place the seed stalks in a paper bag as soon as you cut them. The bag will catch any seeds that fall from the opened pods.

3 Remove chaff from the seeds before storing them in a tightly covered and labeled container.

Echinacea

Echinacea purpurea
PURPLE CONEFLOWER

These sturdy, long-blooming plants are known for their purple-pink daisylike flowers with bronzy brown centers. The plants are upright and branched with coarse-textured, narrowly oval leaves. The centers become elongated as they mature and make excellent additions to dried flower arrangements and winter bouquets.

Hardiness: Zones 3 to 8 or 9.

Blooming Time: All summer into autumn.

Height: 2 to 4 feet.

Spacing: 1½ to 2 feet.

Light: Full sun.

Soil: Well-drained, average to poor fertility.

Moisture: Average to low, tolerates drought.

Garden Uses: Ideal plants for meadows, low-maintenance gardens, and informal beds and borders, purple coneflowers are also seen in herb gardens because of their use as a popular herbal remedy. The flowers attract butterflies.

Comments: Plants are easy to grow and extremely dependable. The leaves can sometimes be disfigured by powdery mildew; problems are most severe when relative humidity levels are high and the plants are crowded enough to impede good air circulation. Divide mature plants every three to five years in the spring or fall.

'Magnus'

Recommended Cultivars: 'Bright Star', 2 feet, bright rose pink; 'Magnus', 3½ feet, deep purple-pink; 'White Swan', 3 feet, white.

'White Swan'

how to

Save Purple Coneflower Seeds

DIFFICULTY LEVEL: EASY

Tools and Materials: Pruning shears or scissors, paper bag, bowl, storage containers

1 To save seeds: let *Echinacea* flowers produce seed heads, and when fully dry and dark-colored, clip them off.

2 Place the seed heads in a paper bag to let them dry completely. After a week or so, shake the bag to loosen the seeds.

3 Pour the contents of the bag into a bowl; separate the seeds from the chaff; and store the seeds in an airtight container.

Filipendula

Filipendula species
MEADOWSWEET

These big sturdy plants have an affinity for damp spots. Their clumps of stems are lined with lobed leaves divided into leaflets that are arranged like fingers on a hand. In summer they are topped by fluffy or plumy clusters of minute, fragrant flowers.

Hardiness: Zones 3 to 9.

Blooming Time: Summer.

Height: 3 to 8 feet, depending on species.

Spacing: 2 to 4 feet.

Light: Full sun to partial shade.

Soil: Average to rich fertility.

Moisture: Even to abundant.

Garden Uses: Meadowsweets are lovely alongside a pond or stream or in a moist meadow or other moist location.

Comments: Plants may suffer from powdery mildew in dry soil. In cold climates they appreciate a winter mulch.

Recommended Cultivars: Queen-of-the-prairie (*F. rubra*), to 8 feet, light peachy pink flowers; queen-of-the-meadow (*F. ulmaria*), 3 to 6 feet, creamy white flowers; 'Aurea' yellow leaves, creamy white flowers; 'Variegata' yellow markings on foliage, white flowers.

Queen-of-the-Prairie

Queen-of-the-Meadow

PERENNIALS

how to

Divide Meadowsweet Plants **DIFFICULTY LEVEL: EASY**

Tools and Materials: Spade or shovel, pruning shears or scissors

1 Propagate new plants by dividing *Filipendula* clumps. Dig up the root clumps, and separate them into sections.

2 Cut back the stems to help plants establish themselves more easily, and replant in their new locations.

'Goblin'

Gaillardia

Gaillardia × *grandiflora*
BLANKETFLOWER

Perennial blanketflowers bear daisylike blooms up to 4 inches across; the flowers have domed, red to red-purple centers and red petals tipped with golden yellow. Plants are upright and branched, with lance-shaped, irregularly notched leaves of medium to deep green; the leaves may be spotted.

Hardiness: Zones 4 to 9.

Blooming Time: Early summer to frost.

Height: 6 inches to 3 feet, depending upon variety.

Spacing: 9 inches to 1½ feet.

Light: Full sun.

Soil: Average fertility, good drainage is important; will not thrive in dense, soggy soils.

Moisture: Average; tolerates some drought.

Garden Uses: These cheerful flowers are most at home in informal gardens because the plants tend to look a bit dishevelled and weedy by late summer. Position blanket flowers according to their mature height, placing smaller cultivars in the front of the garden and taller types in the middle or background. The plants are also nice additions to meadow gardens.

Gaillardia makes a good cut flower, too. Cut blossoms in the morning or early evening while the centers are still tight. Stand the stems in water nearly up to the base of the flowers for several hours before arranging. Add a little sugar or commercial cut flower preservative to the water.

When ready to arrange the flowers, remove the leaves and recut the stems before you place them in a vase.

Comments: Blanketflowers are hardy and can go out into the garden slightly before the date of the last expected frost. Start seeds indoors; sow directly in the garden; or purchase container-grown seedlings to transplant.

Transplant seedlings before they bloom.

If flowers are not dead-headed, the plants may self-sow, but they may not come true from seed. A better way to propagate new plants is to take stem cuttings in early summer. Root them in a soilless medium, and grow in pots until it is time to transplant to the garden, about 30 days before the first expected frost.

Deadhead spent flowers to keep the plants blooming. Plants tend to be short-lived; you may need to replace them after a few years. However, you can often propagate new plants by dividing the clumps in early spring. When you divide a clump, discard the central portion of the plant if it has lost vigor or has died back.

Recommended Cultivars: 'Baby Cole', 8 inches, bright red tipped with yellow, burgundy center; 'Burgundy', 20 to 24 inches, wine red; 'Goblin' ('Kobold'), 1 foot; 'Golden Goblin' ('Goldkobold'), 10 inches, deep golden yellow ray flowers with a brilliant red central disk.

smart tip

CUTTING BACK BLANKETFLOWER PLANTS

Cut back the stems after the plants have finished blooming in the early summer. They will regrow and reward you with a second bloom later in the season.

'Johnson's Blue'

Lancaster geranium

Geranium

Geranium species
CRANESBILL

Hardy *Geranium* plants, also called cranesbills, are a large genus of perennials. These plants should not be confused with the tender geraniums grown as summer annuals, which belong to the genus *Pelargonium*. Most cranesbills are relatively low-growing and sprawling, producing open to slightly cup-shaped flowers on slender, branched stems lined with divided leaves. Flowers come in many shades of pink as well as lilac and blue.

Hardiness: Zones 4 to 10, but varies with species.

Blooming Time: Mid- to late-spring into summer; rela-

tively long-blooming.

Height: 6 inches to 1½ feet.

Spacing: 8 inches to 1 foot.

Light: Full sun or partial shade.

Soil: Well-drained, average fertility.

Moisture: Average; most can tolerate some dryness, but not prolonged drought.

Garden Uses: Plant cranesbills in the front of informal beds and borders. Some are suited to rock gardens; low, spreading types can be used for ground covers in the garden.

Comments: Cranebills are durable, dependable, easy to grow, and charming in informal settings. Deadheading guarantees their bloom for many weeks. Propagate plants by dividing established clumps in early spring or fall.

Recommended Cultivars: *G. cinereum*, 6 to 8 inches, small pink flowers.

 G. endressii 'Wargrave Pink', 1 to 1½ feet, salmon pink.

 'Johnson's Blue', hybrid growing to 1½ feet, with bright blue flowers through most of the summer.

 G. sanguineum, blood-red cranesbill, 10 inches to 1 foot, magenta; var. *striatum* (Lancaster geranium), 6 to 8 inches, pink flowers veined in red, extremely long-blooming; 'Alpenglow', to 1½ feet, carmine, tolerates poor, dry soil.

'Alpenglow'

smart tip

SUPPORTING PLANTS

Cranesbills tend to have floppy, sprawling stems. Support stems with metal hoop stakes or simple wooden frames.

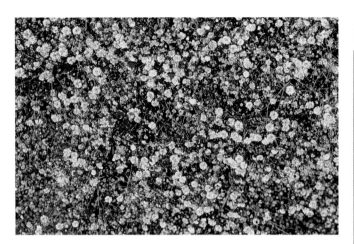

'Pink Star'

Gypsophila

Gypsophila paniculata
BABY'S BREATH

This perennial is named for the lovely clouds of little white or pink flowers that cover the many-branched, narrow-leaved plants. The plants' tiny flowers, slender, sharply angled stems, and small leaves give them a light airy texture in the garden.

Hardiness: Zones 4 to 8.

Blooming Time: Mid- to late-summer; relatively short-blooming.

Height: 1½ feet to 3, depending on cultivar.

Spacing: 1 to 2 feet.

Light: Full sun; appreciates partial afternoon shade in warm climates.

Soil: Fertile, well-drained, neutral to slightly alkaline pH.

Moisture: Average.

Garden Uses: Although it doesn't bloom for very long, baby's breath is a wonderful filler in fresh or dried bouquets, and it can perform the same function in the garden. The plants like to spread out, and they can cover holes left by poppies, spring phlox, or spring bulbs.

Comments: Baby's breath may need staking to support the stems when plants are in bloom; make a supporting structure with four canes and wrap some twine or heavy string around them.

Recommended Cultivars: 'Perfecta', 3 to 4 feet, double white flowers; 'Pink Fairy', 1½ feet, pale pink flowers.

smart tip

DRYING BABY'S BREATH

Baby's breath air-dries beautifully. Gather stems in bunches with rubber bands and hang upside down in an airy location until they are completely dry.

Baby's breath makes an excellent filler in fresh arrangements.

Christmas rose

Helleborus

Helleborus niger,
CHRISTMAS ROSE
Helleborus orientalis, also known as
H. × hybridus, LENTEN ROSE

Christmas roses bear white flowers that turn pinkish as they age; the divided evergreen leaves are a deep green and have toothed edges. The later-blooming Lenten roses bear clusters of drooping bell-shaped flowers in pale greenish white or pale pink to deep maroon-pink. The leaves of both species are glossy green and divided with sharply toothed edges.

Hardiness: Christmas rose, Zones 3 to 9; lenten rose, Zones 3 to 10.

Blooming Time: Christmas roses bloom in the winter in mild climates and in early spring in areas where the soil freezes. Lenten roses bloom in early spring.

Height: Christmas rose, 8 inches to 1 foot; lenten rose, to 2 feet.

Spacing: Christmas rose, 1½ feet; lenten rose, 2 feet.

Light: Partial or light, dappled shade.

Soil: Cool, well-drained, fertile and rich in organic matter, with a neutral to alkaline pH.

Moisture: Average to even.

Garden Uses: Grow these plants in woodland gardens, under deciduous shrubs, or in informal shady beds and border gardens.

Comments: Dig in lots of compost, well-aged manure, or leaf mold when you prepare the planting area, and topdress liberally with one of these amendments once a year to keep the soil in good condition. Plants take a couple of years to get established in the garden. Christmas rose is fairly demanding in terms of its environmental conditions, but the rewards are worth the extra effort. It does best in light, dappled shade and in neutral to alkaline soil. Lenten rose prefers the same conditions but is generally more adaptable to a range of soil types. It tolerates most average garden soils and is easy to grow in all but hot climates.

Once established, the plants spread very slowly, so you probably won't have to divide or move them. It's best to leave them in place because the roots do not like to be disturbed. They are likely to self-sow and form colonies. If you wish to transplant some of the volunteers, do so with great care in spring. The plants go dormant in dry summer weather and should not be disturbed at that time.

The evergreen leaves may dry out in harsh winter winds; if wind is a problem in your garden, you may wish to spray the foliage with an antitranspirant to protect it. In spring, cut off any dried out or tattered leaves to improve the overall look of the plants and make the flowers easier to see. (They can be hidden under the foliage.)

Helleborus is poisonous if ingested, and contact with the sap can cause skin irritation in sensitive individuals. Wear gloves when cutting and arranging them if you don't know whether you are sensitive or not.

Recommended Cultivars: 'Atrorubens', slightly over 1 foot tall, deep plum purple, flowers in late winter or early spring; 'Royal Heritage', 1½ to 2 feet, purple, red, deep maroon, white, green, pink, and yellow, long-lasting when cut.

Lenten rose

Hemerocallis

Hemerocallis cultivars
DAYLILY

Daylilies are one of the most useful garden flowers because they are easy to grow, come in a huge range of colors, and require little care. How could a gardener go wrong with such a plant? Daylilies produce trumpet-shaped flowers on branched stems above a clump of strap-shaped leaves. Each flower lasts only one day, but plants produce many of them in succession.

'Stella de Oro'

'Chicago Regal'

Hardiness: Zones 3 to 10.

Blooming Time: Summer; there are early, mid- and late season cultivars.

Height: 1 to 5 feet.

Spacing: 1½ to 2½ feet.

Light: Full sun to partial shade; pastels hold their color better in partial shade.

Soil: Any ordinary garden soil.

Moisture: Average; can tolerate dryness but need water during prolonged drought.

Garden Uses: Plant groups in beds and borders (low growers in front, taller cultivars in the middle to back according to height), or mass along a driveway or a fence.

Comments: Plants don't need dividing very often. But after several years, they may become crowded. If you notice that the plants are producing fewer flowers than they once did, it's time to divide the clumps of tuberous roots.

Recommended Cultivars: There are far too many cultivars to attempt a listing here. A few beauties: 'Stella de Oro', 2 feet, golden yellow, exceptionally long bloom. 'Hyperion', 4 feet, bright lemon yellow, fragrant; 'Memorable Masterpiece', 1½ feet, pale peach-pink, late-blooming; 'Prairie Blue Eyes', 2 feet or slightly taller, lavender-blue, mid-season.

H. lilio-asphodelus (flava), lemon lily, 2 feet, clear yellow, fragrant.

how to

Divide Daylilies
DIFFICULTY LEVEL: EASY

Tools and Materials: Spade or shovel

1 Divide daylilies in late summer after they finish blooming. Cut back leaves; dig up the clump; and pull apart the tuberous roots with your hands.

2 Check to see that all divisions have both roots and leaves; then replant immediately in the new locations. Water thoroughly.

Hibiscus

Hibiscus moscheutos
ROSE MALLOW

Large, open cup-shaped to saucerlike flowers with prominent fused stamens in the center typify rose mallows. They bloom in shades of pink, rose, pale yellow, or white. The flowers can be 6 or more inches across. Plants have large, oval to nearly heart-shaped leaves on thick stems.

Hardiness: Zones 5 to 10.

Blooming Time: Mid- to late-summer; long-blooming.

Height: 3 to 8 feet.

Spacing: 3 to 6 feet.

Light: Full sun.

Soil: Moist but well-drained, rich in organic matter, with neutral to mildly alkaline pH.

Moisture: Average to moist.

Garden Uses: The huge flowers and lush leaves of rose mallows bring an exotic, tropical feeling to any garden. Plant them in the back of a bed, as a border by themselves, as specimens or focal points in a lawn, or in large tubs.

'Disco Belle White'

'Disco Belle Red'

Comments: The plants are not hardy north of Zone 5; gardeners in these areas grow them as annuals rather than perennials. Start plants about 6 weeks before the frost-free date, or buy seedlings. Set out the plants after all danger of frost is past in spring.

There is a smaller, shrubbier-looking relative, *H. rosa-sinensis* (Chinese or Hawaiian hibiscus), with woody stems and flowers in an assortment of warm shades. This plant is widely available and is not hardy, although it looks like it should be. Unless you live in a frost-free climate, you'll have to bring this species indoors and grow it as a houseplant in winter.

Recommended Cultivars: 'Disco Belle Pink', 2½ feet, pink shading to white; 'Lady Baltimore', 4 feet, pink with red center; 'Lord Baltimore', 4 feet, red; 'Blue River II', flat white flowers.

smart tip

CUTTING BACK DAMAGED STEMS

In early spring, use lopping shears to cut winter-damaged stems to the ground. They will regrow from the crown of the plant and bloom as usual.

PERENNIALS

Hosta

Hosta species
PLANTAIN LILY

Hostas are grown primarily for their foliage, which comes in a range of green shades from chartreuse to blue-green. Many cultivars are variegated in gold or white, in assorted patterns. Some leaves have a puckered, quilted texture; others are smooth. The leaves are oval to elongated and grow in the form of a low rosette. Bell-shaped white or lavender flowers resembling small lilies bloom in clusters on tall stems; some are fragrant.

Hardiness: Zones 3 to 8.

Blooming Time: Mid- to late-summer.

Height: Many sizes, from dwarf 6-inch cultivars to large-leaved plants with flower stems 4 or 5 feet high that rise above a 3-foot-tall mound of foliage.

Spacing: 1 to 3 feet, depending on cultivar.

Light: Partial shade to shade; some can tolerate full sun if the soil is rich and moist.

Soil: Fertile, well-drained, rich in organic matter, with a slightly acid to neutral pH.

Moisture: Even moisture in summer, drier conditions in winter when dormant.

Garden Uses: Hostas are welcome in shady gardens, where, as dictated by their size, they are effective massed in the front or middle of beds or borders. They make excellent ground covers in shady spots because they add needed texture while blocking weed growth.

Comments: Hostas are easy to grow, very hardy, and seldom need division. Deadhead to keep plants looking good.

'Albo Picta'

Recommended Cultivars: New cultivars are continually being developed, with variations in size, leaf color, texture, and variegation patterns.

'Abby', 8 inches, blue-green with gold-green edging; 'Bright Lights', 1¼ feet, puckered golden leaves with blue-green edging, grows well in Zone 9; 'Francee', to 2 feet, deep green

'Gold Standard'

with white edges; 'Gold Standard', to 1¼ feet, yellow-green leaves with darker green edging; 'Krossa Regal', 2 feet, blue-green leaves; 'Royal Standard', 2 feet, light green leaves, fragrant white flowers; 'Sum and Substance', 2½ feet, yellow-green deeply veined leaves.

H. sieboldiana 'Elegans', 2½ feet, wide blue-green leaves; 'Frances Williams', 2½ feet, quilted blue-green leaves irregularly edged in gold.

how to

Divide Hosta Plants
DIFFICULTY LEVEL: EASY

Tools and Materials: Spade or shovel, pruning shears

1 Divide hosta plants when the central stems die out and the clumps appear empty in the center.

2 After blooming, dig up the clump. Use the shovel as a lever to raise the root-ball.

3 Pull or cut apart the clump, discarding the old central portion and retaining the younger outer parts.

4 Cut back the stems to leave only a few inches, and replant the divisions immediately. Water the plants well.

Annual candytuft (*I. umbellata*)

Iberis

Iberis sempervirens
PERENNIAL CANDYTUFT

Candytufts are versatile, easy-to-grow plants with a variety of uses in the garden. They form a low spreading mat of narrow dark green leaves that are evergreen in mild climates. In spring they bear dainty, rounded clusters of tiny pure white flowers.

Hardiness: Zones 3 to 8.

Blooming Time: Mid-spring.

Height: 8 to 10 inches.

Spacing: 1 foot.

Light: Full sun.

Soil: Rich, well-drained.

Moisture: Even moisture produces the best bloom; water during dry spells.

'Improved White Spiral'

Garden Uses: Use candytuft in the front of beds or borders, in rock gardens, along sidewalks or paths, next to driveways, or spilling over retaining walls. Candytuft makes a good companion for tulips and other late-spring bulbs.

Comments: Shearing back plants after the first flush of flowers fades prompts them to bloom again. In cold climates, trim off dead leaf tips at the end of winter to encourage new green growth. Propagate new plants by division or from leaf cuttings taken in late summer. Annual forms of candytuft are also available. While some are only 4 or 5 inches tall, others are up to 8 inches. Unlike perennial candytuft, they are available in shades of rose as well as pure white.

Recommended Cultivars: 'Snowflake', to 10 inches tall, larger flowerheads than the species form; 'Snow White', 6 inches tall, long-lived; 'Purity', blooms over a long season; 'Nana', to 6 inches tall but with a more upright, rather than spreading, habit; 'Autumn Beauty', flowers in spring and reliably in autumn if sheared back after the first bloom.

smart tip

COMBINING PLANTS

Low-growing candytuft makes a good understory plant for shrubs such as this camellia. The combination is particulary effective if the plants bloom at the same time.

PERENNIALS

Iris

Iris species
IRIS

Stately, elegant irises have been favorites among both gardeners and artists for centuries. Most irises grow from rhizomes (some grow from bulbs), but all are distinguished by their straight, tall, swordlike or grassy leaves. Iris flowers consist of narrow, inner, petal-like structures called *style branches*, three upright petals called *standards*, and three drooping outer sepals called *falls*.

Irises are named for the Greek goddess of the rainbow, and they come in a rainbow of colors. The range includes white, ivory, many yellow shades, gold, apricot, orange, pinks, magenta, maroon, brownish red, lavender, blues, purples, violets, and deep purple-black. Many have falls of one color and standards of another; the style branches on others differ in color from the falls and standards.

Irises are divided into a number of classes. Among gardeners, the best-known types are bearded (tall, intermediate, dwarf), spuria, Siberian, Louisiana, and Japanese irises.

Hardiness: Varies with type and cultivar; most don't grow well in the extreme North or South.

Blooming Time: Late spring. Individual cultivars have a

Dwarf iris

Japanese iris

how to

Remove Rhizome Rot
DIFFICULTY LEVEL: EASY

Tools and Materials: Old but sturdy soup spoon, laundry bleach

1 Suspect rhizome rot if leaves begin to yellow and turn brown. Pull back the leaves and carefully examine the rhizome.

2 Use a spoon to scoop out all the soft, rotted portions of the rhizome, cutting just beyond the rot.

3 Pour ordinary laundry bleach on the remaining rhizome. It kills the disease organisms without hurting the plant.

short blooming period—one to three weeks—so plant several types to extend the season. With careful planning, you can have irises blooming until high summer.

Bulbous irises are the earliest to bloom. (See Portraits of Favorite Bulbs, page 167.) Next come the dwarf types, followed by the intermediates (which flower along with tulips). They are succeeded by the tall bearded cultivars. Next come the spurias, then Siberians, and finally, the Japanese and Louisiana types.

Height: 4 inches to 5 feet.

Spacing: 8 inches to 2½ feet, varies with type.

Light: Full sun; some afternoon shade in warm climates.

Soil: Well-drained, humusy, fertile.

Moisture: Average to abundant, varies with type.

Garden Uses: There are irises for the back of beds and borders, rock gardens, bog and water gardens, cutting gardens, and naturalistic gardens. Plant irises in their own beds, in combination with other perennials or annuals, along walks and driveways, in front of a hedge or wall, or in clumps in mixed flower gardens.

Comments: When planting bearded irises, dig a deep hole and make a mound in the center of it. The top of the mound should be level with the surrounding soil. Set the rhizome horizontally on the mound; and spread the roots down over it. Fill the hole with soil; firm it around the roots; and water thoroughly. Don't cover the rhizomes with soil (except in hot climates). Plant with the fan of leaves pointing in the direction you want the plants to grow.

Plant new irises, or dig and divide crowded clumps after their blooming season ends in your area. In warmer zones,

Bearded iris

wait until fall. When dividing, discard the woody inner portion of the root clump and replant the outer portions. Divide bearded iris every three or four years and Siberians whenever clumps become crowded.

Recommended Cultivars: There are far too many excellent iris cultivars to attempt a reasonable listing. Choose cultivars of all types according to your preferences for size and color as well as the plants' blooming season.

how to

Divide Irises
DIFFICULTY LEVEL: EASY

Tools and Materials: Spade, knife, pruning shears

1 Every few years, divide bearded irises in midsummer when they finish blooming. Dig the rhizomes from the ground, taking the roots, too.

2 Examine the rhizomes carefully, and cut them into pieces, each of which has at least one fan of leaves. Discard old, woody pieces of rhizome.

3 Cut back the stems. If your plants have had any fungal diseases, dust the rhizomes with powdered sulfur or another fungicide before replanting.

4 Replant the divisions immediately, setting the rhizomes so that their tops are partially exposed or only very thinly covered with soil.

Siberian iris

PERENNIALS

Kniphofia

Kniphofia uvaria
RED-HOT POKER

A real eye-catcher, these elegant plants get their nickname from their blossoms—vertical spikes of small tubular flowers that may be red, yellow, orange, or shaded from yellow at the base to red-orange at the tip. The plants form clumps of grassy leaves.

Hardiness: Zones 5 to 9, varies with cultivar.

Blooming Time: Late spring to fall, varies with cultivar.

Height: 3 to 6 feet.

Spacing: 3 feet.

Light: Full sun; afternoon shade is helpful in hot, arid regions.

Soil: Well-drained, average to fertile.

Moisture: Average; tolerates drought.

Garden Uses: Red-hot poker is excellent in a garden of hot colors, in one with a tropical theme, or when used as a focal point in a quieter planting.

Red-hot poker

Comments: Good drainage is important, especially in winter. Cut back plants after bloom if the leaves start to look ratty. Plants seldom need division and do better if they are not disturbed.

Kniphofia makes a good cut flower, adding vertical line to an arrangement of round, daisylike, or bell-shaped blossoms, or making a contemporary statement in a vase by themselves. Cut the blossoms when about a third of the tiny flowers in the spike have opened. Morning and evening are the best times to cut. Condition the flowers before arranging by standing the stems in cool water nearly up to the base of the flower heads for several hours. Recut the stems, and cut a vertical slit into the bottom of each one when you place the flowers in the vase.

Recommended Cultivars: Numerous cultivars and hybrids are available, including 'Little Maid', 2 feet, ivory shading to pale yellow; 'Corallina', 3 feet, coral-red; 'Pfitzeri', 2 feet, orange-red; 'Earliest of All', hardy to Zone 5, 2 feet, coral-rose.

Red-hot poker florets open from the bottom of the spike first.

smart tip

PROPAGATING RED-HOT POKERS

Red-hot pokers form offsets from their crowns. Rather than dividing the roots, remove new offsets once they have roots, and transplant them to another spot in the garden.

Lavandula

Lavandula angustifolia
ENGLISH LAVENDER

Lavender flowers range in color from lavender to deep violet, depending on cultivar. Small spikes of the tiny flowers are carried at the top of slender, wandlike stems. The shrubby, sprawling plants have silvery green leaves and stems that become woody as they age. Both flowers and leaves possess a distinctive, refreshing fragrance. There is also a white-flowered form.

Hardiness: Zones 5 to 8.

Blooming Time: Midsummer.

Height: 1 to 3 feet, depending on cultivar.

Spacing: 1½ to 3 feet, depending on the cultivar and growing conditions.

Light: Full sun.

Soil: Light, well-drained, gravelly soil is ideal. Lavender needs a near-neutral pH and does not thrive in dense, soggy soil.

Moisture: Average to occasionally dry.

Garden Uses: Loved for its fresh, clean scent, lavender is as at much at home in the front of a flower garden as it is in an herb garden. It is heavenly planted in masses or along the edge of a path where passersby will brush against it and release the scent.

Comments: Lavender tolerates heat and drought. In the southeastern U.S., especially in Zones 9 to 11, it is best

'Hidcote Blue'

grown as an annual because it doesn't fare well in very humid conditions. In cold windy locations, mulch plants well for winter protection. 'Munstead' often survives in Zone 4 with a deep winter mulch.

Recommended Cultivars: 'Hidcote', 1 foot or slightly taller, deep violet; 'Munstead', to 1½ feet, purple, very fragrant; 'Munstead Dwarf', 1 foot, deep purple; 'Rosea', slightly over a foot, pink; 'Lavender Lady', 8 to 10 inches, traditional lavender, blooms first year from seed but not reliably hardy in cold climates.

smart tip

'Munstead Dwarf'

CUTTING BACK LAVENDER STEMS

Cut back lavender plants in early spring each year to give them a tidy, symmetrical form.

PERENNIALS

Liatris

Liatris spicata BLAZING STAR, SPIKE GAYFEATHER

Blazing stars' straight vertical stems are topped in summer with vertical purplish pink or white spikes that resemble bottle brushes. The tiny flowers clustered along each spike open from the top down. The stems rise above a clump of narrow, pointed leaves shaped like broad blades of grass.

Hardiness: Zones 3 to 9.

Blooming Time: Midsummer into fall.

Height: 2 to 4 feet, depending on cultivar.

Spacing: 1 to 1½ feet.

Light: Full sun.

Soil: Well-drained, humusy, average fertility; good drainage is important in winter.

'Kobold'

Moisture: Average to even.

Garden Uses: A good plant for providing a vertical line or a spiky form in a bed or border, blazing star is also nice in meadow and prairie gardens. The flowers are good for cutting and drying. They attract butterflies, too.

Comments: Blazing stars are easy to grow. Divide plants in early spring if bloom decreases after several years.

Recommended Cultivars: 'Kobold', 2 to 2½ feet, reddish purple; 'Snow Queen', 2½ feet, white.

'Alba'

smart tip

CUTTING *LIATRIS* FOR THE VASE

Liatris is an excellent cut flower. Cut stems when about half the flowers on the spike have opened, as shown in the purple flowers to the right. The white flowers are past their prime and should not be cut.

Cut a vertical slit in the bottom of each stem, and condition in a container of water nearly up to the base of the flower for several hours before arranging.

how to

Save *Liatris* Seed   DIFFICULTY LEVEL: EASY

Tools and Materials: Scissors, storage containers

Save seed from *Liatris* at the end of the season. Wait until the seed spike has dried, but cut the spikes before the seeds scatter.

'Desdemona'

Ligularia

Ligularia species
LIGULARIA

These big, imposing plants have presence in shady gardens. They form mounds of large, triangular or kidney-shaped toothed leaves and bright yellow or orange flowers. Flowers of *L. dentata* are daisylike and carried in clusters; those of *L. stenocephala* appear in an upright spike.

Hardiness: Zones 4 to 8; grows best where summers are cool.

Blooming Time: Early to late summer, depending on cultivar.

Height: 3 to 6 feet, varies with cultivar.

Spacing: 2 to 3 feet.

Light: Full sun to light shade; needs afternoon shade in warmer climates.

Soil: Well-drained, fertile and humusy.

Moisture: Even to abundant.

''The Rocket''

Garden Uses: Use ligularia in the back of beds and borders or in moist, shady spots where you can give it plenty of room. It is lovely when used around a water garden or in a garden at the edge of a woodland. It self-seeds easily and is an excellent choice for a plant to naturalize in moist, partially shaded areas.

Comments: Slugs may be a problem. Trap them as shown below or set out boards next to the plants in the evening. Slugs will crawl under these boards once the sun rises, and you'll be able to catch and dispose of them in the morning. Use kitchen tongs to pick them up if you don't want to touch them.

Water ligularia during spells of dry weather. In cold zones, mulch during the winter.

Recommended Cultivars: *L. dentata* 'Desdemona', to 3 feet, purple stems and leaf undersides, orange flowers; 'Othello', to 3 feet, similar coloration to 'Desdemona', but blooms later.

L. stenocephala 'The Rocket', 5 to 6 feet, yellow flowers.

smart tip

CONTROLLING SLUGS

Stale beer is a good slug trap. Set beer-filled cans flush with the soil surface if possible. However, slugs are so attracted to beer that they may crawl up a can to find it.

PERENNIALS

Lobelia

Lobelia cardinalis,
CARDINAL FLOWER
Lobelia siphilitica,
GREAT BLUE LOBELIA

These *Lobelia* species are both wildflowers native to eastern North America. Cardinal flower bears spikes of brilliant scarlet fringed flowers above a low clump of deep green, lance-shaped leaves. Great blue lobelia has spikes of small blue to violet blossoms similar in form to those of cardinal flower; it, too, has lance-shaped leaves.

Hardiness: Cardinal flower, Zones 2 to 9; great blue lobelia, Zones 4 to 9.

Blooming Time: Cardinal flower, late summer; great blue lobelia, late summer into fall.

Height: Cardinal flower, 2 to 4 feet; great blue lobelia, 2 to 3 feet.

Spacing: 1 foot.

Light: Full sun to light or partial shade.

Soil: Average to fertile, humusy.

Moisture: Even to moist or even periodically wet.

Garden Uses: Both species are lovely in moist meadow gardens, wildflower gardens, and alongside a stream or pond. Cardinal flower attracts hummingbirds.

Cardinal flower

Comments: Plants tend to be short-lived in gardens and may need to be replaced every few years. Great blue lobelia usually takes to domestication better than cardinal flower. Give both species a winter mulch.

Recommended Cultivars: *L. cardinalis:* 'Alba' and 'Gladys Lindley', with white flowers; 'Rose Beacon' and 'Twilight Zone', with pink flowers; and 'Compliment Scarlet', with large scarlet flowers.

    L. siphilitica: 'Alba', with white flowers; 'Nana', a dwarf cultivar with blue flowers; 'Blue Peter', with especially nice blue flowers.

Great blue lobelia

smart tip

MANAGING *LOBELIA* VOLUNTEERS

***Lobelia* species self-seed easily. Thin or transplant the volunteers to new garden spots when they have their first true leaves.**

Monarda

Monarda didyma
BEE BALM

Bee balms produce clusters of tubular flowers surrounded by slender bracts (modified leaves), in shades of red, pink, purple, and white, at the top of their numerous tall, straight stems. Pairs of aromatic, oval, dark green leaves line the square stems.

Hardiness: Zones 4 to 9.

Blooming Time: Summer.

Height: 2 to 3 feet.

Spacing: 1½ feet.

Light: Full sun to partial shade.

Soil: Fertile, rich in organic matter.

Moisture: Even; does not do well in dry soil.

Garden Uses: Bee balm is noteworthy for its unusual flower clusters and fragrant leaves. An attractive plant for the middle or back of the garden, it works best in informal designs. The leaves can be dried and used for tea. Bee balm flowers attract bees and scarlet-flowered types also attract hummingbirds.

The leaves can be dried and used for tea. The flavor is citrusy, containing notes of both orange and lemon. Bee balm leaves give Earl Grey tea its distinctive flavor. You can also add chopped fresh leaves and flowers to green salads or fruit salads, or use the flowers as a colorful edible garnish on salads or dishes where the citrus note will complement the flavors. To use bee balm as a cut flower, cut stems when the first few flowers in the cluster have opened. Strip off the lower leaves; then stand the stems in cool

'Cambridge Scarlet'

'Petite Delight'

water nearly to the base of the flowers for a few hours before arranging.

Bee balm flowers can be dried to use in wreaths and arrangements. Although red ones lose some of their brightness during drying, they still add color to craft projects. Dried leaves and flowers are lovely in potpourris. Hang bunches of flowers upside down in a dark, dry airy place to air-dry them.

Comments: A member of the mint family, bee balm spreads like its relatives and can become invasive. Avoid problems by growing plants in pots that you sink in the garden. Powdery mildew can attack leaves in late summer. Plantings will need division every two or three years.

Recommended Cultivars: 'Gardenview Scarlet', to 3 feet, bright scarlet flowers, mildew resistant; 'Marshall's Delight', to 3½ feet, pink flowers, mildew resistant; 'Petite Delight', slightly over a foot tall, rose pink flowers, mildew resistant.

smart tip

CUTTING BACK BEE BALM

Bee balm is prone to various fungal diseases. If plants begin to look ratty in the late summer, cut back the stems and remove them from the garden. The new growth will be more vigorous.

Nepeta

Nepeta × faassenii
CATMINT

The loose spires of small, tubular catmint flowers can be lavender, purple, mauve, or white. They form at the top of bushy plants with small, oval to heart-shaped toothed leaves of slightly grayish green. The plants have a sprawling, spreading habit, and the leaves have a citrusy fragrance.

Hardiness: Zones 4 to 8.

Blooming Time: Early to late summer; plants bloom almost all summer if deadheaded regularly or sheared back after the first flush of bloom.

Height: 1 to 2 feet.

Spacing: 1 to 2 feet.

Light: Full sun to partial shade.

Soil: Light, sandy, well-drained, average fertility; will also adapt to poor soil.

Moisture: Average, but tolerates some drought.

Garden Uses: Catmint is a lively, exuberant plant for the front of an informal border. It's especially pretty along a path, where the plants can spill onto the walkway. The colors blend well with many other flowers, particularly rose, pink, blue, and yellow shades. It's an excellent plant for hard-to-mow slopes because it protects the soil from erosion and is dense enough to smother out weed seedlings.

Comments: Catmint likes hot, sunny conditions. While not as invasive as other members of the mint family, it does

'Six Hills Giant'

spread. Confine the roots and keep top growth trimmed if that's a problem.

It can also look weedy toward the end of the season. Cut back the plants when they get out of hand; they'll regrow. Where space is limited, divide plantings every few years to keep them under control.

Recommended Cultivars: Look for the species or cultivars of *Nepeta × faassenii*, which you may find labeled (mistakenly) as *N. mussinii*. 'Six Hills Giant', to 3 feet, is taller than other cultivars.

smart tip

Catmint along a walkway

CUTTING BACK

To promote a second blooming, cut back catmint plants after the first flush of bloom. They will regrow and rebloom in late summer.

Oenothera

Oenothera speciosa, SHOWY PRIMROSE

Oenothera fruticosa, SUNDROPS

These are two day-blooming members of the evening primrose clan. Showy primrose bears cup-shaped light pink flowers above bushy mounds of narrow gray-green leaves. The petals are marked with darker pink along the veins and at the margins and have bright yellow stamens that arise from a yellow throat. Sundrops produce the same sort of cup-shaped blossoms, but these are a cheery bright yellow color. They are also slightly taller and more bushlike, with many branched stems. The oval leaves are a deep green color and have smooth margins.

Hardiness: Zones 4 or 5 to 9.

Blooming Time: Both species flower through much of the summer.

Height: 1 to 2 feet.

Spacing: 1½ to 2 feet.

Light: Full sun.

Soil: Well-drained, average to poor fertility.

Moisture: Average; tolerates drought.

Garden Uses: Nice additions to informal beds and border gardens.

Comments: Flowers of both species can coat the foliage when in full bloom, so a mass planting can make a very showy display. However, if they are grown in rich soil, the plants produce lush foliage but fewer flowers.

Both species are easy to start from seed. Plant them indoors about 8 weeks before the frost-free date, and trans-plant them to the garden after all danger of frost has passed.

Divide crowded plants in spring. Showy primrose can be invasive.

Recommended Cultivars: *O. speciosa* 'Rosea', 1¼ feet, clear pink flowers. *O. fruticosa* 'Sonnenwende' ('Summer Solstice'), long-blooming sundrops with burgundy-red leaves in autumn.

how to

Plant *Oenothera* Seeds
DIFFICULTY LEVEL: EASY

Tools and Materials: Seeds, soil mix, flat, plastic wrap, newspaper

Sow seeds as usual in a flat or cell tray. They require darkness to germinate; cover the flat with plastic film, to retain moisture, and then newspaper, to exclude light.

PERENNIALS

Showy primrose

Showy primrose, close-up

Sundrops

Paeonia

Paeonia species
PEONY

Peonies are among the most beloved garden flowers. Their huge single or double blossoms are showy, and sweetly fragrant in some cultivars. The plants are easy-to-grow, dependable bloomers that live long and ask little of the gardener. The flowers come in many shades of red, rose, and pink, as well as cream and white. Peonies die back to the ground in winter, but during the growing season they are large, bushy plants with attractive lobed and divided leaves.

There are a number of flower forms. Single-flowered types have five or more petals with colorful stamens in the center. Japanese peonies, also known as anemone forms, are similar. They have one or two rows of petals and a larger pompom-like tuft of stamens in the center. Double-flowered peonies are the most familiar, with big, full blossoms.

Hardiness: Zones 2 to 8.

Blooming Time: Late spring to early summer.

Height: 1½ to 3½ feet.

Spacing: 2 to 3 feet.

Light: Full sun is best; tolerates partial shade.

Soil: Well-drained, humusy, slightly acidic.

Moisture: Average.

Garden Uses: With foliage that maintains its good looks all season, as well as its graceful form and lovely blooms, peonies are wonderful plants for beds and borders. On their own, they also make a handsome border or divider in the yard, and they are delightful lining a driveway or path. Or use them as specimens or focal points in a lawn. They make marvellous cut flowers.

Cut peonies when the buds are showing color but before the flowers open. Cut the flowers in the morning or early evening. Split the ends of the thick stems in cool water containing a little sugar or some commercial cut flower preservative. Let the flowers stand in the water for several hours to condition them. Recut the stems when you arrange the flowers. Cut peonies are magnificent in a bowl by

'Sarah Bernhardt'

smart tip

SITING PEONIES

Peonies become large bushes in only a few short months each year. Their dark green, lobed leaves and graceful, vase-shaped form make them attractive additions to the landscape, whether they are in bloom or not. Plant them in a location where you want a seasonal focal point.

themselves or in a mixed arrangement with smaller flowers in a variety of shapes.

Comments: Strong winds can damage peony flowers, so plant them in a sheltered location if you can. Don't plant them too shallow or too deep, or they may not bloom—set the crowns 1 to 2 inches below the soil surface. Peonies seldom need dividing. Feed them once a year, in spring, with a balanced all-purpose fertilizer. In cold climate gardens, mulch them for the winter. Plants sometimes need staking to keep them upright.

When you cut peonies for the vase, take buds that are just beginning to open. If you notice ants crawling on the buds, don't be alarmed. They are there to eat a sweet syrup covering the buds. Shake them off any flowers you cut to bring indoors.

Recommended Cultivars: There are many fine peony cultivars on the market. Following are a few of the best: 'Bowl of Cream', 2½ feet, double white flowers, midseason; 'Coral Charm', 3 feet, semidouble, coral flowers, early; 'Festiva Maxima', to 3 feet, double, white flowers, fragrant, early; 'Karl Rosenfield', 2½ feet, double, red flowers, midseason; 'Monsieur Jules Elie', to 3 feet, double, rose-pink flowers, early; 'Sarah Bernhardt', 3 feet, double, light pink, fragrant flowers flecked with red, late blooming.

'Mitama'

PERENNIALS

'Bowl of Beauty'

'Red Charm'

Papaver

Papaver nudicaule,
ICELAND POPPY
Papaver orientale,
ORIENTAL POPPY

Iceland and Oriental poppies are classic late-spring flowers that bloom in a wide range of lovely colors. Their silky, ruffled petals resemble tissue paper. Flowers bloom at the top of tall slender stems that rise above a basal mound of hairy, divided leaves.

Hardiness: Iceland poppy, Zones 2 to 10; Oriental poppy, Zones 3 to 9.

Blooming Time: Late spring.

Height: Iceland poppy, 1 to 2 feet; Oriental poppy, 1½ to 4 feet.

Spacing: Iceland poppy, 1½ feet; Oriental poppy, 2 to 3 feet.

Light: Full sun; partial shade in warm climates.

Soil: Light, sandy or loamy, plenty of organic matter.

Moisture: Average to moist when in active growth.

Garden Uses: Poppies are lovely in mixed beds and borders, where they add color to the middle or back areas. They drop their petals when cut unless you sear their stems in flame just after cutting. The seedpods are interesting in dried arrangements.

Iceland poppy

Comments: Plant Iceland poppies in early spring in most climates and in autumn in the South and Pacific Northwest. Many gardeners prefer to grow them as annuals.

Oriental poppies are grown much like Iceland poppies, but they prefer a somewhat richer soil. Plant bare-root Oriental poppies in the fall. The tall plants may need to be staked. Don't move or divide plants for a few years after planting to allow them time to establish themselves and develop their full beauty. Thereafter, move them in the fall, but only if it's absolutely necessary—they do better when they are not disturbed. Mulch the plants in fall with an inch-deep layer of compost or well-aged manure.

Recommended Cultivars: Iceland poppy, 'Sherbet' series, slightly over a foot tall, pastel peach, yellow and white, or a bright mix of red, orange, rose, and cream; 'Parfum Mix', 1 foot, shades of red, scarlet, orange, pink, yellow, as well as bicolors.

Oriental poppy: 'Helen Elizabeth', 2½ feet, salmon pink flowers with ruffled petals, early blooming; 'Pizzicato Mix', 1½ feet, red, pink, mauve, salmon, or white flowers, grow from seed; 'Raspberry Queen', 2½ feet, raspberry pink flowers with black blotches in the center, midseason; 'Türkenlouis', 3 to 3½ feet, red flowers with fringed petals; 'White King', 3 to 3½ feet, white flowers with purple-black central blotches; early.

how to

Divide Poppies

DIFFICULTY LEVEL: EASY

Tools and Materials: Spade or shovel, mulch

1 Divide crowded oriental poppies in late summer when they produce a new rosette of leaves. Pull clumps apart gently.

2 Replant the divisions immediately in moist, humusy soil. Plant them at the same depth they were growing.

3 Firm the soil around the new plants; water; and mulch with a loose organic material to conserve soil moisture.

Beard-tongue (*P. calcycosus*)

Penstemon

Penstemon species
BEARD-TONGUE

Beard-tongues bloom in shades of pink, blue, violet, red, and sometimes white. There are 250 species and many named cultivars. The tubular, lipped flowers are clustered along slender stems that rise above a low clump of narrow leaves. Though the flowers are delightful, plants tend to be somewhat short lived and may need to be replaced after several years.

Hardiness: Zones 3 to 8.

Blooming Time: Early summer to early autumn, depending on species and cultivar.

Height: 1 to 3 feet.

Spacing: 1 to 1½ feet.

Light: Full sun.

Soil: Very well-drained, sandy or gravelly.

Moisture: Average to low; tolerates drought but not moist soils.

Garden Uses: Grow this in a rock garden or a drought-tolerant bed or border.

Comments: Good drainage is critical for beard-tongues, which are native to the American West from the Rockies to Mexico. They hold up well in hot conditions. Provide a win-

ter mulch in colder zones. Named cultivars tolerate ordinary garden soil somewhat better than the species. In heavy clay soils, plants are susceptible to crown rot.

Recommended Cultivars: 'Rose Elf', 1½ to 2 feet, rose pink flowers; 'Elfin Pink', 1 foot, clear pink flowers; 'Firebird', 2½ feet, bright red flowers, Zones 6 to 9; 'Garnet', 2 feet, garnet red flowers, Zones 6 to 9.

P. digitalis: 'Husker Red', 3 feet, white flowers and red-bronze foliage.

Close-up of *P. australis* flower   *P. barbatus* 'Coccineus'

smart tip

SAVING BEARD-TONGUE SEEDS

To save seed, let some flowers mature and produce seedpods. When the seedpods are dry and dark-colored, cut them off; remove the seeds; and store the seeds in an airtight container.

Perovskia

Perovskia atriplicifolia
RUSSIAN SAGE

This lovely plant has a clump of semiwoody, branched, upright stems that give the effect of a delicate, fine-textured shrub. The stems are lined with gray-green aromatic leaves that are finely cut and divided into narrow, oblong leaflets. The plants are graced with light, airy sprays of tiny tubular purple-blue flowers on silvery stems; in bloom, it looks like a lavender cloud in the garden. The square stems identify Russian sage as a member of the mint family.

Hardiness: Zones 5 to 9.

Blooming Time: Mid- to late-summer.

Height: 3 to 5 feet.

Spacing: 2 feet.

Light: Full sun.

Soil: Well-drained, sandy, average fertility.

Moisture: Average; tolerates drought.

Garden Uses: Plant Russian sage for a soft, misty look in an informal summer bed or border. One interesting way to use it is to plant it in the front of the garden as a scrim through which to view other, bolder flowers behind it. Otherwise, use Russian sage in the middle ground of a large border or in the back of a garden of smaller plants. It is a good choice

Russian Sage

for a seashore garden, especially if you stake the stems to brace them against the frequent winds.

Russian sage is lovely with pink garden phlox (and lavender and white phlox cultivars as well), cosmos, sparkling white shasta daisies, deep blue salvias, golden achillea or rudbeckia, and later on, sedums and chrysanthemums. Ornamental grasses are also excellent companions for perovskia.

Comments: Easy to grow in a well-drained location; holds up well in hot weather. The plants can tolerate dry, alkaline soils. Stake the tall stems if they lean. Propagate from stem cuttings taken in summer. Cut back the stems to about a foot from the ground for winter, and mulch well. Russian sage is seldom bothered by pests or diseases.

Recommended Cultivars: 'Blue Spire', deep blue, finely divided feathery leaves; 'Blue Haze', lighter blue flowers than the species, and the leaves are not as finely cut and divided; 'Filigran', 3 to 4 feet, feathery foliage more finely divided than that of other varieties, and hardy to Zone 4 or possibly even 3.

P. × superba (or *P.* 'Hybrida') is an improved hybrid with darker violet-blue flowers in clusters up to 16 inches long. This plant is more compact than the species, topping out at about 3 feet in height.

how to

Plant Nursery-Grown Russian Sage Plants

Tools and Materials: Spade or shovel

DIFFICULTY LEVEL: EASY

1 Plant container-grown *Perovskia* from a local nursery in spring. Dig the hole; then slide the plant out of its pot.

2 Add or subtract soil from the hole so the plant sits at the same depth as in the pot; then firm the soil, and water well.

smart tip

CUTTING BACK *PEROVSKIA*

Cut back stems in late fall; then mulch when the ground freezes.

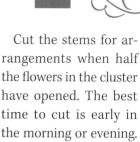

'Starfire'

'Eva Cullum'

Phlox

Phlox paniculata
GARDEN PHLOX

The tall-growing garden phlox is a mainstay of many summer perennial gardens. It blooms lavishly and for a long time, and many cultivars are available in shades of pink, purple, and white. Flowers bloom in conical clusters on top of tall stems lined with lance-shaped leaves.

Hardiness: Zones 4 to 9.

Blooming Time: Summer to early fall.

Height: 2 to 4 feet.

Spacing: 1½ to 3 feet.

Light: Full sun.

Soil: Rich, loamy, with lots of organic matter; well-drained.

Moisture: Even, abundant.

Garden Uses: Garden phlox is a mainstay of summer beds and borders, both formal and informal. Use taller cultivars in the back of the garden and shorter ones in the middle. The flowers are also excellent for cutting and have the added benefit of a wonderfully sweet but not cloying fragrance.

Comments: The plants are very hardy, but they are prone to attack by leaf spot and powdery mildew in hot, humid weather. To help prevent this, space plants far enough apart to allow air to circulate between them, and water the plants at ground level rather than sprinkling leaves from overhead. Thinning the plants, by allowing just three or four shoots to remain on each plant, promotes good air circulation, strong growth, and large, abundant flowers.

Cut the stems for arrangements when half the flowers in the cluster have opened. The best time to cut is early in the morning or evening. Before you arrange the flowers, condition them by standing the stems in a container of cool water nearly up to the base of the flower heads for several hours.

Lift and divide perennial phlox about every three years, when the plants finish blooming, to maintain the vigor of the plants. Cut off the flower clusters as the blossoms fade to keep the plants blooming longer. The plants are heavy feeders and appreciate an annual topdressing of compost or well-aged manure. Scratch some all-purpose fertilizer into the soil around the plants when they start growing in spring.

Recommended Cultivars: 'David', 3½ feet, white, long blooming, mildew resistant; 'Eva Cullum', 2½ feet, pink with red eye, long blooming; 'The King', 2 to 2½ feet, deep purple, long blooming; 'Norah Leigh', 3 feet, variegated leaves edged in cream, pale pink flowers with dark eye; 'Starfire', 2 to 3 feet, cherry red flowers.

PERENNIALS

smart tip

PREVENTING SELF-SOWING

Prevent phlox from self-sowing by cutting off the seed stalks while seedpods are still green. To save seeds, wait to cut until the pods are brown and the seeds are mature.

Physostegia

Physostegia virginiana
OBEDIENT PLANT, FALSE DRAGONHEAD

Obedient plants get their name because you can train the flower spikes to grow in a certain direction simply by moving them into that position; they obediently remain where you put them. The tiny, tubular, two-lipped light purple or white flowers grow in spires that form in a semicircular pattern around the stem. The plants are clump-forming with stiff upright stems clad in pairs of toothed, lance-shaped leaves. Physostegia is native to eastern North America.

Hardiness: Zones 3 to 10.

Blooming Time: Summer into fall.

Height: To 3 feet.

Spacing: 1 to 1½ feet.

Light: Full sun to partial shade.

Soil: Average fertility.

Moisture: Average to moist.

Garden Uses: Grow in beds and borders or in a cutting garden. Cut stems when the lowest flowers have opened, ideally in the morning or evening. Upper flowers will open in the vase. Place stems in a container of water nearly up to the base of the flowers for several hours for conditioning before you arrange the flowers.

'Summer Snow'

Comments: Plants spread quickly in moist, rich soil and may need dividing every two or three years. Divide in early spring before the new growth begins. Obedient plants are easy to grow and well worth the space they take.

Recommended Cultivars: 'Alba' and 'Summer Snow', white flowers; 'Variegata' (subspecies *speciosa* 'Variegata'), pink flowers, green leaves edged in cream; 'Vivid', bright rosy pink flowers; 'Bouquet Rose', light lilac-pink flowers; 'Galadriel', dwarf to 1½ feet high, pale pinkish lavender flowers; 'Rosea', pink flowers.

Flower as seen from the back

how to

Divide Pot-Bound Container Plants

Tools and Materials: Knife, spade or shovel   **DIFFICULTY LEVEL: EASY**

1 If you buy a pot-bound container plant, divide it when you transplant. Cut the entire plant and root-ball into sections.

2 Transplant the divided sections as usual, setting the plant at the same depth it was growing in the pot. Firm the soil, and water immediately.

Platycodon

Platycodon grandiflorus
BALLOON FLOWER

The interesting buds of balloon flowers really do resemble miniature balloons; they open into star-shaped flowers of blue-violet, pink, or white. The erect plants have a clump of straight stems and relatively small, toothed, oval leaves.

Hardiness: Zones 4 to 8.

Blooming Time: Early to late summer.

Height: 1½ to 2 feet.

Spacing: 1 to 1½ feet.

Light: Full sun to partial shade.

Soil: Light, well-drained, moderately fertile.

Moisture: Average to abundant.

Garden Uses: Plant balloon flower in the front or middle of the garden. It is easy to grow and has a long blooming period. The flowers, especially of taller cultivars, are good for cutting and are lovely in the vase with shasta daisies, cosmos, achillea, rudbeckia, spiky salvia, veronica, pink phlox, physostegia, and small fillers such as gypsophila and armeria.

An unopened flower bud

Comments: Balloon flower is reliable, hardy, and easy to grow but does not do well in hot, humid climates. It is late to appear in the spring; don't assume you've lost it until a week or two after the soil has truly warmed.

Cut stems for arrangements when several of the flowers have opened. Early in the morning or evening when they are cool is the best time to cut. The stems bleed sap when cut; this sap fouls water in a vase. Prevent bleeding by dipping the cut stem ends quickly in boiling water or searing them over a candle flame. Then condition the flowers by standing the stems in a container of warm water for several hours.

Recommended Cultivars: 'Alba', white; 'Sentimental Blue', dwarf to 1 foot or slightly higher, flowers a lighter blue than the species; 'Albus' (forma *albus*), white flowers with blue veins; 'Double Blue', double flowers of rich violet-blue; 'Mother of Pearl' ('Perlemutterschale') and 'Shell Pink' both have pink flowers.

Platycodon

smart tip

SEARING *PLATYCODON* STEMS

Seal the stems of balloon flowers before using them in a bouquet. Dip them in boiling water for a second or two, or sear them over a flame until the end has become calloused.

Primula

Primula species
PRIMROSE

Polyanthus hybrids

Botanists have given primroses a family all their own, and it's a large one—there are over three hundred kinds of primroses. Some are difficult to grow, but there are many delightful cultivars that take only minimal care.

Primroses produce their flowers in clusters above a basal mound of oblong leaves. Some species bear their flowers on tall stems; other species have short stems.

Hardiness: Zones 3 to 9, varies with species.

Blooming Time: Early- to mid-spring in cool climates, winter in warm climates.

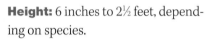

Height: 6 inches to 2½ feet, depending on species.

Spacing: 9 inches to 1 foot.

Light: Partial shade.

Soil: Fertile, well-drained, with an acid pH; rich in organic matter.

Moisture: Average to moist.

Garden Uses: Primroses are lovely planted under trees, alongside a stream or pond, and in the rock garden.

Primula polyanthus, Gold Lace Group

Comments: Lift and divide the plants every few years as soon as they finish blooming. You can also propagate new plants from seed in early- to mid-autumn or in early spring. Sow the seeds indoors or in a cold frame, and move transplants to their permanent garden location in spring, when all danger of frost is past. In the deep South and the Southwest, plants may have difficulty surviving. If so, grow them as annuals.

Massed primroses

Recommended Cultivars: *P. denticulata* (Drumstick primrose): 1 foot, lavender, purple, white, pink, mauve, and red cultivars.

Polyanthus hybrids: 6 to 10 inches, shades of red, pink, mauve, lavender, purple, violet, many with a yellow eye. Often grown as a winter annual in warm climates.

P. japonica (Japanese primrose): 1 to 2 feet, clusters of flowers on tall stems in shades of pink, red, and white.

Drumstick primrose

'Irish Eyes'

Rudbeckia

Rudbeckia fulgida, R. hirta
ORANGE CONEFLOWER, BLACK-EYED SUSAN

Black-eyed Susans supply bright color to any landscape. Wild plants often grow along country roads and woodlands, while domestic cultivars add color to beds and borders. The petals of the daisylike flowers are a golden yellow to an orangy gold color; centers of most cultivars are dark brown to near-black, though one has a green center. The branched plants have lance-shaped to oval leaves.

Hardiness: Zones 4 to 9.

Blooming Time: Midsummer to early autumn.

Height: 2 to 3 feet.

Spacing: 1 to 2 feet.

Light: Full sun is best, but they tolerate some light shade.

Thompson and Morgan Mixed

Soil: Well-drained, and average fertility.

Moisture: Average to moist; will tolerate dry soil.

Garden Uses: The color intensity of these flowers is not to everyone's liking, but black-eyed Susans are good, dependable plants for a meadow garden or the middle ground of an informal cutting garden.

Comments: Easy to grow and

smart tip

SAVING *RUDBECKIA* SEEDS

To save seeds, let some flowers mature on the plants; then cut off the seed heads when they're brown and dry.

durable, the plants tolerate hot weather and some cold, as well. *Rudbeckia fulgida* will spread, especially in light, moist soil, and needs division about every three or four years.

Recommended Cultivars: 'Goldsturm', 1½ to 2 feet, many flowers and one of the longest bloom seasons of any perennial.

R. hirta: 'Gloriosa Daisy', to 2 feet, yellow petals are flushed with varying amounts of mahogany red around the center.

smart tip

CUTTING *RUDBECKIA* FOR THE VASE

When using *Rudbeckia* plants as cut flowers, remove all leaves that would be underwater in the vase before you arrange the flowers, or they will foul the water.

Massed salvias

Salvia

S. × *superba*

SALVIA, VIOLET SAGE, ORNAMENTAL SAGE

This hybrid was created by crossing several salvia species. It's sold under various names, so shop for particular cultivars, including those suggested below. The best-known perennial salvias bear slender upright spikes of tiny violet or purple flowers and have oblong grayish green leaves.

Hardiness: Zones 5 to 10.

Blooming Time: Late spring to summer.

Height: 1½ to 3 feet.

Spacing: 1½ to 2 feet.

Light: Full sun.

Soil: Light, well-drained; thrives in any good garden soil.

Moisture: Average; tolerates some dryness, but needs to be watered during extended dry spells.

Garden Uses: The flowers are a welcome addition to summer flower gardens and cut flower arrangements. They are beautiful paired with soft yellows, such as *Achillea* 'Moonshine' or *Coreopsis* 'Moonbeam'.

Comments: New plants are easily propagated from cuttings, divisions, or seeds. Start seeds indoors, six to ten weeks before the last expected frost. Take cuttings in early fall or early spring. Dig and divide crowded plants in early fall or early to mid-spring.

Salvia is a good cut flower for fresh arrangements and can also be dried. The slender flower spikes add a welcome vertical line to arrangements of round, daisylike, and cup-shaped

Mexican Bush sage, *Salvia leucantha*, is also useful in the home landscape. It can help to anchor a bed or border and is a lovely sight in bloom.

flowers. Cut stems when the lower flowers on the spike have opened. Place the stems in a container of warm water for several hours to condition them before arranging the flowers. The flowers last about a week in the vase.

To dry salvia flowers, hang bunches of stems upside down to air-dry, or lay stems horizontally in silica gel.

Recommended Cultivars: 'Blue Hill', true blue flowers; 'East Friesland', rich blue-violet flowers; 'May Night', deep violet-blue flowers.

smart tip

THINNING SALVIA VOLUNTEERS

Salvia species self-seed easily. Use small scissors to thin the volunteer seedlings when they appear in early spring.

Scabiosa

Scabiosa caucasica
PINCUSHION FLOWER

These plants get their nickname from the structure of their domed lavender-blue or pink flower heads. The blooms consist of outer rings of small-petaled flowers surroundng a rounded center of tiny tubular flowers with prominent stamens that resemble pinheads.

Hardiness: Zones 3 to 8.

Blooming Time: Mid- to late-summer.

Height: 1½ to 2½ feet.

Spacing: 1 to 2 feet.

Light: Full sun.

Soil: Well-drained, humusy, neutral to slightly alkaline pH.

Moisture: Average to even.

Garden Uses: *Scabiosa* is a delightful addition to a cottage garden, perennial garden, mixed bed or border, or a cutting garden. Though not long blooming, the plants add a light, airy texture to the middle ground of a bed or border.

Comments: Pincushion flowers like moisture but do not tolerate wet, soggy conditions. Divide mature plants in spring every four years or so.

Blooms of pincushion flower are excellent cut flowers. The unusual structure of the flowers, in combination with the softness of their colors, adds sophistication to any arrangement. Pincushion flowers last up to a week in the vase. Cut the flowers when at least half of the florets in the flower head have opened. Cut in the early morning or evening if possible. Strip off all foliage that would be below the water level in the vase, and split the stems or cut a few vertical slits up into the bottom of each stem. Condition pincushion flowers by placing the stems in a container of cold water for several hours before arranging.

Recommended Cultivars: *S. caucasica:* 'Alba', white flowers; 'Miss Willmott' also has white flowers. 'Fama', rich true blue flowers to 3 inches across, on 2-foot stems.

S. columbaria: 'Butterfly Blue', dwarf hybrid to 15 inches tall, blooming from spring well into fall, violet-blue blossoms; 'Pink Mist', 1 to 1¼ foot tall, lilac-pink flowers.

'Pink Mist'

Pincushion flower

smart tip

CLEANING CELL-PACKS

Before sowing seeds indoors, clean previously used containers and scrub them with a solution of 1 part chlorine bleach to 9 parts water. Rinse before using.

smart tip

DEADHEADING *SCABIOSA* FLOWERS

Deadhead pincushion flowers promptly to prolong their bloom period and keep the plants looking neat. Pinch or cut off faded flowers along with their stems.

PERENNIALS

Sedum

Sedum 'AUTUMN JOY' STONECROP

'Autumn Joy' produces tight, flattish heads of flowers that start out light green in late summer, change to pink, then rosy red, deepen to a beautiful coppery bronze that's difficult to describe, and eventually darken to a rich rust color. Light green fleshy leaves with scalloped edges grow all along the stems of these upright plants.

Hardiness: Zones 3 to 10.

Blooming Time: Late summer into fall.

Height: 1½ to 2 feet.

Spacing: 1 to 1½ feet.

Light: Full sun; tolerates light shade.

Soil: Average fertility, well-drained, especially in winter when plants are dormant.

Moisture: Plants are healthiest and produce the best blooms if they are kept on the dry side, but they will tolerate moist soil in summer as long as it is not soggy.

Garden Uses: *Sedum* 'Autumn Joy' is a welcome addition to an autumn garden of chrysanthemums and asters, par-

'Autumn Joy'

smart tip

PLANTING STONECROP IN A WALL

Small *Sedum* plants can be tucked into soil-filled niches in a stone wall or rock path. Remember to water the plants periodically.

ticularly if the rusty red tones of *Sedum* complement the colors of the asters and chrysanthemums.

This cultivar is an outstanding garden plant—easy to grow and hard to beat for late-season color in the front to middle of the garden. The changing colors provide a long-lasting display. You can leave the flower heads on the plants all winter if you wish—they are interesting even when dry and brown.

Comments: Plants will grow in poor soil as long as it's well-drained. When plants become crowded, divide them in the spring. To propagate without dividing, take stem cuttings in early summer and transplant them into place at least a month before hard frost.

The stems and leaves of *Sedum* contain sap that can cause skin irritation on contact and stomach discomfort if ingested. Wear gloves when cutting the blooms, taking cuttings, or even dividing.

Sedum plants make great cut flowers. They last more than a week in the vase, and may even form roots while in the water, like stem cuttings. Cut the flowers and place the stems in a container of water nearly up to the base of the flower heads to condition them before arranging. If the stems bleed sap when you cut them, dip the cut ends briefly into boiling water to seal them before you condition them or place them in a vase.

Sedum plants also dry well although the color loses its red tones and becomes more brown. Hang them upside down in small bunches to air-dry.

'Golden Fleece'

Solidago

Solidago cultivars
GOLDENROD

A familiar sight in fields and along roadsides in late summer and fall, goldenrods deserve a place in the garden, too. There are numerous cultivars and hybrids with different sized and shaped flower heads, but all of them are yellow and feathery. The upright stems form clumps and have elongated leaves.

Hardiness: Zones 5 to 9.

Blooming Time: Late summer into fall.

Height: 2 to 3½ feet.

Spacing: 1½ to 2 feet.

Light: Full sun.

Soil: Well-drained, average to low fertility.

Moisture: Average to low; tolerates drought.

Garden Uses: Goldenrod is pretty in a meadow garden, a naturalistic planting, or an informal bed or border. It makes a stunning companion to fall chrysanthemums, asters, and late-blooming annuals such as *Calendula*.

Comments: Contrary to popular opinion, goldenrod does not cause allergies—the culprit is often ragweed, which tends to grow near goldenrod in the wild. Plants spread, and some kinds can be invasive; divide spreaders every few years to keep them in line. Hybrids

'Peter Pan'

smart tip

PLANTING GOLDENROD

Young nursery plants transplant and settle into the garden more easily than larger, older plants. Dig the hole before sliding the plant out of the pot. Water after planting.

PERENNIALS

have larger, brighter colored flowers and don't spread as much as species and wild forms.

Goldenrods are lovely in autumn bouquets and arrangements, especially with asters, mums, dahlias, and monkshoods. Cut them early, when the flowers are just beginning to open. Cut stems in the morning or early evening. Condition the flowers by standing the stems in water nearly to the base of the flowers for several hours before arranging. Goldenrods also dry well. Hang them upside down in bunches to air-dry.

Recommended Cultivars: *S. rugosa* 'Fireworks', 3½ feet, sprays of bright yellow flowers reminiscent of fireworks exploding in the sky.

Hybrids include 'Golden Dwarf', 1 foot, golden yellow flowers; 'Peter Pan', 2 feet, bright yellow flowers; 'Baby Sun', 1 foot, clear yellow flowers; 'Golden Baby', 2 feet, golden yellow flowers.

Goldenrod is at home in a mixed border.

Stachys

Stachys byzantina
LAMB'S EARS

Lamb's ears are grown primarily for their oval, softly fuzzy green leaves covered with silver hairs. Some gardeners also enjoy the small purple flowers that they produce on tall, rather thick stems. The plants have a sprawling, spreading habit.

Hardiness: Zones 4 to 10.

Blooming Time: Midsummer.

Height: Leaves grow to about 1 foot; flower stems 1½ to 2 feet.

Spacing: 1 foot.

Light: Full sun to partial shade.

Soil: Average fertility, good drainage is essential.

Moisture: Leaves will rot if the soil is too wet, but plants need water in dry weather.

Garden Uses: Lamb's ears is attractive in the front of beds and borders; if you want to let the flowers develop, plant a little farther back. The silver-white foliage beautifully complements pink, blue, and purple flowers.

'Countess Helene von Stein'

Comments: If leaves begin to look ratty and brown in hot summer weather, cut them back and new ones will grow. If you don't like the look of the purple flowers, pick off the stems as they form in summer.

Recommended Cultivars: 'Big Ears' ('Countess Helene von Stein') to 3 feet high, large, medium green leaves to 10 inches long, covered with grayish white hairs, flowers are purple; 'Silver Carpet', dwarf to 6 inches high, does not bloom and has very silver leaves.

'Silver Carpet'

smart tip

TRIMMING LAMB'S EARS

Keep lamb's ears looking neat by cutting off flower stalks and trimming away any yellowed, dried, or decayed leaves.

Veronica

Veronica species
SPEEDWELL

Veronica plants are handsome, easy-to-grow hardy perennials with a multiplicity of uses in flower gardens. The plants produce slender, tapered, upright spikes of little blue, purple, rose, pink, or white flowers on stems with oval to oblong leaves.

Hardiness: Zones 3 or 4 to 10, varies with species.

Blooming Time: Summer.

Height: 1 to 4 feet, varies with species.

Spacing: 1 to 1½ feet.

Light: Full sun.

Soil: Prefers reasonably fertile, well-drained soils; tolerates most average garden soils.

Moisture: Average to even.

Garden Uses: Speedwells are excellent plants for the middle of flower beds and borders.

Comments: The plants tolerate both heat and drought, but they're not always hardy in very cold winters. If you live in a cold climate, you might want to dig up the plants in fall and put them in a cold frame over winter, just to be safe.

Most *Veronica* plants aren't grown from seed; order plants from a nursery catalog, or buy locally for spring planting. You can propagate established plants by lifting and dividing them in spring or by taking cuttings in summer. Warm-climate gardeners can divide the plants in early fall after they finish blooming.

Recommended Cultivars: 'Goodness Grows', to slightly over a foot, deep blue, long blooming; 'Sunny Border Blue', slightly over a foot to 1½ feet, deep blue-violet flowers.

V. peduncularis 'Georgia Blue', 6 to 8 inches, deep true blue flowers with a white eye, flowers are larger than most and not gathered into spikes; grow as a ground cover.

V. spicata 'Red Fox', just over a foot, dark rose pink flowers.

smart tip

COMBINING SPEEDWELL IN THE GARDEN

Speedwell works well with spring bulbs such as daffodils.

Veronica spicata

'Red Fox'

'Icicle'

PERENNIALS

PART 3

About Bulbs

A bulb is the swollen underground stem base of a plant that stores nutrients. The plant draws on these supplies during its annual dormant rest period as well as for leaf development. A *true bulb* is a modified flower bud and stem enclosed in thick *scales*, or enlarged overlapping leaf bases. In lilies, the scales are formed like garlic cloves; in tulips and daffodils, they grow like an onion. Bulbs' scales are anchored to a tough *basal plate*, the flat structure at the bottom of the bulb from which the roots grow.

Plant clumps, masses, or "rivers" of bulbs for carefree color year after year. Hardy bulbs like these tulips brighten the garden in spring, paving the way for perennials and annuals that follow.

Tulips, daffodils, and lilies are true bulbs, but the word *bulb* is often used inclusively to refer to other kinds of underground storage organs: *tubers, tuberous roots, corms,* and *rhizomes.*

A tuber (sometimes known as a *tuber-corm*) is a swollen stem that usually grows underground. Roots grow from it, as do *eyes,* or buds, from which new shoots develop. Tuberous begonias, anemones, and caladiums grow from tubers.

Tuberous roots are enlarged roots that have growth buds at the crown, the area where the plant's roots meet the stems. Dahlias have tuberous roots.

A corm is the swollen base of a stem, modified to be a storage organ. Corms are usually flatter than bulbs and store their nutrients in the basal plate more than in their scales. Crocuses and gladiolus are familiar corms.

Rhizomes are underground stems that grow horizontally and produce both roots and shoots. Many plants, including some grasses and perennials, spread by means of rhizomes. Both cannas and bearded irises grow from rhizomes (though bearded iris is usually grouped with perennials rather than bulbs). Other irises, such as *I. reticulata* and Dutch hybrids, grow from bulbs.

Hardy or Tender?

Many plants categorized as bulbs are hardy to temperatures below freezing. Spring-blooming crocuses, daffodils, tulips, hyacinths, and squills are all hardy bulbs.

Other bulbs are tender, meaning that they are damaged or even killed by cold temperatures and frost. As described in "End of Season Activities," page 145, gardeners in cold climates lift these bulbs in autumn. Most summer-blooming bulbs, including dahlias, cannas, tuberous begonias, and gladiolus, are tender. But just because a bulb blooms in summer doesn't necessarily mean it's tender; lilies flower in summer, and many of them are very hardy. The profiles on pages 150 to 177 list the zones in which each bulb is hardy.

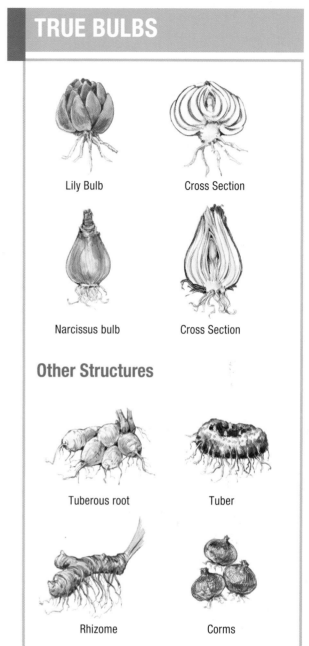

TRUE BULBS

Lily Bulb

Cross Section

Narcissus bulb

Cross Section

Other Structures

Tuberous root

Tuber

Rhizome

Corms

BULBS

MAJOR AND MINOR BULBS

Commercial bulb growers divide bulbs into two categories—major and minor. Major bulbs are the larger, flashier, more commercially important bulbs—daffodils, tulips, lilies, gladiolus, dahlias, cannas, and tuberous begonias.

The smaller and less expensive minor bulbs include grape hyacinths, squills, and species crocuses. Some catalogs now call these specialty bulbs instead of minor bulbs. By either name, minor bulbs are individually less showy than the majors, but they are still an important source of springtime color. Plant them in a mass so that their colors can merge to make an impact.

What Bulbs Do in the Garden

Early bulbs welcome spring to many gardens. From the first snowdrops and species crocuses to the elegant hybrid tulips of midspring, bulbs are unequalled as a source of early color. They bloom in many colors, sizes, and shapes, and you can mix and match them in endless combinations. Once planted, they come back year after year with only minimal maintenance

Designing with Bulbs

The smaller, or minor, bulbs—crocuses, scillas, grape hyacinths, and snowdrops among them—are lovely massed to form carpets of color. Plant them in areas that can be left unmowed while the foliage matures—in lawns, open woodlands, under deciduous trees, or on slopes and banks. These little charmers look good in beds and borders, too, if you plant dozens or scores of them rather than clumps of threes or fives. Like undisturbed daffodils, many spread and form colonies that expand and eventually cover whole swaths of ground. This process is called naturalizing.

Using Major Bulbs. The larger bulbs—daffodils, tulips, and crown imperials, for instance—are most at home in beds and borders, especially in combination with shrubs, perennials, and annuals. One way to bring color to the garden from spring to fall is to plant annuals among and around the spring bulbs to hide their maturing foliage and carry on the show throughout the summer. Spring perennials such as candytuft and columbine also make good companions for bulbs.

Bulbs add color to summer gardens too. Here, gladiolus 'Violetta' blooms along with catmint and 'Sparrleshoop', a climbing rose.

Bulbs are lovely naturalized in a lawn where the grass can be left unmowed in spring until the bulb foliage ripens. This lawn is graced by tulips, daffodils, anemones, and spring starflowers (*Ipheion uniflorum*).

Bulbs in Summer and Fall

Although many gardeners associate bulbs with spring, numerous lovely summer flowers also grow from bulbs. In Zone 7 and cooler, most summer bulbs must be planted each spring, dug each fall, and stored indoors over the winter. But the result is worth the extra work.

Cut flowers. Plant gladiolus every two weeks or so for armloads of tall, spiky cut flowers throughout the summer. Hardy alliums send up their big starry globes of purple, white, or yellow from early to midsummer, and dahlias light up the garden with their huge variety of colors, sizes, and flower forms in late summer and fall.

In beds and or borders. A classic in summer beds and borders, lilies offer a wide assortment of flower sizes, colors, and blooming times. Lily flowers are more-or-less trumpet shaped; the petals vary in width, and some lilies have reflexed, (backward curving) petals. Many lilies are fragrant, and some are flushed or spotted with a second color. Best of all, many lilies are very hardy and can be left in the garden year-round.

Tuberous begonias bring bold bursts of color to shady summer gardens and container plantings. Their big blossoms may be shaped like camellias or roses, or fringed like carnations.

For a touch of the tropics, turn to cannas or caladiums. Late bloomers include colchicums, autumn crocuses, and hardy cyclamen.

Planting Bulbs

In colder climates, daffodils, tulips, and other hardy spring-bloomers should be planted in early- to mid-autumn, before the first hard frost. In warm climates, plant bulbs in November (or even December where winters are very mild). To stimulate blooming in warm climates, you may need to refrigerate hardy bulbs for six to eight weeks before you plant them. Ask a gardening friend or the local Cooperative Extension Service if this is necessary in your area.

For the best display, plant the bulbs in drifts or in clusters of 12 or more. Plant lots more if the bulbs are small.

Preparing Bulb Sites. Hardy bulbs thrive in almost any well-drained soil, in full sun or partial shade. Ideally, you should amend their site a season before planting. But if you haven't prepared the area in advance, begin by loosening the soil and digging in an all-purpose fertilizer or a special bulb formula and plenty of organic matter. Add some gypsum and rock phosphate or superphosphate for long-term supplies of calcium and phosphorus. If your soil is sandy or contains a lot of clay, be sure to add extra leaf mold, compost, or peat moss; abundant organic matter will help improve these soils. Then rake the soil surface smooth.

If you're planting a small number of bulbs, make holes of the required depth with a trowel or a bulb planter. But to plant a lot of bulbs in the same area, it's easier to excavate it all at once with a shovel.

Placing the Bulbs. Plant the bulbs with their pointed ends up. Set one bulb in each hole or, in a larger planting, place them at the correct spacing on the bottom of the excavated area. To make the planting look more natural, gently toss them onto the area and plant them where they land.

Set the bulbs firmly in the soil at the correct depth. (See the table below.) Bury them with soil; water thoroughly; and cover the bed with a 2- to 3-inch layer of shredded leaves or other loose mulch.

Buying and Storing Bulbs

Handle bulbs with care. Even though they're dormant when you buy them, they are still alive and are affected by their environment. If they get too wet, they'll rot; if left in hot sunlight, they'll dry out; and if sealed in a plastic bag, they'll suffocate. Such compromised bulbs won't bloom well and may not even survive. So treat newly purchased bulbs with respect.

Shop wisely, too. If you buy bulbs locally, examine them carefully. If you order by mail, unpack the bulbs as soon as they arrive and look them over. Most healthy bulbs are firm to the touch. Anemone tubers look shriveled and dried up even when healthy, but most bulbs should be full and plump. You should feel no soft spots or see any evidence of rot or mold. The basal plate on the bottom of the bulb should be firm and solid and show no mold or other damage. If the basal plate is damaged, the bulb may fail to flower or, at best, will bloom poorly.

Always buy nursery-grown bulbs, never those that have been wild-crafted or collected from sites where they grow naturally. Wild-crafting depletes the populations of these bulbs, sometimes to the point of endangerment. Look for a "Commercially Propagated" label on bags, or ask the supplier about the bulbs' origins. Be particularly careful when buying Anemone blanda, Cyclamen species, Eranthis, and small or species Narcissus.

If you can't plant your new bulbs right away, store them in a cool, airy location away from direct sun. Good air circulation is important. Store the bulbs in mesh bags (like the kind in which onions are sold); put them in paper bags with plenty of room; or—if you have the space—spread them out on open shelves in a dark area.

BULBS

Bulb-Panting Depths

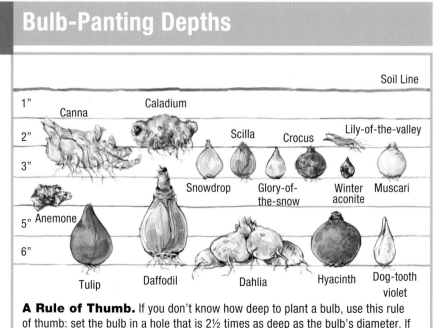

Soil Line

1" — Canna, Caladium
2" — Scilla, Crocus, Lily-of-the-valley
3" — Snowdrop, Glory-of-the-snow, Winter aconite, Muscari
5" — Anemone
6" — Tulip, Daffodil, Dahlia, Hyacinth, Dog-tooth violet

A Rule of Thumb. If you don't know how deep to plant a bulb, use this rule of thumb: set the bulb in a hole that is 2½ times as deep as the bulb's diameter. If you're planting in clay soil, don't plant so deep. In light, sandy soil, plant deeper.

Naturalizing Bulbs

Naturalizing bulbs means planting them in a lawn or ground cover and then allowing them to multiply on their own and spread out. Many of the smaller bulbs are great for naturalizing. The usual procedure is to naturalize bulbs in a lawn for a cheerful, informal effect that looks as if the bulbs had come up on their own.

Quantity matters when it comes to naturalized bulbs. It takes a minimum of a dozen or so major bulbs in every clump and 18 to 24 minor ones to show up well. Keep your costs down by looking for lower-cost packages of slightly smaller bulbs for naturalizing. With good care, they soon catch up to higher-priced bulbs.

If you're planting in an existing lawn, use a sharp pointed trowel to punch holes for the bulbs. It's a time-consuming process, but it creates the most natural look. Alternatively, you could strip the sod from the area, plant the bulbs, then either replace the sod or overseed a new lawn. Sprinkle a little rock phosphate for phosphorus and gypsum for calcium into the bottom of each planting hole or the excavated area. Scratch these amendments into the soil before setting in the bulbs. Remember that any fertilizer you put on the lawn will also affect the bulbs; a high-nitrogen lawn fertilizer could hinder the bulb's flower production. Use a more balanced formula (one with more equal numbers) for the areas where bulbs grow.

Species crocuses naturalize beautifully. Plant groups of crocuses in a lawn for a meadowy look in early spring.

Planting Tools for Bulbs

Bulb planters are specially designed for planting bulbs. There are both long- and short-handle types, and most have the depth in inches marked on the outside. To use them, just push the tool into the soil, twist it, and pull it up with the excavated core of soil inside.

A pointed trowel can also make a perfectly good planting hole and often works better than a bulb planter in heavy soil. If you have a favorite trusty trowel, by all means use it!

trowel

short-handle bulb planter

long-handle bulb planter

RODENT PROTECTION

Some bulbs, such as crocuses and tulips, are candy to chipmunks and other small rodents. Keep them away from your bulbs by excavating entire bulb planting areas and lining the bottom and sides

with hardware cloth. After planting, cover the bulbs with a sprinkling of soil and a double layer of chicken wire before adding enough soil to cover the bulbs to the correct depth. A top layer of wire gives further protection from the rodents. Or plant bulbs they won't eat, such as daffodils.

BULBS FOR NATURALIZING

Autumn crocus (*Colchicum autumnale*)
Checker lily (*Fritillaria meleagris*)
Daffodil (*Narcissus* species and hybrids)
Dwarf iris (*Iris reticulata*)
Glory-of-the-snow (*Chionodoxa luciliae*)
Grape hyacinth (*Muscari* species)
Grecian windflower (*Anemone blanda*)
Ornamental onion (*Allium* species)
Siberian squill (*Scilla siberica*)
Snowdrop (*Galanthus nivalis*)
Spanish bluebell (*Hyacinthoides hispanica*)
Species crocus (*Crocus* species)
Trout lily (*Erythronium* species)

Start tuberous begonias indoors unless you live in a warm climate with a long frost-free growing season. Plant the tubers in a flat or pots of moist potting mix, with their concave side facing upward.

Use pots of daffodils, as shown above, for a shot of bright color. Small cultivars and species narcissus grow especially well in pots. Shown here are 'Tête-à-Tête', 'Minnow', and 'Jumblie'.

Containers of `Ice Follies' daffodils line a walkway and glow cheerily against the evergreen shrubs behind them (above right).

Planting Tender Bulbs

Tender bulbs are planted like hardy bulbs, except you plant them in spring, after the danger of frost is past and the soil is warm. Prepare the soil as described under "Preparing Bulb Sites," page 141. Set the bulbs at the depth recommended in the profiles on pages 150 to 177.

If you live where the frost-free growing season is short, get a jump on the season and start some of your tender bulbs indoors. Tuberous begonias, especially, benefit from an indoor head start. Plant them in pots or flats as described below. Keep the potting mix moist but not soggy. When shoots appear, give the young plants bright light. Move them outdoors when the danger of frost is past.

Planting in Containers

Bulbs are ideal for containers. Plant pots of a single type, such as daffodils or tulips, or mix several types together.

Plant the bulbs in pots, deep flats, tubs, or planters. The containers should have drainage holes in the bottom and be at least 5 to 6 inches in diameter; flats should be 4 to 5 inches deep. Use a 5-inch bulb pan (a wide, shallow pot) to force crocuses, irises, squills, or grape hyacinths. Leave about 1½ inches between the bulbs when you plant them. They should be close together but not touching. A 6-inch pot will hold five to six tulip bulbs, three hyacinths, or three double-nosed daffodils. (A bulb's nose is the tip where stems emerge. A double-nosed bulb has two tips, usually because the bulb has propagated itself but the bulbs have not yet fully separated from each other.)

If you're reusing old pots, scrub them thoroughly and soak them in a disinfectant solution of one part liquid chlorine bleach to nine parts water before you plant. Soak clay pots in water overnight.

All bulbs need loose, crumbly soil with good drainage. A potting mix of equal parts of garden loam or potting soil, compost, peat moss, and sand is ideal. If you will discard the bulbs after they bloom, they don't need any fertilizer. They already contain the nutrients they need to produce their flowers. However, if you plan to keep the bulbs or transplant them to the garden, use a half-strength liquid fertilizer every two weeks after the shoots first appear.

In large containers outdoors, bulbs need to be planted at their regular depth. Allow ½ inch between the soil line and the rim of the pot to allow for watering.

BULBS

PLANT A DISH GARDEN

It's easy to create a pretty dish garden of blooming spring bulbs. Buy several small potted bulb plants that are already in bud. Replant them in a bulb pan or a decorative ceramic dish, using a combination of large and small bulbs with flowers at different heights.

An alternative is to arrange the pots in a basket. Hide them by covering the soil and rims with long strands of sphagnum moss (the kind that hasn't been ground up). For a decorative look, tie a colorful bow on the handle of the basket.

Caring for Bulbs

Although bulbs are easy to grow, they do need some care. They appreciate a dose of fertilizer and compost once a year. To keep them blooming vigorously and increase your stock of plants, divide them after several years in the same location or whenever blooms start to diminish.

During and After Flowering

As the blossoms fade, clip them off so the bulb can channel its energy into enlarging and developing bulblets rather than pro-ducing seeds. Deadheading isn't feasible for grape hyacinths, crocuses, and other small bulbs that you grow by the dozens, but it is helpful for larger daffodils, tulips, and other major bulbs.

Most bulbs produce leaves along with their flowers, and these are an important source of nourishment for the plants. Unless you plan to dig and discard the bulbs after they bloom (as many people do with the short-lived hybrid tulips), it's essential to leave the foliage in place until it turns yellow and begins to dry out. Planting annuals or bushy perennials close to the bulb plants will help to hide the fading bulb leaves.

In the case of crocuses, grape hyacinths, and other small bulbs that you've naturalized in a lawn, wait at least six weeks after they flower before you mow the lawn where they are growing.

Fertilizing Bulbs

Small bulbs don't need to be fertilized, but larger ones benefit from feeding once or twice a year. Apply a balanced, all-purpose fertilizer as soon as the young shoots emerge from the soil, and again after the plants have finished blooming. Or you can fertilize in autumn by applying a rich compost,

an all-purpose organic fertilizer blend, or a slow-release bulb fertilizer. If you don't mulch, topdress with an inch of compost or leaf mold every year to maintain a good level of organic matter in the soil.

Bulbs don't need to be watered except during prolonged dry spells when you'd normally water perennials and shrubs. They seldom suffer from pest or disease problems either, as long as they are not too crowded and grow in soils with good drainage and the appropriate pH.

DIVIDING BULBS

Bulbs reproduce by means of underground offsets called bulblets that form on the outside perimeter of the bulb's basal plate. Some lilies produce bulbils— small, round structures that form in the leaf axils. Both bulblets and bulbils can be removed and planted; they eventually grow into full-size bulbs capable of producing flowers.

Corms go through an annual renewal cycle; a new corm forms on top of the old one each summer. The old corm shrivels, and the roots on the new one pull it down into the hole left by the first. Small cormlets or cormels form at the base of the new corm or, in some cases, on aboveground stems.

Tuberous roots and rhizomes are easy to divide. In the case of tuberous roots such as those of dahlias, the old tuber deteriorates as the new ones form. The new replacements can be cut into pieces, each with a bud or eye, to produce new plants. Clumps of tuberous roots can be divided like clumps of perennials.

Tubers (or tuber-corms), such as those of tuberous begonias, get larger with age. Propagate them by cutting them into large pieces, making certain that each piece has an eye or two. Let the cut surfaces callus over in the open air for a day or so before replanting.

Daffodils light up a border in spring when they tower above their companions (below left).

The same border in summer when zinnias, rudbeckia, and phlox are blooming (below right).

End-of-Season Activities

Autumn brings some special tasks to the bulb gardener. Hardy bulbs can be planted for bloom the following spring, tender bulbs can be lifted and stored safely away, and other bulbs can be prepared for forcing into winter bloom.

Lifting Tender Bulbs

When the first frost strikes, it's time to dig up tender bulbs, corms, and tubers from the outdoor garden and put them in storage for the winter. You can wait to dig most bulbs until the foliage has started to turn brown or has been softened by a light frost. Exceptions to this rule are tuberous begonias and tuberoses, which can't tolerate even a light frost. Dig them early. If you delay digging any of the tender bulbs until you get a heavy frost, the plant crowns or the bulbs themselves may be damaged.

The basic procedure for lifting bulbs of tuberous begonias, dahlias, gladiolus, and most other tender plants with fleshy top growth is shown in the box below, "How To Lift Tender Bulbs."

Mulch bulb plantings in late fall after the soil has frozen to prevent heaving damage.

how to
Lift Tender Bulbs

DIFFICULTY LEVEL: EASY

Tools and Materials: Spade, pruning shears, peat moss or dry leaves, cardboard boxes

1 Wait until autumn to lift plants such as this dahlia. Loosen the soil, and lift the entire root-ball.

2 Using a sharp pair of pruning shears, cut back the stems to several inches above the tubers.

3 Using your fingers, gently remove as much soil as possible from around the tubers and roots.

4 Label the tubers as to cultivar and color, and store them in peat moss or dry leaves in a cool, dark area.

BULBS

Forcing Bulbs, Corms, & Tubers for Winter Flowers Indoors

Many spring-blooming bulbs can be forced into bloom indoors during the bleakest part of winter. The first step is purchasing the best-quality bulbs you can find when they become available in autumn. Top-quality exhibition-grade bulbs produce the best flowers. Bulbs that have been specially prepared for forcing are widely available. These bulbs are prechilled and don't need a cold period between planting and the time you start the forcing process.

If you get the bulbs before it's time to plant them, store them carefully. In a warm climate, put them in the refrigerator; in cooler climates, store them in mesh bags or spread them out on an open shelf where air can circulate freely around them. Cool, but not freezing cold, temperatures are best for storing bulbs.

To have flowers in winter, you must begin the process in autumn. Plant the bulbs in pots as described in "Planting in Containers," page 143. To enjoy continuous bloom over a long period, stagger your plantings. A good rule of thumb is to plant in September for late December or January flowers, in October for flowers in February, and in November for flowers in March. As you plant, label each pot with the type of bulb, flower color, and date of planting. When the bulbs bloom later on, make a note of the date to help you plan next winter's display.

Water the bulbs thoroughly but gently when you finish planting. After the bulbs are planted, they need several weeks of darkness and cold storage—at temperatures from about 35° to 48°F—before you can actually force them into bloom. This period is essential for root formation; rooting takes 10 to 14 weeks for most bulbs. Depending on your climate and conditions, you can store the bulb pots in the basement, an insulated coldframe, an unheated garage or shed, or even the refrigerator (well wrapped to exclude light). Cover the pots with burlap to keep the soil moist, and check them once a week. Water if the soil is dry; keep it moist but not wet.

how to

Plant for Forcing

DIFFICULTY LEVEL: EASY

Tools and Materials: Bulbs, pot, soil mix

1 Crowding forced bulbs does not interfere with growth or blooming.

2 Cover daffodil bulbs for forcing with only an inch or so of soil mix.

Freesias

Lily-of-the-Valley

Planting Instructions for Different Bulbs

Anemone coronaria / Florist's or Poppy Anemone

In September or October, soak the tubers overnight in lukewarm water to prepare them for planting. When they're soft enough that you can dent them with your fingernail, they're ready to plant.

Plant three tubers in each 6-inch pot. Water well, and store the pots in a moist, cool location where the temperature is 45°F to 50°F for six to eight weeks. Move the pots to a bright airy location, also with temperatures around 50°F. (A south-facing window in a cool room works well.) Water freely as the plants grow.

Convallaria majalis / Lily-of-the-Valley

Lily-of-the-valley pips are usually shipped from mail-order houses in fall. You can buy them preplanted or plant them yourself, using three or four pips to each 6-inch pot. Generally all you need to do is add water and you'll have flowers in two or three weeks. Keep them watered and fertilized all winter, and plant the pips out in the garden in spring. They will bloom in successive years.

Crocus hybrids / Crocus

Plant Dutch crocus corms in mid- to late autumn, 1 to 2 inches deep and 1 inch apart. Six corms will fit in a 4-inch pot. The pot should be at least 3½ inches deep to accommodate the roots. Give the potted corms eight weeks of cold storage. Water sparingly until the plants are full grown; then keep the soil moist but not waterlogged.

Freesia × hybrida / Freesia

Plant freesia corms in September or October, six to a 5-inch pot. Position the corms 2 inches apart and just below the soil line. Chill for six to eight weeks. Feed once a month with an all-purpose houseplant fertilizer until buds are set.

After the rooting period, move the pots to a bright, sunny but cool (60°F to 65°F) location. The temperature should drop at least 10 degrees at night. The plants will bloom in about three months. The weak stems usually need staking.

When the flowers are finished blooming, keep watering and feeding the plants until late spring and then stop. When the foliage dies, store the pots on their side in a dark, dry place until it's time to replant them in fall. Unlike most bulbs, freesias can be forced repeatedly if they are fed and stored correctly.

Hyacinthus orientalis / Hyacinth

For flowers in January and February, pot the bulbs in September or October; water them well; and store them outside in a box or cold frame, covered with straw, until mid-December. Pot bulbs for early spring bloom in November or early December and keep them outdoors all winter, covered with straw. You can also force hyacinths in bulb glasses. Keep the bottom part of the glass filled with clean water. Give them a cold period by filling the glass with water so that it just touches the bulb's basal plate. Put the glass in a foil-lined insulated bag; tie the top shut; and keep it in your refrigerator for 12 to 15 weeks or until the shoot is about 4 inches high. Then bring the glass into bright, indirect light, such as a well-lit north window.

Cool temperatures of 60°F to 65°F are best. Keep the soil moist (or the bulb glass filled with water to the bottom of the bulb) until the flowers have finished blooming. If the bulb is in soil, put the pot in a sunny spot; let the foliage develop naturally; and keep the soil moist until the leaves yellow. Then gradually let the soil dry until the foliage yellows and dries. Save the bulbs to plant outdoors. (A bulb that has been forced in a glass container is best discarded.)

Iris species / Iris

The small bulbous irises are the best kind to force. *Iris reticulata* will give you violet-purple flowers and *I. danfordiae* will give you yellow ones. Plant the rhizomes in mid-fall to have flowers in mid- to late-winter. Plant them 2 to 3 inches deep and 3 inches apart. Give the potted rhizomes eight weeks of cold storage. When the plants bloom, keep them in a sunny but cool spot.

(continued on page 148)

how to

Force Hyacinths
DIFFICULTY LEVEL: EASY

Tools and Materials: Bulbs, hyacinth glass, water

Bulbs ready for cooling; the water comes only to the basal plate, not above it.

Blooms just starting to open. Set them in a place with bright, indirect light.

BULBS

(continued from page 147)

Lilium 'Enchantment' / Enchantment Lily

'Enchantment' is a particularly vigorous Asiatic lily, which is why it responds well to forcing. Plant three bulbs in a 12-inch pot that is twice as tall as the bulbs. Put 2 inches of pebbles in the bottom of the pot before adding soil—excellent drainage is critical. Plant the bulbs 1 inch deep. Water well, and set the pot in a cool (60°F to 65°F), dark place—such as a basement—where there is some humidity. Keep the soil evenly moist.

When shoots appear (in about three weeks), move the pot into full sun and keep the soil moist. Feed the plants once a month with an all-purpose houseplant fertilizer. The plants will bloom in about six weeks. Stake the tall stems to help them support the flowers.

When the last flowers die, cut off the stem right below the lowest blossom. When the leaves die, cut off the stem at ground level. Remove the bulbs from the pot, and store them in dry peat moss until planting time next year. 'Enchantment' lilies can be forced repeatedly.

Narcissus cultivars / Daffodil and Narcissus

For winter flowers, pot daffodils in early October. Double-nosed bulbs will give you the most flowers. Plant three bulbs in a 6-inch pot, four or five in a 12-inch pot. The top of each bulb should be 1 inch below the soil surface. Keep the pots in cold storage until late December or for 12 to 14 weeks.

smart tip

PROLONGING BLOOMS

Bulb flowers last longer indoors if the pots are kept in a cool area with bright but indirect light.

Iris reticulata **and *Iris danfordiae***
have been forced for winter bloom.

Crocuses

Narcissus tazetta 'Paperwhite' / Paperwhite Narcissus

Paperwhite narcissus bulbs are available in autumn and can be planted anytime after you get them. They need no cold storage period and don't even need soil.

You can plant the bulbs in pots of soil or perlite, in bowls of pebbles, or in a bulb glass. To plant in soil, perlite, or pebbles, fill the container halfway with the medium of your choice. Set the bulbs on top, about ½ inch apart. Add more of the medium until the bulbs are about one-third covered. Water the soil or perlite thoroughly, or add water to the pebbles until it just touches the bottom of the bulbs. If planting in water, fill the glass until the bottom of the bulb is in water but the entire bulb is not submerged.

Some gardeners like to set the containers in a dark place for two or three weeks before moving them into a bright place. But you can simply leave your pots of paperwhites on a bright windowsill until they bloom. The best thing about paperwhites is their speed—they give you flowers about four weeks after you plant them. They bloom readily anytime from November to April, though bulbs planted in December and January will bloom more quickly than bulbs planted in November. For continuous bloom, start new bulbs every two weeks. You can save some bulbs to force in late winter and early spring by refrigerating them.

After the plants finish blooming, gardeners in Zones 8 to 10 can plant the bulbs outdoors. Everywhere else, they should be discarded because they can't survive cold weather.

how to

Plant in Pebbles

DIFFICULTY LEVEL: EASY

Tools and Materials: Bowl, pebbles, bulbs

Paperwhite narcissus will bloom in a bowl of pebbles. Keep the water level up to the bottom of the basal plates for the best results.

Mixed potted lilies that have been forced into bloom.

Anemone coronaria

Tulipa hybrids / Tulips

Planting pots of early-, mid- and late-season tulips will give you flowers over a period of several weeks.

Plant five or six bulbs to a 6-inch pot, with the flat side of the bulb facing toward the outside of the pot. (The flowers always turn towards the flat side, so that placement gives the nicest display.) Plant the bulbs as soon as they arrive from the nursery because they bruise easily. Set them so that their tops are ½ inch deep. They need 12 to 15 weeks of chilling.

To bring tulips into bloom, give them good ventilation and plenty of light, but keep them out of direct sun. Keep the soil moist but not soggy.

BULBS

Lily leek

Allium

Allium species
ORNAMENTAL ONION

The genus that gives us so many indispensable seasonings—onions, garlic, shallots, and chives—also boasts a number of ornamental species with pretty round clusters of small starry flowers. The flowers come in a range of colors (blue, purple, rose-purple, white, and yellow) and the plants in a range of sizes. All have narrow, grassy leaves and carry their blossoms at the top of straight, slender stems.

Hardiness: Zones 4 to 8, varies with species.

Blooming Time: Late spring to midsummer, depending on the species.

Height: 4 inches to 4 feet, varies with species.

Depth and Spacing: 4 to 8 inches deep, 3 inches to 1½ feet apart, varies with species.

Light: Full sun to partial shade.

Soil: Fertile, well-drained, and sandy. (*A. neapolitanum* tolerates heavier soils.)

Moisture: Abundant, even.

Garden Uses: Ornamental onions are attractive planted in clumps in beds and borders,

Persian onion

especially surrounded by other summer bloomers that can hide their foliage. Some make good cut flowers. Shorter-growing species are at home in a rock garden or container.

Comments: Plant alliums in fall. Divide them when the clumps become crowded and the plants begin producing fewer flowers. Tall-growers may need staking. *A. moly* and *A. neapolitanum* self-sow; deadhead to prevent unwanted seedlings.

Recommended Cultivars: *A. aflatunense*, Persian onion: 2 to 3 feet, deep violet-purple.

A. caeruleum, Blue-of-the-Heavens: 2 feet, clear blue.

A. christophii, Star of Persia: 1 to 2 feet, large silvery purple globes.

A. moly, Lily leek 'Jeannine': 1 foot to 1¼ feet, bright yellow.

A. neapolitanum, Daffodil garlic: to 1¼ feet, fragrant, white.

A. karataviense: to 9 inches, pale pink flowers with purple midribs.

A. sphaerocephalum, Drumstick allium: 2 to 3 feet, purple-pink egg-shaped flowerheads, naturalizes well.

A. triquetrum, Three-cornered leek: 1 foot, loose clusters of dangling white, bell-shaped flowers, naturalizes well.

A. karataviense

Star of Persia

Anemone

Anemone blanda,
GRECIAN WINDFLOWER
A. coronaria,
FLORIST'S ANEMONE,
POPPY ANEMONE

Grecian windflowers (*Anemone blanda*) are small plants that open their daisylike blue, pink, or white flowers early in the growing season. Florist's or poppy anemones (*A. coronaria*) produce big, poppylike blossoms in brilliant red, scarlet, rose, pink, blue, purple, and white; the flowers have a dark center.

Hardiness: Grecian windflower, Zones 5 to 9; florist's anemone, Zones 7 to 10.

Blooming Time: Grecian windflower, early- to mid-spring; florist's anemone, mid-spring.

Height: Grecian windflower, 6 to 8 inches; florist's anemone, 1½ feet.

Depth and Spacing: Grecian windflower, 4 inches deep, 3 to 4 inches apart; florist's anemone, 2 to 3 inches deep, 3 inches apart.

Light: Full sun to partial shade.

Soil: Well-drained, humusy, average to good fertility.

Moisture: Average to moist; anemones can't tolerate drought.

Garden Uses: Let Grecian windflowers spread and naturalize in an open area, grow them in the front of beds and

A. De Caen tubers

borders, or place them in a rock garden. They are delightful as a carpet under taller growing tulips and daffodils.

Plant florist's anemones in beds and borders or in a cutting garden. They also grow well in containers and can be forced for winter flowers indoors.

Comments: Florist's anemones can't tolerate frost; except in very warm climates, wait until all danger of frost is past to plant the tubers in the garden. Dig them before frost in the fall, and store them indoors over winter. Plant Grecian windflowers in autumn, when you plant other hardy bulbs.

Recommended Cultivars: Grecian windflowers are often sold by color—mixed colors or blue shades, for instance. Individual cultivars are also available: 'Blue Star' blue; 'Charmer', deep rose; 'Pink Star', light pink; 'Violet Star', violet; 'White Splendour', white.

Florist's anemone: The De Caen group is a brilliant mix of scarlet, blue-violet, and white; 'Bride', white flowers; 'His Excellency', scarlet; 'Mr Fokker', violet-blue; 'Rosea', rose. The St. Brigid group is double and blooms in scarlet, rose, blue, and white; 'Admiral', double, rose; 'Lord Lieutenant', double, blue; 'Governor', semi-double, bright red.

smart tip

Grecian windflower

PLANTING WINDFLOWER TUBERS

Soak the wrinkled anemone tubers in water to soften them before planting.

Begonia

Begonia Tuberhybrida hybrids
TUBEROUS BEGONIA

Red and yellow begonias mix with browallias in a shady garden bed.

Spectacular plants for shade, tuberous begonias produce their big, splashy blossoms in brilliant warm colors and show them off against contrasting dark green leaves. The flowers of various cultivars are formed similarly to camellias, roses, or carnations.

Hardiness: Zones 10 and 11; elsewhere, dig and store indoors over winter.

Blooming Time: Midsummer to fall.

Height: 8 inches to 1½ feet.

Depth and Spacing: Set the top of the tubers at soil level, 10 to 15 inches apart.

Light: Partial to medium shade; need shade at least part of the day.

Soil: Well-drained, fertile, humusy, deeply dug.

Moisture: Even but not soggy.

Garden Uses: Tuberous begonias grow and bloom beautifully in shady or partly shady gardens. Many are cascading or trailing and work wonderfully in pots, tubs, window boxes, or hanging baskets on shady porches or patios.

Comments: Begonias need a long growing season; if you live in a cold climate, start the tubers indoors in February or March, as shown on page 143. Plant or transplant outdoors when all danger of frost has passed, and fertilize monthly with an all-purpose fertilizer until blooming begins. Switch to a low-nitrogen fertilizer or compost once plants have flowers. Because the flowers are large and heavy, all but the cascading types usually need staking.

In cold climates, dig begonia tubers after the first frost; in warm areas, wait until the leaves yellow and start to turn brown at the end of the season. After digging, spread out newly dug tubers and let them dry in the sun for a few days. Then cut off the stems an inch above the tops of the tubers. Shake off the soil; lay the tubers in a shallow box or tray; and cover them with peat moss or dry sand. Pack tubers of the same flower color together, and label the boxes so that you know what you're planting in spring. The best storage temperature is 40°F to 50°F.

Recommended Cultivars: Camellia-flowered begonias have red, pink, yellow, or white flowers shaped like camellias. Picotee, Crispa, and Marginata hybrids have petals edged in red, pink, or orange. Cascade begonias have a trailing habit and bloom in red, pink, yellow, white, and mixed pastel shades. Non Stop begonias produce double flowers continuously all summer in red, pink, orange, or white. Carnation (Fimbriata group) begonias have fringed petals in red, orange, yellow, or white.

how to

Store Begonia Tubers
DIFFICULTY LEVEL: EASY

Tools and Materials: peat moss, box

Store tubers over winter, concave side up, in a single layer in dry peat moss or sand.

smart tip

HARDENING OFF

Harden off plants by exposing them gradually to the outside.

'Apricot Lace'

'Postman Joyner'

Caladium

Caladium bicolor
FANCY-LEAVED CALADIUM

These familiar foliage plants are aptly named. Their arrowhead-shaped leaves are veined, flushed, edged, and splotched in varying combinations of red, rose, pink, green, and white. With large leaves and lush colors, caladiums bring a tropical look to summer gardens.

Hardiness: Zones 10 and 11; elsewhere grow as an annual or dig and store tubers indoors over winter.

Blooming Time: Midsummer to fall.

Height: 1 to 1½ feet.

Depth and Spacing: 2 inches deep, 8 inches to 1 foot apart.

Light: Partial to full shade.

Soil: Well-drained, humusy, slightly acidic.

Moisture: Even.

Garden Uses: Caladiums bring a flash of exotic color to shady beds and borders. They look best planted in clumps or drifts, but they can be difficult to combine with summer flowers. One solution is to plant drifts of caladiums by themselves along a fence or walkway. They also grow well in shaded pots and window boxes.

'Candidum'

'Pink Beauty'

Caladium complements this mixture of coleus, amaranth, nasturtium, and elephant ears.

Comments: Don't plant outdoors until all danger of frost is past in spring; where the growing season is short, start tubers indoors. Dig the bulbs in fall, and store them in a cool indoor location over the winter. Pack them for storage in dry peat moss or vermiculite.

Recommended Cultivars: 'Candidum', white leaves with green veins; 'Freida Hemple', red leaves with green edges; 'Pink Beauty', green leaves blotched with pink. Often sold as mixed colors and patterns.

smart tip

CONTAINER-GROWING

Caladiums grow well in containers, making them an ideal plant for a shady entranceway into your home.

BULBS

Canna

Canna × generalis

Big and bold, *Canna* is undeniably dramatic in the garden. The large, brightly colored flowers resemble gladiolus; they bloom at the top of stout stems that rise from large, oblong, deep green leaves. *Canna* plants have long been known for their brilliant, assertive red or orange flowers, but newer cultivars have expanded the palette to include soft yellow, pink, peach, and bicolors. Some cultivars have boldly colored or variegated leaves.

how to

Lift and Store *Canna* Rhizomes
DIFFICULTY LEVEL: EASY

Tools and Materials: Spade or shovel, pruning shears

1 After the first fall frost, dig the rhizomes and cut back the stems, leaving several inches.

2 Divide clumps by pulling apart the rhizomes so that each piece has roots and stems.

3 Clean the divided rhizomes, brushing off any loose soil around the roots.

4 Store the rhizomes in a single layer in a cardboard box in a frost-free area.

Hardiness: Zones 10 and 11 (Zones 8 and 9 if mulched well); elsewhere, dig and store the bulbs indoors over winter.

Blooming Time: Midsummer into fall.

Height: 2 to 5 feet.

Depth and Spacing: 2 to 4 inches deep, 1 to 2 feet apart.

Light: Full sun.

Soil: Fertile, with high organic matter content.

Moisture: Even; water during dry spells.

'Embassador', front, 'Striata', rear

Garden Uses: *Canna* is bold, bright, and exotic. The plants are good additions to a tropical-style garden, but they also make a statement in a foundation planting or massed along a walk or driveway. Some kinds, notably the Longwood Hybrids, can grow in standing water; these are beautiful in water gardens or along the edge of a pond. Dwarf cultivars do well in containers.

Comments: Don't plant *Canna* outdoors until the temperature no longer dips below 50°F; it flourishes in hot, humid weather.

In Zones 6 and colder, start rhizomes indoors in spring. Plant the rhizomes in flats of moist peat moss or a peat/vermiculite starting mix. When shoots appear, transplant each rhizome to a 4-inch pot of moist but well-drained garden loam or soil-based potting mix. When all danger of frost is past, transplant to the garden, setting plants so that the tubers are planted 3 to 4 inches deep.

After the first fall frost, cut off the plants at ground level; dig up the roots; let them dry for a few days; then store over the winter in a cool, dry, frost-free location.

Recommended Cultivars: 'Red King Humbert', bronzy red-purple leaves, red flowers; 'Yellow King Humbert', red-dotted yellow flowers, green leaves; 'The President', classic red flowers, green leaves; 'City of Portland', rose flowers; 'Rosemond Coles', red flowers edged in yellow; 'Pretoria' green-and-yellow striped leaves and orange flowers; 'Picasso', dwarf, yellow blossoms covered, with red spots; 'Brilliant', dwarf, red flowers; 'Tropical Rose, dwarf, rose flowers.

For pools and ponds, look for Longwood Hybrids and other cultivars in water garden catalogs.

Chionodoxa

Chionodoxa luciliae
GLORY-OF-THE-SNOW

These delightful little plants produce star-shaped flowers in shades of lavender-blue, pink, or white early in the year. In suitable environments and with well-drained soil, they multiply rapidly. Even if you do not divide and replant them, they will eventually carpet an area with their flowers.

'Alba'

Hardiness: Zones 3 to 8.

Blooming Time: Late winter to early spring, depending upon climate.

Height: 5 to 6 inches.

Depth and Spacing: 2 to 3 inches deep, 3 inches apart.

Light: If you live in a cool climate where summers are mild, plant glory-of-the-snow in full sun. If your summers are hot, choose a site that receives partial shade, in the afternoon if possible, during late spring and summer.

Soil: Well-drained, high in organic matter.

Moisture: Even; water regularly during the growing and blooming seasons if rains are sporadic in your area. Taper off watering when the foliage browns and begins to die back.

Garden Uses: Use glory-of-the-snow in rock gardens, the front of borders and garden beds, or naturalize them under shrubs and trees. They grow well with and complement the appearance of the earliest miniature daffodils.

Comments: Mice, moles, or squirrels generally don't eat glory-of-the-snow. The plants spread from both self-sown

Glory-of-the-snow

how to

Plant
DIFFICULTY LEVEL: EASY

Tools and Materials: Trowel, wire cage, bulbs

Plant bulbs 2 to 3 inches deep and 3 inches apart. Cage them only if mice bother tulips or other bulbs in the same area.

seeds and by forming bulblets. Every few years, the plants will become crowded; they lose vigor and both flower quality and quantity declines. Mark their location in the spring; dig them up in early autumn; separate them; and replant. These tough flowers stay open through rain and cold weather. In fact, rain can help to pollinate the flowers. The foliage disappears soon after the flowers fade.

Recommended Cultivars: *C. luciliae:* 'Alba', white flowers; 'Pink Giant', pink blooms; 'Gigantea' has blue flowers larger than those of the species.

smart tip

NATURALIZING GLORY-OF-THE-SNOW

Glory-of-the-snow is an ideal plant for naturalizing under trees because it can tolerate shade by the time the trees leaf out.

Colchicum

Colchicum
COLCHICUM SPECIES

Colchicums bloom with autumn crocuses and have similar chalice-shaped flowers, although colchicum flowers are larger. They aren't widely grown by American gardeners, but they should be. They are reliable and easy to grow, and their beautiful flowers are a welcome addition to fall gardens. Colchicums bloom in shades of pink, rose, lilac, and white.

Hardiness: Zones 5 to 9.

Blooming Time: Early- to mid-fall.

Height: 6 inches to 1 foot.

Depth and Spacing: 3 to 4 inches deep, 6 to 10 inches apart.

Light: Full sun to partial shade.

Soil: Any well-drained soil of average fertility.

Moisture: Average.

Garden Uses: Colchicums are lovely naturalized in a lawn if you have an area that you can leave unmowed in spring when the foliage grows. You can also plant them in beds and borders or in rock gardens, but plant them behind something that will hide their fading foliage in the late spring.

Spring foliage

Comments: Colchicum plants grow from corms that are planted in late summer and burst into bloom just a few weeks later. Most species send up their autumn flowers on leafless stems; the foliage does not appear until the following spring. The leaves grow about a foot high and die back in late spring or early summer along with the foliage of spring-blooming bulbs.

Colchicum bulbs are shipped from mail-order nurseries in July or August. This is the season when they are dormant. Plant them as soon as you receive them.

Recommended Cultivars: 'Waterlily', large double flowers with pointed petals, warm rosy pink; 'The Giant', 1 foot, large lavender-pink flowers.

C. autumnale: 'Album', white flowers; 'Plenum', double lilac-pink flowers.

C. byzantium: large rosy lilac flowers.

C. speciosum: blooms later than the rest, with fragrant, rosy lavender-pink flowers.

how to

Plant Colchicum Bulbs
DIFFICULTY LEVEL: EASY

Tools and Materials: Shovel or spade, rake, bulbs

Plant bulbs 2 to 3 inches deep and 3 inches apart. Cage them only if mice bother tulips or other bulbs in the same area.

Double colchicum

Convallaria

Convallaria majalis
LILY-OF-THE-VALLEY

Lily-of-the-valley is a carefree perennial that grows from small, pointed, bulblike structures known as "pips." The waxy bell-shaped little flowers dance along small slender stems for an all-too-brief couple of weeks each year, perfuming the air with an unmistakable sweet fragrance. The large, elliptical leaves, about 8 inches high, grow from the base of the plant; they remain until late summer, when they begin to turn brown and die back.

Hardiness: Zones 3 to 9.

Blooming Time: Late spring.

Height: 8 inches to 1 foot.

Depth and Spacing: 2 inches deep, 4 inches apart.

Light: Filtered sun to light shade.

Soil: Well-drained, humusy, average fertility; tolerates a range of soils.

Moisture: Average to even.

Lily-of-the-valley

Garden Uses: Lily-of-the-valley likes to spread, so it is not a good addition to an orderly bed or border. Instead, give it a place of its own along a sidewalk or massed in a corner of the yard, or grow it as a ground cover in an informal shady or woodland garden.

In autumn, lily-of-the-valley leaves turn yellow before turning brown. Placed in a rock garden, as they are here, their color adds vibrancy to the autumn landscape palette.

The fragrant flowers are good for cutting and useful as fillers in bouquets and arrangements, although they only last a few days in the vase if cut when fully open. To get the longest life in the vase, cut when the topmost buds on a stem have turned white, but before the flowers open. If you have cut the stem low enough that the white base of the stem is visible, recut the stem to remove the white portion. Condition the flowers before arranging them by standing the stems in a container of water nearly up to the base of the flowers for several hours.

C. majalis var. *rosea*

Comments: Lily-of-the-valley is too invasive for some people. If it grows where you don't want it, you'll need to dig it up to remove it. The leaves tend to turn straggly and brown around the edges in a hot, dry summer. Trim off ragged or brown leaves if necessary to keep plants looking neat. If you can't accomodate its foibles in your yard but still want to enjoy the flowers, try forcing the pips indoors in winter. (See page 147 for forcing directions.)

Recommended Cultivars: 'Fortin's Giant', to 12 inches, white, large flowers; 'Plena', double white flowers; C. majalis var. rosea, pink blooms. 'Albostriata' has leaves with thin, creamy white stripes running along their length and white flowers; 'Aureovariegata' has white flowers and leaves with yellow stripes. 'Hardwick Hall' has broad leaves with narrow pale green margins and large flowers.

Ripe seedpods show off colorful display in autumn.

BULBS

Crocus

Crocus species and cultivars

There are two groups of crocuses—spring bloomers and fall bloomers. The earliest spring species flower in late winter and early spring. The larger Dutch hybrids also bloom in early spring, but a bit later than many of the species. Autumn crocuses, as the name implies, send up their welcome blossoms in fall. All crocuses have chalice-shaped blossoms and narrow, grassy leaves. The color range of the flowers includes various shades of purple, lavender, yellow, and white, and some are striped or bicolored. Most autumn crocuses flower in shades of purple.

Hardiness: Zones 4 to 8, varies with species.

Blooming Time: Late winter to spring or in autumn, depending on species and cultivar.

Height: 4 to 6 inches.

Depth and Spacing: 3 to 4 inches deep, 3 to 4 inches apart.

Light: Full sun.

Soil: Well-drained; average fertility.

Moisture: Average.

Garden Uses: Crocuses welcome spring to many gardens. Plant them in the front of beds and borders, in containers, and along a path or sidewalk. Or let them naturalize in a part of the lawn you can leave unmowed for eight weeks after they finish blooming.

'Purple Giant'

The lilacs, lavenders, and purples of autumn crocuses offer a lovely counterpoint to the warm, earthy tones of orange, russet, gold, bronze, and beige of the mums, pumpkins, and ornamental grasses that are so abundant at this time of year.

Comments: Wherever you plant crocuses, plant lots of them, and give them room to spread. Crocuses love the sun; they thrive when their dormant bulbs can bake in soil warmed by it during the summer. When the plants become crowded after several years, they will produce fewer flowers. Revive the planting by lifting and dividing the corms in fall or late spring after the foliage has died back. Plant bulbs for spring bloomers in autumn and those for autumn bloomers in late summer. Stigmas of the fall-bloomer *C. sativus* are otherwise known as the spice saffron.

Recommended Cultivars: Spring bloomers: snow crocuses (*C. chrysanthus cultivars*), the usual range of crocus colors plus some unusual blue-and-yellow and red-brown-and-yellow bicolors; tommies (*C. tommasinianus*), several shades of purple, red-purple, and lavender; Dutch crocus (*C. vernus*), larger flowers in a pretty range of crocus colors. Dutch hybrid crocuses are the most widely grown type because they are easy to grow, dependable, and inexpensive.

Autumn bloomers: saffron crocus (*C. sativus*), purple with bright red-orange stigmata; *C. goulimyi*, good for warm climates, pale to deep purple; *C. kotschyanus*, good for cold, damp climates, pale lilac with darker purple veins and a soft yellow throat; *C. speciosus*, lilac-purple, blooms early, good for gardens where winter snow comes early.

An early spring bloomer

smart tip

BUYING CORMS

Purchase unsprouted corms whenever possible. Corms that have sprouted before planting will be weakened and may not bloom their best during the first year.

smart tip

PLANTING CROCUS BULBS

Plant crocuses in large groups for maximum visual impact. Space corms 3 to 4 inches apart for best growth.

Cyclamen

Cyclamen hederifolium (C. neapolitanum)
HARDY CYCLAMEN

This outdoor version of the classic winter houseplant has lovely flowers whose reflexed petals give them a form reminiscent of shooting stars. Shooting star is, in fact, a nickname for the plant. Cyclamen flowers come in pink or white, with a darker eye; some are slightly fragrant. The plants have attractive heart-shaped leaves.

Hardiness: Zones 6 or 7 to 9.

Blooming Time: Late summer to autumn.

Height: 2 to 6 inches.

Depth and Spacing: Set the tops of the tubers even with the soil surface, 6 inches to 1 foot apart.

Light: Partial to light shade.

Soil: Well-drained, humusy.

Moisture: Needs ample moisture during the growing season and even moisture the rest of the year.

Garden Uses: Hardy cyclamen is lovely along a path in a shady garden; it's also nice in a wooded area or shady rock garden. Grow hardy cyclamen with other small bulbs, such as species crocus, snowdrops, and glory-of-the-snow.

Comments: Plant tubers in midsummer. Place them so the dimpled side points up and the roots point down; if roots have not yet grown, plant with the smooth sides down. Cyclamen doesn't reach its full blooming potential for a few years after planting, so be patient. Once established, the plants flower lavishly. Plants self-sow and spread if left undisturbed; in fact, they do not like to be disturbed. So choose their location carefully so that they have space to spread. Don't deadhead the flowers or divide the tubers. The tubers do not produce bulblets, but they do grow larger over the years, and the plant size increases correspondingly.

Hardy cyclamen

Mice and squirrels may attack the tubers; if rodents are a problem in your garden, cyclamen may not be a good choice for you. Screen cages, as shown on page 176, may be effective barriers.

Cyclamen are endangered in their native habitats, but many are still collected from the wild and exported for sale in North America. To be absolutely sure you are not planting wild-collected tubers, buy your cyclamen from a mail-order nursery that guarantees that their corms are nursery-propagated.

Individual blooms

Recommended Cultivars: There are numerous hardy cyclamen species. In addition to *C. hederifolium*, consider the following: *C. cilicium*, 2 to 4 inches high, fragrant flowers in white or shades of pink with a dark red eye, round to heart-shaped leaves with silver markings; both flowers and leaves appear in fall.

C. coum, to 3 inches high; deep purple-pink flowers; rounded leaves may be solid green or marked with silver; blooms in early spring in most areas but winter in warmer climates. '*Album*' has white flowers. Suited to Zones 5 to 8.

how to

Plant Cyclamen   DIFFICULTY LEVEL: EASY

Tools and Materials: Trowel, amendments

Plant hardy cyclamen in midsummer, with the roots downward and the dimpled side up.

BULBS

Dahlia

Dahlia × *pinnata* cultivars

Members of this genus of tender tuberous plants have been extensively bred into thousands of flamboyant, large-flowered cultivars. The flowers resemble chrysanthemums, and they come in a wide range of warm colors, flower forms, and sizes. The American Dahlia Society recognizes 17 different flower classes: formal decorative, informal decorative, semi-cactus, straight cactus, incurved cactus, laciniated, ball, miniature ball, pompom, waterlily, peony, anemone, collarette, single, mignon single, orchid, and novelty (forms that don't fit into any of the other categories).

Hardiness: Zones 7 to 11; elsewhere dig tubers in fall and store indoors over winter.

Blooming Time: Late summer into autumn; in many areas dahlia plants peak in September.

Height: 10 inches to 7 feet.

Depth and Spacing: 6 inches deep, 2 to 3 feet apart.

Light: Full sun (at least six hours of sun a day to produce the best flowers).

Soil: Loose, rich, loamy soil with good fertility and excellent drainage.

Moisture: Even; plants like lots of moisture but do not tolerate soggy soil.

'Alabaster'

Garden Uses: Plant dahlias in groups in beds and borders. Shorter cultivars go in the front of the garden and very tall ones in the back.

Comments: Plant dahlia tubers in spring as soon as the danger of frost is past. In very cool climates (Zones 3 to 5), start them indoors in pots to get earlier flowers. All but the dwarf cultivars will need staking. To avoid damaging the tuberous roots, set the stakes in place before planting.

When planting, lay the root horizontally in the hole with the eye, or growing point, facing upward and toward the stake. Cover the tuber with 2 to 3 inches of soil, leaving a depression. As the shoots grow, gradually fill in around them with more soil, until just a very shallow depression remains; this will hold water for the plant.

Allow only the one or two of the strongest shoots to develop on each plant—cut back the rest at ground level. From

smart tip

Dahlias respond to regular deadheading by prolonging their bloomtime by several extra weeks. Make it a habit to deadhead every three or four days.

early summer until autumn, cultivate lightly once a week to keep the soil well-aerated. About the middle of August, give the flowers a nutrient boost. Scratch a handful of all-purpose fertilizer into the soil around each plant, or mulch with compost and then water with a mixture of liquid seaweed and fish emulsion.

In warm parts of Zone 7 and Zones 8 to 11, dahlias can overwinter under a thick mulch. Elsewhere, after a heavy frost has blackened the plants in autumn, cut back the stems to 4 inches above ground level. Dig up the clumps of tubers, and store them indoors over the winter in dry peat moss in a cool (40°F to 50°F), dry place. Divide the clumps before replanting in spring.

Recommended Cultivars: Choose cultivars based on your preferences for height, flower form, and blossom color. All present-day cultivars perform well under a variety of circumstances.

Dahlias are classed by the appearance of their flowers. Some common classes include:

Anemone	Collarette	Cactus

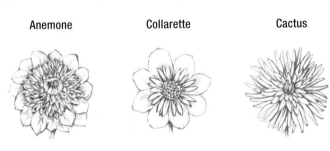

Eranthis

Eranthis hyemalis
WINTER ACONITE

The buttercup-yellow flowers of winter aconites bloom along with snowdrops and early crocuses, both of which make nice companions for them. The plants grow just a few inches high. The large flowers have flat, broad petals that are pointed at the tips—they resemble buttercups in form as well as color. The flower stalks arise from a basal mat of finely divided leaves.

Hardiness: Zones 3 to 8.

Blooming Time: Late winter to early spring.

Height: 3 to 4 inches.

Depth and Spacing: 3 to 4 inches deep, 4 inches apart.

Light: Full sun to light shade.

Soil: Any reasonably fertile, well-drained soil.

Moisture: Average to evenly moist.

Garden Uses: Plant winter aconites in the front of beds and borders, or let them naturalize in a woodland garden—they are charming under deciduous trees and shrubs. To get visual impact from these diminutive flowers, plant them in masses, and give them a place where they can be left undisturbed to spread and colonize the area.

Comments: Winter aconite often starts blooming as the last snows of winter are melting away around it. The leaves appear after the flowers. The plants go dormant in summer, like other spring-blooming hardy bulbs, but don't stop watering them during spells of dry weather. Winter aconite likes moisture, even during its summer dormant period.

Winter aconite will grow everywhere except in very warm climates. It doesn't demand much. As long as it gets winter cold and moisture during the growing season, it should thrive. It grows well in shade, a characteristic that increases its versatility. Even better, the plants can

An early spring bloomer

Winter aconite and snowdrops are naturalized in a wooded area.

Winter aconite

be left undisturbed for years as they spread; in fact, you don't ever have to divide winter aconite unless you want to propagate new plants.

If you do want to propagate the tubers, dig them when the plants finish blooming in spring; break them into pieces; and then replant immediately. The plants self-sow, and you may find them popping up in a nearby lawn when the colony has become well established.

Be careful to purchase winter aconite from a reliable nursery that sells only propagated stock, and not bulbs collected from the wild. This is extremely important because winter aconite is endangered in its native habitat as a result of overcollection. Plant the bulbs in late summer or very early autumn.

Recommended Cultivars: A related species, *E. cilicica*, has somewhat larger flowers and leaves that are more finely divided than those of the more common *E. hyemalis*. The leaves of *E. cilicica* are bronze when they first emerge, then turn green.

BULBS

Fritillaria

Fritillaria species
FRITILLARY, CROWN IMPERIAL, CHECKERED LILY

Fritillaries bear bell-shaped flowers that hang downward on slender stems. Their leaves are narrow and grassy. The most imposing member of the genus is the tall crown imperial (*F. imperialis*). Its yellow or red-orange flowers are clustered around the top of a tall, bare, straight stem and are surmounted by a "crown" of vertical leaves. The checkered lily, or guinea hen flower (*F. meleagris*), is smaller and more delicate-looking, with nodding bells of purple or white checkered in burgundy or purple-brown. *F. persica* has more slender blossoms of deep purple on stems 1 to 4 feet high.

'Aurora' and 'Lutea'

Hardiness: Zones 3 to 8, varies with species.

Blooming Time: Mid- to late-spring.

Height: 8 inches to 4 feet, varies with species.

Depth and Spacing: 3 to 6 inches deep; 4 inches to 1 foot apart, depending on species.

Light: Full sun to partial shade.

Soil: Moist but well-drained, humusy, fertile.

Moisture: Crown imperial: evenly moist when in active growth, average while dormant; checkered lily and *F. persica*: average moisture.

Garden Uses: Plant crown imperial in beds and borders, behind bushy, leafy plants that can hide its bare stems. Checkered lily is lovely in a woodland or rock garden or along a shady path. *F. persica* is stunning in a bed or border containing light pink, yellow, or white flowers.

Comments: Plant fritillaries in fall, when they become available from nurseries. They thrive in soils rich in organic matter.

smart tip

SITING CROWN IMPERIALS

Crown imperial is equally at home growing in the front border or beside a small stream—just give it moist, well-drained soil.

Checkered lily

Recommended Cultivars: Crown imperial, 3 feet: 'Aurora', orange-red veined in purple; 'Lutea' and 'Lutea Maxima', lemon yellow; 'Premier', soft orange; 'Rubra Maxima', orange flushed with red.

Checkered lily, 8 inches to 1 foot: *F. Alba*, solid white flowers ; 'Charon', light purple with black checkering.

Snowdrop

the hot summer sun. Planted under deciduous trees and shrubs, snowdrops usually thrive; the leaves of the woody plants give them dappled shade during the weeks when they most need it.

Plant snowdrops in autumn. The bulbs don't need to be divided very often. When they appear crowded or blooms start to diminish, dig and divide them right after the flowers fade in spring. Transplant the bulbs carefully, and give them plenty of water after you replant them.

Naturalized snowdrops and winter aconite announce springtime.

Recommended Cultivars: 'Lady Elphinstone', gray-green leaves and double flowers with yellow rather than green markings; 'S. Arnott', large, honey-scented blooms with an inverted V-shaped mark on each inner petal. A related species, the giant snowdrop (*G. elwesii*), is larger—to 8 inches tall—and blooms with honey-scented flowers even earlier than *G. nivalis*.

Galanthus

Galanthus nivalis
SNOWDROP

Among the earliest and most welcome heralds of spring in cold climates, snowdrops can be seen blooming in woodlands before the last snow has melted. Their bell-shaped white flowers dangle from slender stems above narrow, grassy leaves. The inner parts of the small flowers are often tipped in green.

Hardiness: Zones 3 or 4 to 8.

Blooming Time: Late winter to early spring.

Height: 3 to 6 inches.

Depth and Spacing: 3 to 4 inches deep, 4 inches apart.

Light: Full sun to partial shade.

Soil: Average to well-drained; tolerates heavier soil than most bulbs.

Moisture: Evenly moist; water when rainfall is sparse.

Garden Uses: Snowdrops can be planted in beds or borders but are best used in rock gardens, under deciduous trees and shrubs, or naturalized in unmowed grassy areas. They bloom at the same time as winter aconite, and the two plants make an attractive combination in the garden.

Comments: Snowdrops like lots of sun when they are growing and blooming, but they need to be shaded from

how to

Divide Snowdrops   DIFFICULTY LEVEL: EASY

Tools and Materials: Spade, shovel, or trowel

Rejuvenate a crowded clump of snowdrops by digging and dividing the clump when flowers fade in spring. Replant the bulbs right away, and water them well.

BULBS

Gladiolus

Gladiolus × *hortulanus* **cultivars**

The bold, brightly colored flower spikes of gladiolus are a familiar summertime sight in backyards, flower stands, and farmer's markets. The color range of today's gladiolus hybrids includes practically every warm color imaginable plus various shades of lavender, an unusual lime green, white, and bicolors. The flowers bloom along sturdy upright stems; plants have stiff, sword-shaped leaves.

Hardiness: Zones 8 to 11; in other zones, dig and store indoors over winter.

Blooming Time: Early summer to fall, if plants are planted in succession.

Height: 2 to 6 feet.

Depth and Spacing: Large corms (an inch or larger), 6 to 8 inches deep; medium-size corms (½ to 1 inch) 4 to 5 inches deep; smaller corms 3 inches deep; plant all corms 6 to 8 inches apart.

Light: Full sun.

Soil: Deep, loose, rich soil.

Moisture: Even.

Garden Uses: Gladiolus are classics for cutting gardens. Put the tall, spiky plants in the back of display gardens.

Gladiolus

Comments: Gladiolus is a fairly demanding plant when it comes to nutrient and moisture levels. To ensure high soil fertility, incorporate plenty of organic matter into the bed and mix some gypsum, rock phosphate, and all-purpose fertilizer in the bottom of the planting holes or trenches. When the flower spike appears, make sure the plants get plenty of water. During dry weather water deeply every two or three days.

For a succession of bloom, plant gladiolus in batches two weeks apart from just after the last frost until midsummer. This ensures that some plants will be blooming from midsummer until early fall.

Gladiolus spikes grow quite tall and often need staking. There are also smaller-growing miniature cultivars on the market.

At the end of the growing season, dig the corms. Even warm climate gardeners often lift them because they can become weedy if left in place. Unlike spring bulbs, gladiolus corms can be dug before the leaves die; you can start lifting the frost-tender corms a month to six weeks after the plants have finished blooming. As soon as you dig the corms, cut off the leaves to the top of the corm. Destroy the old foliage because it can harbor pests and diseases that will winter over and attack plants the following year. Separate the smaller bulblets when you can pull them off easily. Store them over the winter in a cool, dry, well-ventilated place. If you live in a warm climate, place the corms in cold storage to ensure that they enter dormancy.

Recommended Cultivars: All present-day gladiolus cultivars perform well under a variety of circumstances. Choose cultivars based on your color and height preferences. In addition to the fancy cultivars, try the following species:

G. byzantinus, to 3 feet, pink, white, burgundy, or rosy purple with white stripe; *G. cardinalis*, to 3 feet, bright red blooms marked with white; *G. nanus*, to 2 feet, red, pink, white, and bicolors, hardy, mulch well for winter in Zones 3 to 5; *G. tristis*, to 2 feet, fragrant white flowers streaked with purple, open at night.

how to

Storing Gladiolus Corms
DIFFICULTY LEVEL: EASY

Tools and Materials: Spade or shovel, laundry bleach, cardboard box

1 Dig corms in fall, before frost, and cut off the leaves.

2 Brush all loose soil from the corms with your fingers.

3 Dip corms in a 10 percent solution of chlorine bleach.

4 Dry and store in a single layer in a cardboard box.

Hyacinthoides

H. hispanica
(Endymion hispanicus, Scilla campanulata),
SPANISH BLUEBELL
H. non-scripta
(Endymion non-scriptus, Scilla non-scripta),
ENGLISH BLUEBELL

Charming little bell-shaped flowers of violet-blue, pink, or white cluster along the stem tips of Spanish bluebells. The leaves are straplike rather than grassy. English bluebell flowers are deep violet-blue and are fragrant. Though somewhat less showy than their Spanish cousins because there are fewer flowers, English bluebells add vibrant color to the landscape.

Hardiness: Spanish bluebell, Zones 3 or 4 to 8; English bluebell, Zones 5 to 7.

Blooming Time: Mid- to late-spring.

Height: Slightly over a foot to 1½ feet.

Depth and Spacing: 3 to 6 inches deep, 4 to 6 inches apart.

Light: Partial to full shade. (Spanish cultivars tolerate full sun in cool climates.)

Soil: Well-drained, fertile, humusy, acid to a neutral pH.

Moisture: Evenly moist to damp while growing and blooming; drier while the plants are dormant.

Garden Uses: All bluebells are lovely planted in masses and allowed to naturalize in a woodland garden or other naturalistic shade garden, but this is particularly true of Engish bluebells. Spanish bluebells look good in informal and cottage gardens or a rock garden. Grow them in a shady spot.

You can also plant bluebells to naturalize in a lawn, provided you can leave the grass unmowed as the bulb foliage matures.

Comments: Plants spread by bulblets and also self-sow; don't deadhead flowers if you want the plants to multiply. To keep them more confined, deadhead faded flowers before they go to seed.

Spanish bluebell

These Spanish bluebells are naturalized in woodland.

These bulbs rarely if ever need dividing. If you do want to propagate new plants, dig the bulbs in summer; remove the smaller bulblets; then replant the parent bulbs and bulblets immediately.

Neither bluebell species does well where summers are hot, but English bluebells are more finicky than Spanish bluebells. In extreme situations, they may die out.

Bluebells can cause skin irritation on contact in sensitive individuals, so wear gloves when handling the bulbs or any other parts of the plants. They will also cause stomach upset—which may be severe—if ingested, so be warned if your household includes small children.

Recommended Cultivars: Most of the available cultivars are hybrids between the two bluebell species, making them a bit more tolerant of hot weather than English bluebells. 'Blue Queen', light blue; 'Danube', deep blue; 'Excelsior', violet-blue; 'Rosabella', pink; 'Rose Queen', deep rose-pink; 'White City', white; 'White Triumphator', white, taller than other cultivars.

English bluebell

BULBS

Hyacinthus

Hyacinthus orientalis cultivars
HYACINTH

Most of the hyacinths found in American gardens are hybrid bulbs that were grown in the Netherlands and bred from the common garden species, *H. orientalis*. Their star-shaped flowers cluster together in a dense, fat spike at the top of a thick stem. The color range has expanded beyond the traditional pink, white, and blue to include red, yellow, apricot, and deep purple. The intense, sweet fragrance of the flowers provokes strong reactions—some people love the scent and others detest it, but it's hard to ignore.

Hardiness: Zones 3 to 9.

Blooming Time: Mid-spring.

Height: 10 inches to 1 foot.

Depth and Spacing: 6 inches deep, 6 to 9 inches apart.

Light: Full sun.

Soil: Well-drained.

Moisture: Average.

Garden Uses: Hyacinths aren't easy to integrate into a garden with other flowers, but you can plant them in groups in beds and borders. They also grow well in containers. They're easy to force indoors in winter. (See page 146.)

Comments: To overwinter hyacinths in Zones 3 and 4, mulch them well after the top inch of the soil has frozen. Gardeners in Zones 3 and 4 can also plant the bulbs in very early spring and dig them in fall like dahlias and gladiolus. Store them over the winter in a cardboard box filled with peat moss; place them in a single layer; and cover with more peat moss before placing them in the dark.

The stems may need staking to support the weight of the flowers in the first year; in subsequent years, the flower spikes tend to be less heavy and dense (and prettier, depending on your taste).

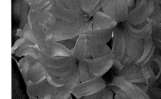

'Pink Pearl'

Recommended Cultivars: 'Blue Jacket', deep violet-blue; 'Bolero', apricot-pink; 'Champagne', light bluish pink; 'City of Haarlem', light yellow; 'Distinction', unusually slender, open flower clusters in a deep red-purple; 'Hollyhock', double, bright red; 'Gipsy Queen', apricot-orange; 'Jan Bos', carmine; 'Lady Derby', rosy pink; 'L'Innocence', white; 'Peter Stuyvesant', purple-blue; 'Pink Pearl', deep pink; 'Sheila', pale pink; 'Sky Jacket', light blue; 'Blue Giant', light blue; 'Woodstock', purple-red.

how to
Plant for Forcing Hyacinths

Tools and Materials: Pot, soil mix, bulbs   **DIFFICULTY LEVEL: EASY**

1 For forcing indoors, place several bulbs in a 4-in. pot, ½ inch apart.

2 Cover the bulbs with porous potting mix and water well; then place in cold storage.

Heirloom hyacinth cultivars

I. reticulata

Iris

Iris species and cultivars
BULBOUS IRISES

I. xiphium

Irises have long been favorite garden flowers. Most gardeners are familiar with the lovely bearded irises that bloom in late spring and grow from rhizomes. (See "Portraits of Favorite Perennials," pages 80 to 137.) But there are also smaller irises that grow from bulbs and flower earlier in spring. The earliest to bloom outdoors are the bulbous *I. histrioides, I. danfordiae,* and *I. reticulata*; these are sometimes called dwarf or rock garden irises because their small stature suits them to planting in a rock garden. All of these have the classic iris form with standards and falls. *I. histrioides* comes in shades of blue and purple, some with contrasting yellow flushes and deeper blue markings. *I. danfordiae* is bright yellow. *I. reticulata,* the best known of the three, is available in several blue and purple shades as well as yellow, white, and bicolors.

Another bulbous iris is the later blooming Dutch iris (*I. xiphium* × *I. tingitana*), which has slender, graceful flowers in shades of blue, purple, pink, and white, along with some lovely bicolored combinations. Dutch irises have a limited hardiness range and don't do well in either cold climates or the lower South.

Hardiness: *I. histrioides, I. danfordiae,* and *I. reticulata,* Zones 5 to 9; Dutch iris, Zones 6 to 9.

Blooming Time: *I. histrioides, I. danfordiae,* and *I. reticulata,* late winter to early spring; Dutch iris, late spring to early summer.

Height: Dwarf species, 4 to 6 inches; Dutch iris, 1½ to 2 feet.

Depth and Spacing: Dwarf species, 4 inches deep, 4 to 5 inches apart; Dutch iris, 6 inches deep, 6 inches apart.

Light: Full sun.

Soil: Well-drained, average fertility.

Moisture: Average; dwarf species can't tolerate soggy soil, especially in summer.

Garden Uses: Plant dwarf irises in large groups in the front of beds and borders, in the rock garden, or in containers. They are easy to force indoors for winter bloom. (See page 146 for directions.)

Dutch irises are lovely in the middle ground of beds and borders and make good companions for roses and peonies. They are long-lasting as cut flowers.

Comments: Plant dwarf species in fall, when you plant other early-blooming bulbs. Many of the dwarf irises are fragrant, a quality that makes them especially delightful when forced indoors.

Plant Dutch irises in spring in cool climates and fall in warm areas. They usually need a good winter mulch in Zone 6. You can also dig the bulbs in fall and store them indoors over winter as you would dahlias or gladiolus.

To enjoy Dutch iris as cut flowers, cut the stems when the buds are plump and let them unfurl indoors.

Recommended Cultivars: *I. reticulata:* 'Springtime', sky blue flowers; 'Harmony', blue flowers with yellow and white markings; 'Ida', blue falls with lighter blue standards; 'J.S. Dijt', purple standards with red-purple falls; 'Natasha', palest blue-white blooms; 'Pixie', blue-black flowers.

I. histrioides: 'George', deep purple; 'Katharine Hodgkin', blue standards with greenish falls blotched with yellow; 'Major', deep blue flowers on vigorous plants.

Dutch iris: 'Blue Magic', blue-violet; 'Sky Beauty', light blue; 'Marquette', white standards with yellow falls; 'Silvery Beauty', pale blue-and-white; 'Bronze Beauty', bronze with gold splotch on falls; 'Cream Beauty', creamy white standards with yellow-and-orange falls; 'Telstar', violet standards with blue falls; 'White Wedgwood', white; 'Golden Harvest', yellow; and 'Rosario', purple-pink.

I. danfordiae

I. reticulata bulbs

Lilium

Lilium species and cultivars
LILY

Unlike daylilies, with which they are sometimes confused, true lilies have traditionally been considered hard to grow. Yet today's hybrids are sturdier than their predecessors and bloom beautifully if you give them the growing conditions they prefer. The mostly trumpet-shaped flowers come in a range of colors, sizes, and blooming times. They grow on tall, straight stems lined with narrow, pointed leaves.

Hardiness: Zones 4 to 8.

Blooming Time: Summer.

Height: 2 to 8 feet, depending on species or cultivar.

Depth and Spacing: 4 to 8 inches deep (or three times as deep as the bulbs are tall), 1 to 1½ feet apart.

Light: Filtered or not-quite full sun.

Soil: Light and loamy, with absolutely perfect drainage.

Moisture: Evenly moist before and during bloom, average afterwards.

Garden Uses: Plant lilies in groups in mixed beds and borders, or grow them in a cutting garden.

Comments: Try to plant lilies in a spot with filtered sun for most of the day; full sun bleaches out the colors of some lily flowers. Most lily bulbs are planted in fall, but some of the late-blooming types can be planted in spring. Gardeners in Zones 9 to 11 can dig and refrigerate the bulbs for two months before planting in spring.

The plants are heavy feeders and benefit from one to two applications of an all-purpose fertilizer in spring. Also top-dress with compost or leaf mold to make sure their soil is rich in organic matter.

During dry weather, water the plants once a week until

'Herald Angel Yellow' trumpet lily

they bloom. After they finish flowering, the plants like drier conditions. Lilies cannot tolerate moisture standing around the bulbs. They also do not like hot soil, so you need to either mulch them or overplant them with annuals or ground covers to shade the roots and help keep the soil cool.

Many lilies grow tall—6 feet or more—and need to be staked. It is a good idea to stake all cultivars that grow taller than 3 feet. The stakes need to be far enough away from the plants so that they don't touch the bulbs. For appearance's sake, insert the stakes just before the first flowers open. To prevent the stems from being damaged as they move with the breeze, attach them to the stakes loosely, with ties that form figure eights that cross between the stem and stake.

Every few years, when the plants become crowded, lift and divide the bulbs. After the plants have finished blooming and the foliage has died back in fall, carefully dig up the clumps, leaving as many of the roots intact as you can. Very gently separate the bulbs, and replant them immediately. Keep the bulbs out of the soil for only the briefest possible time so they do not dry out.

Lilies propagate themselves with small bulblets and, as shown in the box opposite, aboveground bulbils and seeds.

Recommended Cultivars: Many lilies are available, both hybrids and species. A few of the best include:

Asiatic Hybrids (bloom in early summer): 'Connecticut King', 2½ to 3 feet, golden yellow; 'Coral Sunrise', 3 to 4 feet, coral-pink flushed with peach and yellow; 'Enchantment', 3 to 4 feet, red-orange; 'Luxor', 3 to 4 feet, light yellow flushed with apricot; 'Marissa', 2 to 3 feet, peach flushed with apricot and gold; 'Shirley', 3 to 4 feet, white brushed with pink at center; and 'Sorbet', 3 to 4 feet, white with burgundy edges and spots.

Oriental Hybrids (large flowers in late summer, most with reflexed petals, often fragrant): 'Blushing Pink', 5 feet, soft pink; 'Casa Blanca', 4 feet, large, white, very fragrant; 'Dolce

'Casa Blanca' oriental lily

Tiger lily

Vita', 3 to 4 feet, rose-pink; 'Emmely', 3 to 5 feet, pink with white edges and a deeper pink stripe down the center of the petals; 'Mediterranee', 2½ to 3½ feet, rich pink; 'Pink Paramount', 3 to 3 1/2 feet, clear pink, fragrant; 'Sans Souci', 2 feet, crimson with white edges and darker spots; 'Silver Elegance', 4 to 5 feet, white with red spots; 'Star Gazer', 2½ to 3 feet, deep reddish pink with white edges.

Trumpet Lilies (derived from Asiatic Hybrids, very fragrant, trumpet shaped): 'Herald Angel Yellow', 3 to 5 feet, yellow with darker yellow throat, very fragrant.

L. speciosum var. *rubrum*, late summer, 3 to 5 feet, very fragrant, reflexed petals, light crimson-and-white with crimson spots.

L. tigrinum, tiger lily, mid- to late summer, 2 to 5 feet, reflexed

'Connecticut King' Asiatic lily

how to

Propagate Lilies

DIFFICULTY LEVEL: EASY

Tools and Materials: Spade or trowel, bowls, storage containers

Propagate Asiatic lilies by dividing them in fall or collecting and planting bulbils when they form in leaf axils.

Collect seeds of trumpet lilies when seedpods are dry. Plants grown from seed will combine traits of parent plants.

Propagate tiger lilies by digging, separating, and replanting small bulblet that form underground. They grow to blooming size in three years.

BULBS

Lycoris

Lycoris squamigera, MAGIC LILY
Lycoris radiata, SPIDER LILY

These relatives of the amaryllis are usually called resurrection or magic lilies, and magical they certainly are. The plant leaves grow rapidly in spring but die back and completely vanish in summer while the plant goes through a dormant period. In late summer, flower stalks suddenly burst through the soil, springing up as if magically resurrected.

The fragrant, funnel-shaped magic lily flowers, mostly in shades of pink and lilac-pink, closely resemble those of amaryllis, but they are more delicate in their size, shape, and colors. Spider lilies are rosy red to crimson. Petals of both species are long and narrow, but the flowers of spider lily have long, spidery stamens that curve and twist out into space from the center of the flower.

Hardiness: Magic lilies, Zones 5 to 9; spider lilies, Zones 8 to 10.

Blooming Time: Late summer to early fall.

Height: Magic lilies, 2 to 3 feet; spider lilies, to 1½ feet.

Depth and Spacing: Just below the soil surface, 1 foot apart.

Light: Full sun.

Soil: Well-drained.

Moisture: Evenly moist in spring, dry in summer.

Garden Uses: The fanciful, exotic forms of magic and spider lilies lend a touch of grace to gardens or patios. Plant magic lilies in beds and borders, or grow them in pots on patios and terraces. The tender spider lilies can be grown in pots and moved indoors for the winter in areas where they are not hardy.

Magic lily

Comments: These bulbs are planted during their summer dormant period. The plants seldom need to be dug and divided unless you want to move them or propagate new plants. Treat them differently from most other plants in one important respect: do not water them in summer—they need a dry dormant period rather than a cold one. Water them regularly until their leaves die back, but keep them dry until the flower stalks appear. Resume watering while they are blooming.

Recommended Cultivars: *L. aurea*, golden spider lily, Zones 9 to 11, yellow flowers.

smart tip

PLANTING *LYCORIS* BULBS

Plant magic lilies and spider lilies in midsummer, while they are still dormant.

Spider lily

Muscari

Muscari species
GRAPE HYACINTH

Grape hyacinths bear conical to oblong spikes of tiny round to elongated bell-like flowers on top of slender stems. Most look like an upside down bunch of tiny grapes on a stem, but there are also double-flowered forms, and a cultivar with fringed flowers that look as if they exploded. The leaves are narrow and grassy.

Hardiness: Zones 4 to 8 or 9.

Blooming Time: Early- to mid-spring.

Height: 4 to 8 inches.

Depth and Spacing: 3 inches deep; 2 to 4 inches apart.

Light: Full sun to light shade.

Soil: Well-drained, average to poor fertility.

Moisture: Average to even.

Garden Uses: Plant grape hyacinths in masses in beds or borders; let them naturalize in a woodland garden; grow them in the rock garden; or put them in pots. They make an excellent companion plant for spring-blooming shrubs such as lilacs and can also give needed contrast to a bed of yellow daffodils or tulips. Their form is slightly reminiscent of a miniature hyacinth, and they look good when massed at a front of a bed where these bulbs are growing. To force them indoors, see pages 146 and 166.

M. botryoides 'Album'

Comments: Grape hyacinths are ridiculously easy to grow—they need no attention after you plant them. They spread quickly, both by self-sown seeds and bulblets, and are great for naturalizing. New plants are likely to pop up in a lawn nearby the garden. Grape hyacinths adapt to a variety of situations and bloom reliably year after year.

Recommended Cultivars: *M. armeniacum* (common grape hyacinth), deep blue; 'Christmas Pearl', light violet-blue, early blooming; 'Blue Spike', double, loosely grouped flowers.

M. azureum, bright blue; 'Album', white.

M. botryoides 'Album', white.

M. comosum 'Plumosum', large, feathery, fringed violet flowers.

M. latifolium, two-toned flower spikes are deep blue at the bottom and lighter blue on top.

M. neglectum, deep blue-black, with lower flowers sporting a white rim.

M. 'Valerie Finnis', light blue.

Common grape hyacinth

smart tip

CHOOSING GRAPE HYACINTH BULBS

Grape Hyacinth bulbs should be firm to the touch with smooth, unbroken skins. Choose bulbs that have not yet sprouted and have a healthy-looking basal plate.

Narcissus

Narcissus species and cultivars
DAFFODIL

There are many kinds of daffodils. For simplicity, the plants can be divided into two major groups—the small-growing species and their derivatives (which are grown in rock gardens and in the front of the garden), and the vast group of larger cultivars and hybrids.

Daffodils can be grown in most climates, but different types perform better in different places. In very cold climates, small-cupped, poeticus, and jonquil types work best. In Zones 8 and warmer, try small-cupped, jonquilla, triandrus, and tazetta types. Stay away from late-blooming cultivars if you live in a warm climate because the weather will be too hot for them when they bloom.

Hardiness: Varies with species and cultivar.

Blooming Time: Early- to mid-spring.

Height: 6 inches to 1½ feet.

Depth and Spacing: Small species and cultivars 3 to 5 inches deep, 4 to 5 inches apart; larger ones 6 inches deep, 6 inches apart.

Light: Full sun to partial shade.

Soil: Well-drained, rich in organic matter.

'King Alfred'

'Ice Follies'

Moisture: Evenly moist during growth and blooming, average the rest of the year.

Garden Uses: Daffodils are delightful in beds and borders and also grow well in containers. Plant them along paths, tuck them into foundation plantings—put them wherever you'll see their welcome flowers in spring.

Smaller triandrus and cyclamineus types are good additions to rock gardens and make bright spots in a woodland garden.

For an early taste of spring, force various types of daffodils and some of the delightful paperwhite narcissus into bloom indoors in winter, as directed on page 146.

---

how to

Divide Daffodils

DIFFICULTY LEVEL: EASY

Tools and Materials: Spade or shovel, cardboard box

1 Dig daffodil bulbs for division after the leaves die back in late spring. Pull off the bulblets around the bulb's base.

2 Replant the bulbs immediately, at the correct depth and spacing, or store and replant in fall.

'Edna Earl'   *N. cyclamineus*

Comments: Plant bulbs in fall, at least a month before you expect the first frost. Feed the plants once a year with compost or an all-purpose fertilizer.

If you want the plants to naturalize but don't want to divide them often, plant them deeper than normal—they won't spread as quickly and will be maintenance-free for a longer time. When in doubt, plant the bulbs deeper rather than shallower.

In beds and borders, daffodils need to be lifted and divided every four years or so. Dig the bulbs after the foliage dies back in late spring or early summer. Let them dry in the shade. Don't divide them until the offsets break off easily; otherwise you risk damaging the basal plates. You can replant the divided bulbs right away or store them until autumn in a cool, dry, well-ventilated place.

Recommended Cultivars: There are many excellent narcissus species and cultivars. See Types of Daffodils, below, for a sampling.

TYPES OF DAFFODILS

Narcissus and daffodils are divided into 12 groups or divisions according to their flower type.

Division 1: Trumpet daffodils have one flower to a stem. The central trumpet, or corona, is as long as or longer than the length of the outer petals (the perianth). The flowers may be all yellow, all white, or bicolored. Good cultivars include: 'King Alfred', all yellow; 'Mount Hood', creamy white; 'Empress of Ireland', pure white; 'Arctic Gold', all yellow; 'Rinjveld's Early Sensation', yellow, very early blooming; 'General Patton', white perianth with yellow trumpet.

Division 2: Large-cupped daffodils have large coronas, but they aren't as long as those of the trumpets. Stems bear only one flower. The flowers usually have a yellow or white perianth and a colored (often orange) cup, though some are all white or yellow. Good cultivars include: 'Accent', white perianth with salmon-pink cup; 'Roseworthy', white with orangy pink cup; 'Salome', white with pinkish yellow cup; 'Ice Follies', white with yellow cup that turns white as it matures; 'Carlton', all yellow.

Division 3: Short-cupped daffodils also have only one flower to a stem. In these, the corona is smaller and substantially shorter than the perianth. Good cultivars include: 'Barrett Browning', white perianth with orange cup; 'Polar Ice', all white, fragrant; 'Segovia', white with yellow cup.

Division 4: Double daffodils can grow with one or more flowers to a stem. Doubling can occur in the perianth, the corona, or both. Good cultivars include: 'Acropolis', white perianth, corona flushed orange in center; 'Erlicheer', clusters of fragrant, ivory-yellow flowers; 'Cheerfulness', clusters of fragrant, creamy white or yellow flowers; 'Ice King', white perianth with creamy yellow ruffled cup; 'Tahiti', yellow perianth and corona with orange in center.

Division 5: Triandrus daffodils usually bear two or more pendent flowers on each stem. The perianth petals are reflexed. Good cultivars include: 'Thalia', white, fragrant; 'Hawera', light yellow, fragrant.

Division 6: Cyclamineus daffodils bear only one flower to a stem and are distinguished by their highly reflexed petals. Good cultivars include: 'February Gold', all yellow; 'Jack Snipe', white petals with yellow cup; 'Jenny', white petals, corona opens pale yellow and turns white.

Division 7: Jonquilla daffodils, the jonquils, have one to three flowers on each stem. The flowers are fragrant and petals in the perianth spread out. The corona can be small, so some of these resemble the small-cupped types. Good cultivars include: 'Baby Moon', pale yellow, miniature; 'Suzy', red-orange cup, yellow perianth; 'Quail', bronzy yellow.

Division 8: Tazetta types usually carry 3 to 20 highly fragrant blooms on each stem. The perianth petals spread out, and the corona is short. Good cultivars include: 'Geranium', white with orange cup, very fragrant; 'Cragford', white with orange cup, fragrant and *N. papyraceus*, paperwhite narcissus, not hardy north of Zone 9 but easily forced, clusters of white, fragrant blooms.

Division 9: The Poeticus group includes both species and hybrids, all of them recognizable by their large white perianth petals and contrasting small, flat corona with a green or yellow center and a red rim. The flowers are fragrant. Look for: 'Actaea', white perianth, yellow cup edged in red, fragrant, tolerates moist locations.

Division 10: Species, Wild Forms, and Natural Hybrids can be single or double, fragrant or unscented. Their unifying charactristic is that they were discovered growing in the wild. Look for: *N. bulbocodium* var. *conspicuus*, hoop petticoat daffodil, yellow, funnel-shaped flowers.

Division 11: Split Corona daffodils have a corona that is split for about half its length or more, giving the bloom a somewhat flattened appearance. Good cultivars include: 'Broadway Star', orange corona, white perianth; 'Lemon Beauty', lemon yellow corona, white perianth.

Division 12: Miscellaneous daffodils include those that do not fit into one of the other divisions, such as 'Tête-à-Tête' and cultivars of *N. bulbocodium*.

Polianthes

Polianthes tuberosa
TUBEROSE

Tuberoses are among the most fragrant flowers on earth and have been an important ingredient in perfume formulas for generations. The plants bloom late in the season when most other fragrant flowers are long gone. The flowers aren't terribly striking, although they are attractive. They are waxy, white, and borne in clusters near the tops of the tall stems. The leaves are long and grassy.

Hardiness: Zones 8 to 11; elsewhere grow as a tender bulb.

Blooming Time: Late summer into autumn.

Height: 2½ to 3⅓ feet.

Depth and Spacing: 2 inches deep, 4 to 6 inches apart.

Light: Full sun.

Soil: Rich, well-drained, acidic; rich in organic matter.

Moisture: Even to damp. (Water regularly when the leaves appear.)

how to

'The Pearl' double tuberose

Garden Uses: Warm-climate gardeners can grow tuberoses in beds and borders; those in cool climates may prefer to plant them in pots. But no matter where you live, containers are perfect for tuberoses. They grow well when confined, and you can also move the containers to a spot where you can most enjoy their lovely perfume.

Comments: Tuberoses can be grown in cold climates if you dig the rhizomes in fall and store them over the winter.

The flowers bloom in late summer and early autumn, and the plants need a long, warm growing season in order to produce them. In cool climates (Zones 3 to 6), start the rhizomes indoors about six weeks before the last frost date to guarantee blooms before frost. In warmer areas, plant after all danger of frost has passed.

When the leaves start to turn yellow in fall, stop watering the plants, and let the soil dry out. When the leaves are dead, dig up the plants or remove them from their pots. Do not let the rhizomes freeze. Cut off the dead leaves, and let the rhizomes dry for two weeks in a dry, airy place. Then store them as you do other tender bulbs, in dry peat moss in a cool (40°F to 50°F), dry place.

Recommended Cultivars: 'The Pearl' has double flowers.

Single tuberose

Store Tuberose Rhizomes
DIFFICULTY LEVEL: EASY

Tools and Materials: Peat moss or sawdust, cardboard box

Store tuberose bulbs by burying them in a mixture of sawdust and peat moss in a covered cardboard box.

Scilla

Scilla species
SQUILL

Squills are among the most productive and charming of bulbs. They bloom lavishly and spread quickly, carpeting the ground with their little blue flowers. The most familiar kind, Siberian squill, has small, starry flowers of vivid blue, with several flowers to a stem. Persian squill (*S. mischtschenko-ana*) blooms earlier with pale blue-white flowers with a blue stripe on the petals. *S. bifolia* blooms earliest, with bright lavender-blue flowers.

Hardiness: Zones 5 to 8 or 9, depending on species.

Blooming Time: Late winter to early spring.

Height: 4 to 7 inches.

Depth and Spacing: 3 to 4 inches deep, 3 to 4 inches apart.

Light: Partial shade.

Soil: Any well-drained, loamy, humusy soil; slightly sandy is best.

Moisture: Average.

Garden Uses: Because they spread so rapidly, squills are excellent plants to naturalize in lawns, especially beneath

Siberian squill

the branches of deciduous trees. Their inconspicuous grassy leaves die back before the lawn needs to be mowed in spring. You can also plant squills in beds, borders, and rock gardens.

Comments: Squills are extremely easy to grow. An annual topdressing of an inch or so of compost or leaf mold in fall will ensure that the soil stays rich in organic matter and contains plenty of nourishment for the bulbs.

Squills need very little care after planting. You can divide the bulbs every four years or so, but they do well if you just leave them alone to naturalize. In addition to spreading by means of bulblets formed on the bulbs, the plants also self-seed, and the seeds grow into blooming-size bulbs in just a few years.

Recommended Cultivars: *S. siberica:* 'Alba', white flowers; 'Spring Beauty', deep blue, fragrant long-lasting flowers.

how to

Divide and Replant *Scilla* Bulbs   DIFFICULTY LEVEL: EASY

Tools and Materials: Spade or shovel, cardboard box

1 To increase your stock, dig and divide bulbs after foliage dies back in spring.

2 Separate the offset bulblets, and replant at the correct depth and spacing.

BULBS

Tulipa

Tulipa species and cultivars
TULIP

Tulips have cup-shaped blossoms with pointed petals. The petals of some types remain cupped, but in others they open wide like stars. Tulips bloom in many warm shades as well as purples, white, and bicolors. Flowers top straight, slender stems that rise above oblong, pointed leaves of varying widths.

Thousands of tulip cultivars are available. You'll find a wide selection of heights, colors, and blooming times and several different flower forms. Botanists have divided tulips into 15 divisions, as described in the box on the facing page.

Parrot tulips

'Tarda'

how to

Protect Tulips from Rodents
DIFFICULTY LEVEL: EASY

Tools and Materials: Hardware cloth, wire cutters

1 Rodents love tulips; line planting areas with screen cages where they're a problem.

2 Dig the soil to the correct depth, and line the bottom and sides with metal screening.

3 Set the bulbs in a layer of soil at the bottom of the cage, at the correct depth and spacing.

4 Cover with soil and water. For extra protection, cover with another piece of mesh and mulch.

When you buy bulbs, you'll find that most nurseries also use these categories to describe their stock.

Unfortunately, many hybrid tulips are not reliably perennial or are short-lived, especially in warm climates, so many gardeners prefer to treat them as annuals, digging and discarding the bulbs when they finish blooming and replanting the space with summer annuals. Species tulips often last longer in the garden.

Hardiness: Zones 4 to 7 or 8.

Blooming Time: Mid- to late-spring.

Height: 4 inches to 2½ feet.

Depth and Spacing: 3 to 6 inches deep (deeper to encourage hybrids to rebloom in subsequent years); 3 to 6 inches apart. Planting depth and spacing vary with the type and size of bulb. Follow the directions that come with the bulbs you buy.

Light: Full sun.

Soil: Deep, rich, well-drained soil with a neutral to slightly alkaline pH.

Moisture: Average.

Garden Uses: Plant tulips in groups in beds and borders, in cottage gardens, and along paths and walkways. Smaller species and hybrids, such as the Kaufmanniana hybrids, are at home in rock gardens, too. And, as described on page 146,

tulips can be forced for winter flowers indoors.

Comments: Hybrid tulips are often not reliably perennial, so many gardeners prefer to treat them as annuals even where they are hardy, pulling them up when they finish blooming. If you wish to treat your tulips as perennials, deadhead the flowers after they fade, and leave the foliage in place until it yellows and dries. In warm climates, treat them as annuals, or dig the bulbs after they finish blooming and keep them refrigerated until you replant them in fall.

Recommended Cultivars: There are many good cultivars. For suggestions, see the box below.

TYPES OF TULIPS

Division I. Single Early tulips, the first group, bloom early (along with hyacinths), are usually short-stemmed (10 to 18 inches tall), and come in a range of colors. Good cultivars include: 'Apricot Beauty', salmon-pink; 'Beauty Queen', apricot-rose; 'Bellona', yellow; 'Christmas Dream', reddish pink; 'Princess Irene', orange flushed with purple; 'Purple Prince', pinkish purple; 'Flair', buttercup yellow with orange-red feathered strips.

Division II. Double Early tulips bloom slightly later than the single early, are 10 to 12 inches tall, and are double in form. Good cultivars include: 'Monte Carlo', yellow; 'Peach Blossom', rosy pink; 'Schoonoord', white.

Division III. Triumph hybrids bloom right in the middle of the tulip season, in mid-spring. Plants range from 16 to 24 inches tall, and the color range is mostly red, white, and shades of pink. Many of the flowers have a second color flamed onto the petals. Good cultivars include: 'Arabian Mystery', deep purple with white edge; 'Cream Perfection', pale yellow; 'Bastogne', deep red; 'Golden Melody', buttercup yellow; 'Ile de France', deep red; 'Negrita', dark plum purple; 'Peerless Pink', rich pink; 'White Dream', white.

Division IV. Darwin hybrids are large-flowered plants that range in height from 22 to 34 inches tall. They bloom in mid-spring in a range of bright colors and often have a black blotch at the base of the petals. Good cultivars include: 'Apeldoorn', bright red; 'Cream Jewel', creamy white; 'Daydream', opens yellow, turns apricot-orange; 'Elizabeth Arden', purple-pink to salmon-pink; 'General Eisenhower', rich red; 'Ivory Floradale', opens pale yellow, turns ivory; 'Orange Sun', bright orange; 'Pink Impression', pink and rose blend; 'President Kennedy', yellow flushed with red.

Division V. Single Late tulips used to be called cottage tulips. This group also includes what used to be called Darwin tulips, which are not the same as the newer Darwin hybrids.

Ranging in height from 9 to 32 inches, they have pointed petals and long stems. Good cultivars include: 'Aristocrat', purplish rose with light edge; 'Bleu Aimable', bluish lilac; 'Dreamland', purplish red flamed with cream; 'Duke of Wellington', white; 'Kingsblood', deep cherry red; 'Pink Jewel', pale pink flamed with cream; 'Pink Supreme', dark pink; 'Queen of the Night', deep maroon-black.

Division VI. Lily-flowered tulips have pointed petals and a gracefully curving shape. They range from 20 to 30 inches tall and come in colors representing the entire tulip range, except for dark purples and maroons. They hold well in the vase. Good cultivars include: 'Ballade', purple-rose with broad white edge; 'Ballerina', light yellow flamed with scarlet; 'Elegant Lady', ivory with pale purple-pink edge; 'White Triumphator', white.

Division VII. Fringed tulips have petals that are cut into fringe at the edges. Plants range from 10 to 26 inches tall and bloom late. Good cultivars include: ''Burgundy Lace', wine red; 'Fringed Elegance', primrose yellow with thin red edging; 'Swan Wings', white.

Division VIII. Viridiflora tulips have green stripes or markings on their petals. Plants are 10 to 20 inches high and bloom late. Good cultivars include: 'Golden Artist', golden yellow feathered with green; 'Greenland', soft rose striped with green; 'Spring Green', ivory feathered with green.

Division IX. Rembrandt tulips are no longer commercially available. These are the tulips with broken colors as a consequence of a viral disease; it's illegal to sell these as they can contaminate healthy tulips.

Division X. Parrot tulips are distinguished by fringed, curled, twisted, or narrow petals. Many of the large flowers are streaked with a contrasting color and sometimes droop on the stems. Plants are 12 to 30 inches tall and

flower late. Good cultivars include: 'Apricot Parrot', apricot tinged with yellow, green, pink, and white; 'Black Parrot', deep purple-black; 'Flaming Parrot', bright yellow flamed with red; 'White Parrot', white.

Division XI. Double Late or Peony tulips have multiple petals and hold in the garden for long periods of time. They range from 16 to 24 inches tall and bloom late. Good cultivars include: 'Angélique', soft pink edged in cream; 'Blue Diamond', deep violet-purple; 'Lilac Perfection', lilac-purple; 'Miranda', bright red.

Division XII. Kaufmanniana hybrids are sometimes called water-lily tulips because of their open habit. They bloom about mid-spring. Their foliage is often mottled or striped, and they grow to about a foot tall. Good cultivars include: 'Ancilla', rosy red and soft pink, white interior; 'Gaiety', white with broad red stripe; 'Heart's Delight', red with pale pink edging and interior; 'Stresa', red with yellow edge.

Division XIII. Fosteriana tulips bloom in mid-spring. The plants grow a foot to almost 1½ feet tall; the foliage can be mottled or striped; and the flowers are quite large. Good cultivars include: 'Orange Emperor', rich orange; 'Pink Emperor', reddish pink; 'Red Emperor', bright red; 'Sweetheart', yellow with white edging; 'White Emperor', white.

Division XIV. Greigii hybrids grow from 6 to 12 inches tall and have foliage that is streaked and mottled with purple. They bloom in mid-spring, after Kaufmanniana hybrids. Good cultivars include: 'Donna Bella', carmine with wide ivory edging and interior; 'Garden Show', rich red; 'Oratorio', coral to rose; 'Red Riding Hood', carmine; 'Sweet Lady', pink.

Division XV. Other Species. Tulips that don't fit into any of the above divisions are classified as Division XV plants. Examples include: *T. clusiana* (the candy-stick tulip), *T. praestans*, *T. saxatilis*, *T. sylvestris*, and *T. turkestanica*.

Garden Design

The secret of successful gardening is to grow plants that are naturally suited to the garden's environment. That allows you to work with—rather than against—the plants' natural inclinations. When you understand the growing conditions in your garden-to-be, you can choose plants that will thrive in it. Always assess the characteristics of a garden site before rushing out to buy plants.

Assessing Your Site

If you're starting a new bed or border, the first decision is where to place it. The best location for a flower garden is not necessarily the most obvious one. Consider the following factors when choosing a spot.

Light. A location that receives full sun—unobstructed sunlight for at least five or six hours a day—affords the broadest choice of plants. However, quite a few flowers prefer, or at least tolerate, light or dappled shade. Other plants, particularly spring bulbs, like plenty of sun when they are in bloom but can take some shade when they are dormant.

Wind. If your location is subject to strong prevailing winds, you will probably need to install a windbreak to protect your plants. The windbreak can be living—a row of evergreen shrubs, for example—or it can be a wall or fence. Walls and fences used as windbreaks are most effective when made with an open construction that allows some air to pass through them. A solid wall can create damaging airflow patterns that may be as detrimental to plants as unobstructed winds.

Soil. The ideal soil for most plants is porous and crumbly. It contains plenty of organic matter and drains well while still retaining moisture. Light, sandy soils drain too quickly and do not hold moisture and nutrients long enough for roots to fully absorb them. Heavy clay soils pose the opposite problem—they are sticky and dense, difficult for plant roots to penetrate, and they drain so slowly that roots can become waterlogged and oxygen-starved. Few garden sites are initially blessed with ideal soil, but any soil can be improved.

If you've never conducted a soil test or had one performed by a laboratory, it's best to have your soil analyzed for nutrient content and pH. A number of home soil test kits are available, and some U. S. Department of Agriculture (USDA) Cooperative Extension offices provide a soil-testing service or can otherwise direct you to commercial labs. A search on the Internet should help you locate a Cooperative Extension office or commercial soil-testing lab in your area.

Moisture. Soil moisture levels are largely determined by regional climate, but local factors can also be important. If your soil is dry, add compost, choose dry-loving plants, and mulch the beds. If your soil is generally moist, plants that prefer wet conditions, such as irises and astilbe, will do well. If your soil is almost continuously wet, build raised beds to improve drainage.

Temperature. Consider how hot your summers can be and how cold your winters are—your average maximum and minimum temperatures. You also need to know the usual dates of the last spring and first fall frosts. Think about whether snow lingers longer or melts away more quickly in your yard than in your neighbor's. Slow melting usually indicates the presence of a cold pocket. Cold pockets often form at the bottom of slopes, because cold air tends to collect there. If you're new to gardening, or new to the area, your local Cooperative Extension office can give you information on the climate in your

Choose plants whose needs match the conditions in your garden. In this shady border, the pink lockets of bleeding heart are set off by greenish hellebores, golden doronicum, and other shade-tolerant flowers.

Where soil is poor or slow to drain, you can solve the problem by building raised beds and filling them with an improved soil mix.

locality and tell you which hardiness zone you live in. Also consult the USDA Hardiness Zone Map and the Heat Zone Map on pages 10–11. (Note: When using these maps, be aware that conditions vary from year to year and that every garden has its own unique environments, called microclimates. The only way to really understand your property's microclimates is to observe them over a period of years.)

Ratings of both the degree of cold (hardiness zone) and amount of heat (heat tolerance zone) that plants can stand are approximate. You may find that conditions in your garden allow you to grow some plants not considered hardy in your area or, conversely, that some plants zoned to survive in your area just can't tolerate your temperatures. You will come to know the microclimates in your garden and learn which kinds of plants grow best for you.

After you've assessed the growing conditions on your property, you will know where the best spot for your garden is—wherever the best combination of conditions exists. But remember that you can have a successful garden almost anywhere by improving the growing conditions and by selecting plants known to grow and bloom in the conditions you have to offer.

The straight lines of a formal garden, with neatly edged beds bordering a long brick path, draw the eye to the house, which features a filigree of vines on its facade.

TESTING SOIL LIFE

Plants depend on microorganisms to make many of the nutrients in soil available to them, so it's wise to test the soil for biological activity. A reliable but expensive test is available for gardeners. You can locate it by searching the Internet for the words soil+life+test. Here, the blue test patch has turned green-brown, indicating high—but not excessive—biological activity.

Fitting the Garden into the Setting

Flower gardens should relate in terms of scale and style to the rest of the landscape and fit comfortably into their setting. Gardens that "work" on a property usually complement the architectural style of the house and its surroundings. For example, if the other elements on a property are formal, the garden should probably echo that feeling; if the house has a casual feel, an informal garden looks best. The garden should relate well to the other architectural features on the property, too—the garage, sidewalks, fences, and walls. You'll also need to think about the viewing angle or vantage point from which you want the garden, and the flowers in it, to be most visible—from inside the house, the yard, or the street. Because the most satisfactory gardens accommodate your lifestyle as much as they please your aesthetic sense, also design your garden according to your needs—will you use it primarily as a place for reading and relaxation or entertaining and dining?

Garden Shapes and Sizes

Flower gardens come in various shapes and sizes. Edgings and dividers between areas are usually long and narrow, while garden islands, foundation plantings, or complements to architectural features can take any size or shape.

Traditionally, all ornamental plantings (except for cottage gardens) were formally laid out and required armies of gardeners to tend them. But today, the old, rigidly formal styles have largely given way to looser, more free-flowing designs, and the grandiose scale has shrunk to proportions more in keeping with present-day lifestyles and smaller properties.

Start Small. After determining location, size is the next factor to consider in laying out your garden. Gardeners always want to have more flowers than they can realistically handle. But nothing is sadder or more frustrating than finding yourself completely overwhelmed in June or July by spent plants with dead flowers still clinging to the stems, weeds overrunning the ornamentals, and blooming plants all but hidden in the wreckage.

It's best to start small. If this is your first garden, grow just a few different kinds of plants in a simple scheme of one or two colors. It's more effective to have several specimens of a few plants than one or two specimens of many different plants. Coordinating colors and blooming schedules is also easier when you're working with fewer kinds of plants. Repeating an uncomplicated plant grouping two or three times gives even a small garden a sense of continuity and a finished, well-planned look. Simple designs also make garden care simpler.

Siting for Access. When laying out your garden, consider the practicalities of tending the plants while also thinking about aesthetic concerns such as viewing angles. Remember that you will need easy access to every plant in the garden in order to weed, fertilize, deadhead, and divide. Unless your garden is less than 2 feet wide, you'll need to be able to reach into it from both front and back in order to get to all plants. If you plan to install a border along a wall or hedge, allow for a little walkway along the back of the garden so that you can reach all the plants.

Making the Most of Limited Space. If your available space is only a courtyard or small backyard, consider designing a garden as a series of multilevel raised beds. Instead of making one flat garden bed, you can make a raised bed that has two or three different levels and grow flowers on all the levels. This terracing creates an illusion of more space and allows you to grow more plants than you could in a single flat bed. Terracing is also a good solution to the problems posed by a steep hillside.

If you have no ground space for your garden and will be growing your flowers in containers on a patio or rooftop, it's still important to plan the layout carefully. You can group containers in various configurations and on different levels to create both height and depth, and even to serve as a screen. A well-planned container garden can look every bit as lush and colorful as an in-ground bed or border.

smart tip

GOOD GARDEN DESIGN

- Start small and simple.

- Keep the plantings in scale with their site.

- Follow your instincts.

- Plan for a succession of bloom.

- Plan the flower garden to have some complementary flowers blooming when nearby trees and shrubs are flowering.

- Plant drifts of color, not single plants, and let the colors melt into one another.

- Have a gradation of heights, front to back, but let a few plants float in and out of their groups for a softer, more integrated look.

- Use a variety of plant forms and flower shapes: round or clustered flowers, flat daisylike flowers, trumpet-shaped flowers, tall spires and spikes, branching forms.

- Be willing to change next year what you don't like this year.

- Remember to include a bench or chairs in your garden so you can sit and enjoy your flowers.

This sinuous garden seems to hug the terrain and flow around the rocks in the landscape.

Gracefully curving beds and borders (above) are ideal for an informal-style house. Add a bench to enjoy the profusion of color.

On a steep slope where space is at a premium (right), a series of terraces created by retaining walls makes more room for plants.

Garden Styles

Choose your garden style based on the setting and the architecture of your home. Formal gardens complement Georgian, Colonial, or sleek contemporary houses; informal gardens suit ranch, cottage, or salt-box homes.

Formal Gardens. Formal gardens, like classical paintings, are built around controlled forms. Beds usually take the form of precise squares, rectangles, or triangles with straight paths passing between them. They may be edged with low, clipped hedges of boxwood or other small-leaved evergreens, or they may have edgings of brick or stone.

Formal gardens exude an air of elegance and stability, thanks to symmetrical and balanced elements. Formal beds are often arranged along axes that draw the eye to a feature at their end—the house, perhaps, or a beautiful view, or maybe a sculpture. Some gardens have two axes, usually at right angles to one another. Planting beds are arranged along either side of the axis or axes, and plants and colors are often repeated from one bed to another to create both symmetry and unity. Paths in a formal garden are straight, with sharply defined edges, and paved with materials such as brick, bluestone, flagstone, and concrete pavers.

The plants in formal gardens should be displayed in perfect or even an idealized form. Formal gardens are the place for evergreen topiaries—balls, cones, pyramids, or even animal shapes. This is the kind of garden where a fuchsia or lantana trained as a standard can take the place of a small tree as a vertical accent. (Standards are pruned to have a central stem that acts as a trunk.) At the very least, the plants in a formal garden should be neatly maintained—

promptly deadheaded, meticulously weeded, and trimmed to keep them in their place.

Some plants are inherently more formal looking than others. Lilies, irises, hyacinths, delphiniums, and peonies—though they can also be at home in informal designs—possess an elegance, mass, and upright presence that is perfectly suited to formal gardens.

An understated color scheme usually works best in a formal garden. Blue and white flowers can be very serene, and a garden of all-white flowers looks crisp and fresh.

Formal gardens are neat and symmetrical, laid out in geometric shapes defined by careful edging. Here the small, carefully trimmed hedges emphasize the shape of the brick path that enhances the formal feeling. The raised brick around the central garden bed, the statue, and the subdued color scheme also contribute to the formal feeling.

Plants in an informal garden can tumble together in happy abandon, leaning into their neighbors, clambering over fences or bushes, or trailing over the ground beneath the feet of taller neighbors.

Informal Gardens. Informal gardens rely more on flowing curves than on straight lines; curved lines are natural and give a feeling of movement and dynamism. To design an informal garden, create your beds in graceful ovals or freeform shapes, and plant them so that low edging plants spill over and blur the edges.

Paths may lead off at angles or disappear around a corner to beckon you onward. In an informal garden, paths look best when they are paved with informal materials like wood chips and pebbles. Or you might prefer to use stepping-stones or even build a boardwalk.

You can use harmonious or contrasting colors in informal gardens. (See "Working with Color," page 17.) Or you might opt for a multicolored (or polychromatic) color scheme. Arrange the plants in fluid drifts of color, and allow them to assume their natural forms. You will still need to stake some tall-stemmed flowers, but this is not the place for garden elements such as meticulous obelisks or lollipop standards.

Cottage Gardens. The original cottage gardens were planted in front of modest homes in England and Europe. Early settlers brought them to North America. The colonists grew vegetables and herbs in their cottage gardens, as well as flowers for use in dyes, medicines, and seasonings. Typically a cottage garden was enclosed by a fence, in the old days, to exclude wandering animals.

Plants in cottage gardens are chosen for their individual attributes rather than their contribution to an overall design. This garden is the perfect place to grow "one of these and two of those." The old-fashioned flowers your grandmother grew—foxgloves and sweet William, bleeding heart

Cottage garden plants are chosen for their individual qualities rather than their contribution to an overall design.

Old-fashioned flowers such as columbines, lupines, and forget-me-nots are ideal for cottage gardens.

and rose moss—are perfect for a cottage garden. So are the cuttings and offshoots you receive from neighbors and friends. The serendipity of self-sowing plants is especially welcome here—let them come up where they will.

Gardeners today are creating cottage gardens in all sorts of regional vernacular styles. In the arid Southwest for example, a cottage garden might be full of native wildflowers and cacti, and enclosed with an ocotillo fence. In New England, the garden might contain daisies, delphiniums, and phlox behind a dry stone wall. What defines a cottage garden is the absence of rigidity and the presence of those plants the gardener loves best. In addition, many people add informal decorative touches such as a birdbath, sundial, or small bench.

PLANTS FOR A COTTAGE GARDEN

Aster (*Aster* species)
Bachelor's button (*Centaurea cyanus*)
Balsam impatiens (*Impatiens balsamina*)
Bellflower (*Campanula* species)
Bleeding heart (*Dicentra spectabilis*)
Columbine (*Aquilegia vulgaris*)
Crocus (*Crocus* species)
Crown imperial (*Fritillaria imperialis*)
Daffodil (*Narcissus* species)
Flowering tobacco (*Nicotiana* species)
Forget-me-not (*Myosotis* species)
Foxglove (*Digitalis* species)
Garden Phlox (*Phlox paniculata*)
Garden pinks, sweet William (*Dianthus* species)
Globe amaranth (*Gomphrena globosa*)
Heliotrope (*Heliotropium arborescens*)

Lavender (*Lavandula* species)
Lily (*Lilium* species)
Lily-of-the-valley (*Convallaria majalis*)
Love-lies-bleeding, Joseph's coat (*Amaranthus caudatus*)
Peony (*Paeonia* species)
Pot marigold (*Calendula officinalis*)
Poppy (*Papaver* species)
Primrose (*Primula* species)
Rocket Larkspur (*Consolida* cultivars)
Salvia (*Salvia* species)
Snapdragon (*Antirrhinum majus*)
Spider flower (*Cleome hassleriana*)
Squill (*Scilla* species)
Sweet alyssum (*Lobularia maritima*)
Tulip (*Tulipa* species)
Johnny-jump-up (*Viola tricolor*)

CUTTING FLOWERS

The best time to cut flowers is early in the morning before the dew has dried. Plants contain the most water then, so stems, leaves, and flowers are fresh and turgid. Early evening is the next best time. Although the blossoms contain less water after spending a day in the sunshine, the plants have been manufacturing food for themselves throughout daylight hours. Blossoms cut in the evening are well supplied with nutrients, which helps them hold their looks in the vase.

When you cut, take a pail of warm (110°F) water out to the garden with you, and plunge the flower stems into it as you cut them. Be sure your cutting tools are sharp—dull tools can crush the capillaries in stems, making it difficult for the flowers to draw up water.

As a general rule, don't cut tightly closed buds or fully opened flowers. Most flowers last longest if cut when the buds are about half open and showing color. Some exceptions to this rule are asters, mums, marigolds, and zinnias, which should be cut when they're fully open. In all cases, take only flowers that are in perfect condition; those damaged by disease or insects probably won't last long. Cut the stem right above a bud, or at the point where two stems meet; that way, you'll encourage the plant to send out a new shoot.

When you get your flowers into the house, they'll benefit from having their stems recut under water. When flowers are out of water for even a few seconds, their stems seal off. Recutting the stems allows your delicate flowers to again draw up water.

In a cutting garden, plan for easy access by planting flowers of varied shapes and colors in rows or blocks. While not usually designed to be ornamental, these gardens can be quite beautiful at different times during the season.

Cutting Gardens. One of the greatest rewards of flower gardening is having lots of blossoms to cut for bouquets and arrangements. If you enjoy bringing fresh flowers indoors, consider growing a cutting garden. These gardens differ from ornamental ones in that they are meant to be productive rather than decorative. Easy-to-access rows make maintenance and harvesting easy, and you can include all the colors and flower types you'll want for arrangements.

Most people put their cutting gardens along the border of their property or in an out-of-the-way corner, where they're out of sight. But if you're not concerned about appearance, put this garden close to the house so the upkeep will be easier. Vegetable gardeners often include a few rows of cutting flowers in the food garden where their color is a welcome sight and their pollen and nectar can feed beneficial insects. Herb gardeners sometimes mix flowers and herbs in the same plot.

Siting the cutting garden in full sun gives you the greatest plant selection. If the garden site gets less than five or six hours of sun, grow shade-tolerant flowers; you'll have a wider range of choices than you might imagine. See pages 24–67, 96–137, and 150–177 for plant descriptions.

FLOWERS FOR CUTTING GARDENS

Annuals

Bachelor's button (*Centaurea* species)
Blanket flower (*Gaillardia* species)
Candytuft (*Iberis umbellata*)
China aster (*Callistephus chinensis*)
Cockscomb, plume flower (*Celosia argentea*)
Flowering tobacco (*Nicotiana* species)
Globe amaranth (*Gomphrena globosa*)
Gloriosa daisy (*Rudbeckia hirta*)
Pot marigold (*Calendula* species)
Salvia (*Salvia* species)
Snapdragon (*Antirrhinum majus*)
Spider flower (*Cleome hassleriana*)
Stock (*Matthiola* species)
Verbena (*Verbena* species)
Zinnia (*Zinnia* species)

Perennials & Bulbs

Aster (*Aster* species)
Astilbe (*Astilbe* species)
Baby's breath (*Gypsophila* species)
Coneflower (*Echinacea* species)
Daffodil (*Narcissus* species)
Dahlia (*Dahlia* species)
Garden pinks (*Dianthus* species)
Gay-feather (*Liatris* species)
Gladiolus (*Gladiolus* species)
Lavender (*Lavendula* species)
Lily (*Lilium* species)
Lupine (*Lupinus* species)
Ornamental onion (*Allium* species)
Peony (*Paeonia* species)
Phlox (*Phlox* species)
Tickseed (*Coreopsis* species)
Tulip (*Tulipa* species)
Yarrow (*Achillea* species)

smart tip

PLANNING FOR CUTTING

The following guidelines will help you plan a cutting garden:

• Put plants with similar cultural needs together.

• Lay out the garden by flower color, planting in blocks or rows of red, purple, yellow, and so forth.

• Choose flower colors that will go with your decorating scheme indoors.

• Grow a mix of plant forms to use in arrangements: tall, spiky flowers; rounded shapes; and small, airy "filler" blooms.

• Put the tallest plants at the back (ideally the north side), so they won't shade shorter plants. Place medium-size plants next and the shortest ones in front.

• Leave enough space between rows or blocks of plants to cut flowers, pull weeds, and perform other routine chores.

• In between the rows or beds, cover pathways with a good layer of mulch, or plant grass to keep down weeds and make it easy to get in and cut flowers without getting your shoes dirty.

• If the garden includes perennials, try to plan for bloom in different seasons.

• Stagger succession plantings of the same annuals two weeks apart to provide flowers through the season.

Making Good Use of Containers

Plants in pots dress up a window, provide a front-door welcome, and create the perfect setting for relaxing on a deck or city rooftop. Place large tubs of bright flowers next to the front door or set smaller pots with just one or two plants on all or some of the steps leading to the door.

Porches are another good place for containers of flowers if you place them where they'll get some light. Suspend hanging baskets at varying heights along the underside edge of the porch roof to create a pleasant effect. For a living privacy screen, or to shade the porch, let long trailers dangle from hanging baskets or train potted climbing plants on trellises.

Other good places for container plants include balconies, the paving around swimming pools, and the edges of driveways and paths. If you have several plants in small individual pots, group them on a fern stand or in a window box or tub to create a massed effect.

Container Designs. Planning a container garden is just like planning a garden bed or border, but on a smaller scale. A well-planned design, whether it consists of many different containers of plants or several plants in a large tub or window box, still takes into account variation of plant heights and compatibility of forms, textures, and colors. The most successful color schemes for container gardens are generally those built on just a few colors. Pleasing polychromatic schemes can be more difficult to achieve in the confines of a container garden. But containers encourage experimentation, allowing you to try different color combinations that you can easily change the next year.

Caring for container-grown plants is different in an important way from caring for plants in the ground—the plants are much more dependent on you to supply water, nutrients, and the proper environment. When you cover the tops of containers with unmilled sphagnum peat moss or sheet moss to hide their rims, for example, you are also helping them to conserve water. For other watering information, see "Watering Plants in Containers," page 196. Fertilizing information is given in "Caring for Annuals," page 20.

A window box of petunias and geraniums, with lobelias and pansies cascading over the front, strikes a romantic note.

GOOD CONTAINER PLANTS

Sunny Locations:

Annual candytuft (*Iberis umbellata*)

Dwarf dahlia (*Dahlia* species)

Edging lobelia (*Lobelia erinus*)

Garden pinks (*Dianthus* species)

Geranium (*Pelargonium* species)

Marigold (*Tagetes* species)

Nasturtium (*Tropaeolum* species)

New Guinea Impatiens (*Impatiens* New Guinea Group)

Pansy (*Viola* species)

Rose moss (*Portulaca grandiflora*)

Salvia (*Salvia* species)

Spider flower (*Cleome hassleriana*)

Sweet alyssum (*Lobularia maritima*)

Verbena (*Verbena* species)

Wax begonia (*Begonia* Semperflorens-Cultorum Hybrids)

Zinnia (*Zinnia* species)

Shady Locations:

Bedding impatiens (*Impatiens* species)

Edging lobelia (*Lobelia erinus*)

Flowering tobacco (*Nicotiana* species)

Fuchsia (*Fuchsia* cultivars)

Wax begonia, tuberous begonia (*Begonia* species)

Hanging Baskets:

Cascading petunia (*Petunia × hybrida*)

Edging lobelia (*Lobelia erinus*)

Fuchsia (*Fuchsia* cultivars)

Ivy geranium (*Pelargonium peltatum*)

Licorice plant (*Helichrysum petiolaris*)

Nasturtium (*Tropaeolum* species)

Sweet potato vines 'Blackie' or 'Margarita' (*Ipomoea batatas*)

Trailing lantana (*Lantana montevidensis*)

Tuberous begonia (*Begonia × tuberhybrida*)

Working with Color

Figuring out your color scheme can be the most challenging—and enjoyable—part of planning. Although there's no substitute for experience when combining garden colors, your own tastes should be your guide. This section offers basic guidelines for working with color. But don't be afraid to bend the rules. Let yourself play with color combinations on paper, and experiment with them in your garden.

Consider the colors of elements in the landscape outside the garden, too—trees, shrubs, walls, fences, and paving, as well as outbuildings and your house. The colors in your garden should work with these other background colors in order to look good in their site.

Types of Color Schemes

On a color wheel, harmonious colors are located adjacent or close to one another, while contrasting colors are opposite or far apart.

Plan the color scheme in your garden to reflect your own taste. Do you tend to prefer harmonious, subtle combinations of colors, or do you like contrasts? What is the color scheme in your home? You may choose to repeat it in the garden, especially if you'll be growing flowers for cutting. Do you want a single color to dominate the garden all season, or would you rather have several colors working together?

Harmonious Color Schemes. Gardens planted in related, or analogous, colors are quite harmonious, but they can also be surprisingly dramatic. (Analogous colors are those that lie near each other on the artist's color wheel as illustrated at right.) Consider a sunny yellow, yellow-orange, and orange bed of daylilies, cosmos, nasturtiums, Mexican sunflower, and marigolds. Or try an autumn garden of mixed orange, bronze, red, and russet chrysanthemums, perhaps accented with a little purple. A beautifully soft mixture of related hues is blue, violet, red, and warm pink—colors found in flowers such as asters, bachelor's buttons, and petunias.

One way to achieve a harmonious mix of colors is to grow several cultivars of one type of flower—delphiniums, phlox, or Oriental poppies, for example. The colors among cultivars may differ in intensity and in hue, but they usually harmonize with one another. Or try different kinds of flowers in the same color, for example, coreopsis with golden cultivars of yarrow, cockscomb, and marigolds.

Complementary Color Schemes. Complementary colors, those that lie opposite one another on the color wheel, create contrasts. Orange and blue are complementary, as are yellow and purple, and red and green.

These color schemes can be unpleasantly jarring, or lively and jazzy. Pure complementary colors are the most jarring; for example, pure purple and clear yellow look harsh next to each other. But when the purple is deepened toward violet-blue and the yellow is soft and light, the combination is exquisite, as demonstrated by a pairing of *Salvia* 'Victoria' and *Coreopsis* 'Moonbeam'.

Cool blues and violets create a feeling of calm and serenity—a respite from a busy world.

Contrasting colors are lively and active. Complementary colors, here orange geum and blue borage, are the strongest contrast of all.

Contrasting

Contrasting Color Schemes. There are any number of ways to create contrast in the flower garden. The most obvious include pairing light and dark colors, pastels with intense hues, or complementary colors. Contrasting color schemes often look best when you use a paler version of one of the two colors. Use the brighter color sparingly as an accent, and use the less-intense color over a larger area to balance the brighter color. For example, if you want to combine red tulips with blue forget-me-nots, you'll get the best results by planting lots of forget-me-nots among and surrounding the tulips. And you need only a few dark rose cosmos to add spark to a garden of pale pink flowers. To tone down contrasting colors, introduce neutral, or blender, tones as discussed below.

Monochromatic Color Schemes. Relying on one color to dominate the garden all season is probably the least complicated approach and the most successful for new gardeners. If you choose yellow, for instance, you might have daffodils and basket-of-gold in spring, yellow irises and potentillas in late spring and early summer, rudbeckia and yellow daylilies in summer, and buttery or gold dahlias and chrysanthemums in fall. Against the succession of yellow flowers that form the backbone of the garden, other colors can come and go. The other colors serve to accentuate—not compete with—the yellow flowers.

Monochromatic schemes generally work best in small gardens, where they give a sense of added space and openness. Those based on a light color can brighten a partially shaded garden. Single-color gardens need not be boring. You can vary flower sizes, shapes, and tones of color (pale, bright, or dark) in addition to plant heights, shapes, and textures.

Polychromatic Color Schemes. Some gardeners like a polychromatic, or multicolored, scheme. Cottage gardens, with their cheerful riot of colors, are a good example of the polychromatic style. In a mixed-color garden, the variety of colors included depends entirely on the gardener's taste. Sometimes they work, and sometimes they don't. When designing, remember that strong colors modify one another when planted together. Blue flowers seem to cast a yellowish shadow on neighboring blossoms; red flowers tend to have more of an orange appearance when they appear next to white flowers.

Blender Colors

A useful trick for integrating a garden and harmonizing colors that might otherwise be unsettling is to include blender colors. Groups of creamy white or pale yellow flowers make effective harmonizers for groups of stronger colors. Deep-green foliage can be used to harmonize bright colors such as red and orange. Gray or silvery white foliage pulls together soft blues, lavenders, and pinks. And distance also tends to blend colors that are otherwise quite contrasting when viewed close up.

Monochromatic

Polychromatic

Warmth and Coolness in Colors

Warm colors (pink, orange, yellow, and red) project themselves toward you, seeming to be closer than they are. And cool colors (blue, violet, and green) recede, appearing to be farther away. To create an illusion of depth and space in a small garden, try planting warm shades in the front and cool shades behind them.

Warm colors are also stimulating and active—even aggressive if they are strong— while cool colors are restful and quiet. For a peaceful, subtle effect, plant your garden in blues and purples. The cool colors will also create a feeling of distance. For a cheerful but not aggressive feeling, plant warm shades of apricot, salmon, and pink accented with touches of red and purple. Shades on the borderline between warm and cool—yellow-green, for instance, or rosy purple—may convey the cheerfulness of the warm colors and the calmness of the cool colors.

Finally, be aware that warm colors harmonize with other warm colors while cool colors harmonize with other cool shades. This can be important in multicolor gardens because the warmth or coolness of a particular tint can make or break the color scheme. For example, if you're using pink with violet (which can be quite beautiful), choose a cool (bluish) shade of pink. On the other hand, a warm (orangish) shade of pink will be more effective with yellow or red.

Cool and blender colors

Warm colors

smart tip

USING COLOR EFFECTIVELY

- Use simple colors that relate to the landscape and site.

- Plant in generous groups of color for the best effect; single plants here and there get lost in the design. Even flowers used for accent colors should be planted in groups of at least three.

- In all but the smallest gardens, plant in drifts instead of straight rows. Also plant a few flowers of each color over the boundary between adjoining drifts so that the colors melt into each other.

- Avoid bicolored flowers in multicolored gardens (unless you really know what you're doing). Flowers in solid colors will usually produce a more sophisticated look, and they are far easier to work into a design.

- Dark colors are best seen close up. From a distance or in the shade, they seem to disappear.

- Pastel and white flowers can appear to light up shady areas, where they gleam against the dark background. They are especially wonderful in gardens used at night or viewed as the sun goes down. At dusk, light-colored flowers take on a special glow.

- Strong, bright colors are especially effective in very sunny gardens. Pastels and dark colors are overpowered by strong sunlight, but hot colors are only subdued by it. Brilliantly colored flowers can also be quite striking against dark foliage, a point to keep in mind if you have foundation plantings of evergreens.

APPENDIX

Working the Soil

Digging new beds and borders is the hardest work in gardening, but it accomplishes several goals. First and foremost, digging loosens the soil so that plant roots can push through more easily. It also allows you to mix in ample quantities of organic matter to help keep the soil loose, fluffy, and easy to work. If a soil test shows you need lime or sulfur, you'll distribute it evenly if you mix it into the soil when you dig.

Test the moisture level in your soil before working it. Take a small handful and squeeze it in your palm. It should hold together but not show your fingerprints.

How to Tell When Soil Is Workable

All gardeners are anxious to get into the garden in spring, but digging too early isn't good for the soil. In fact, you can break down soil structure and cause compaction if you dig while the ground is still half-frozen or wet. To tell whether your soil is ready to work, scoop up a handful and squeeze it into a ball inside your palm. Then open your fingers. If the soil ball sticks together when you poke it gently (as shown in the photo below left), the ground is still too wet to work. But if the ball crumbles easily when you poke it, you can start digging. If it's really powdery and dry, run a sprinkler until the top inch or two is moist. Wait a few hours before digging or tilling.

Tap the soil ball lightly with your finger. If it crumbles apart into irregularly sized pieces, it is just right, but if it compresses further, it is too wet to work.

Dig Garden Beds

DIFFICULTY LEVEL: MODERATE

how to

Tools and Materials: Trowel, plastic bag, and a soil-testing kit

1 Remove the sod in the area where you are planning to make a garden bed by cutting through the root layer, in shovel- or spade-shaped blocks, skimming off the layer of roots and grass.

2 Remove the top foot of soil from a 2-foot wide trench along the length of the bed. Place this soil on a tarp. When you are finished making the bed, you'll use it to fill the last trench you dig.

3 Loosen the subsoil at the bottom of the trench with a spading fork. If the soil has average to poor fertility, sprinkle a layer of amendments on the trench bottom before using the spading fork.

4 Fill the trench with soil that you dig from the next trench. Continue in this way, removing a foot of soil, using the fork to loosen the soil, and filling the trench, until the bed is completely formed.

Digging

For most gardens, simple but thorough digging is all you need in the way of soil preparation. Remove any existing turf or weeds, as shown in the illustrations at right. Using a tiller, spading fork, or shovel, loosen the soil to a depth of at least 12 inches—18 inches is even better. Then spread about 3 inches of compost or well-aged manure over the surface of the entire bed, and dig it into the top few inches. Rake the soil smooth before planting.

If you suspect drainage problems or have very heavy soil, you may need more-elaborate soil preparation, called double digging. This produces a beautifully porous, fine-textured planting area. But it is comparatively heavy work, and unless your soil is severely compacted and nutrient-poor, it's probably not necessary. Double digging involves removing the top layer of soil from the garden about a spade deep, loosening the subsoil below to another spade's depth using a garden fork, and enriching the topsoil with compost, manure, or another form of organic matter as you return it to the bed.

Power Tilling. A power tiller can be a labor-saving device for turning over new ground. But most power tillers won't dig more than 7 or 8 inches deep, so you'll still need to loosen the underlying soil using a garden fork. Stop tilling as soon as you have clods the size of a golf ball; you can level these with a rake before planting. Caution: Grinding soil to a fine powder with a tiller destroys the vital air channels needed for good drainage. Also, using a power tiller routinely every spring to prepare annual beds can bring many weed seeds nearer the surface and encourage their germination.

Maintaining Good Soil

Once the garden is established—especially if you're growing perennials—you'll be able to do less digging and rely more on the work of soil-improving organisms such as earthworms. If fed annually with topdressings of organic matter, soil organisms will maintain good soil structure and help ensure even distribution of applied fertilizers.

Established gardens benefit from the addition of a 1-inch layer of compost each year. When working compost and fertilizers into perennial beds, scratch them in lightly around the plants' crowns (the area where roots and stems meet). Do not disturb the roots themselves. Also, be careful not to get chemical fertilizers on plant crowns because these concentrated materials can injure delicate plant tissues.

Starting Plants from Seed

Growing your own seedlings affords you a greater choice of plants and cultivars for your garden than purchasing plants from the local garden center. And seeds are much cheaper than plants sold by mail-order nurseries. You can sow seeds for hardy plants directly in the garden. But tender plants and slow-growing ones are often started indoors to produce plants that flower earlier than they would if sown outdoors.

Before you plant any seeds, be sure the containers and tools you plan to use are clean because seedlings are easy prey for disease-causing organisms. If you are reusing starting containers, scrub them out with a 10-percent bleach solution, and let them dry before filling them with soil.

Many people start seeds in a sterile soil mix or growing medium. A number of commercial seed-starting mixes are available, but you can make one from equal parts of peat moss, vermiculite, and perlite. Add two parts of fully finished, good compost to this basic mixture if you want the potting soil to supply nutrients for the first few weeks. Although compost is not sterile, it usually contains enough beneficial microorganisms to combat injurious ones.

Sow seeds that are large enough to easily handle one or two at a time into flats, cell packs, peat pots, or other containers of moist potting mix.

Planting Seeds

Most seed packets carry instructions for planting depth and spacing. A general rule of thumb is to plant seeds at a depth that is two to three times their diameter. Tiny seeds (those of begonias or snapdragons, for example) can be mixed with sand to help separate them and make them easier to handle; sprinkle this mixture on top of the potting mix. Most tiny seeds need light to germinate, so it's important not to cover them after planting. When you mist the soil surface to water them, they'll work themselves into tiny niches that will keep them moist. Plant larger seeds in individual holes, or make furrows as you do in the outdoor garden.

Some gardeners cover their seeds with a thin layer of fine sphagnum moss to protect the seedlings from damping-off (a lethal fungal disease). Sphagnum moss has fungicidal properties. If you use it in your seed flats, make sure it stays moist at all times. When the moss dries out it becomes hard and stiff and tender seedlings may have difficulty penetrating it. Although it was used to dress wounds during World War II because of its fungicidal properties, some people experience skin irritations if it gets into cuts or scratches; wear gloves when you work with it.

Temperature. The best temperature for germination varies from plant to plant. Generally speaking, tender (frost-sensitive) plants usually sprout best in warm temperatures of 70°F to 75°F. Cool-season flowers germinate better in cooler temperatures around 60°F to 65°F. Some perennials need a period of freezing or cooling at temperatures of 35°F to 40°F before they can germinate. Seed packets often supply this information.

Carefully cover seeds that don't need light to germinate by sprinkling fine, loose, moist potting mix over them to the correct depth.

Fluorescent lamps provide ideal light for seedlings. Use daylight tubes or a combination of cool white and warm white, and keep the seedling tops a few inches below the lamps. Adjust the height of the containers as the plants grow, keeping them 5 in. from the leaf tips.

Light. Seedlings need plenty of light as soon as they break through the soil surface. Fluorescent fixtures are the best way to supply light for indoor seedlings. Their light is very even, and the plants don't need to be turned to grow straight. You can use special "grow light" tubes, full-spectrum daylight lamps, or a combination of warm white and cool white tubes. Set the lights on a timer so they're on for 16 hours a day. The tops of the seedlings should be no more than 3 or 4 inches below the lights for the first couple of weeks; later you can gradually raise the lights to 5 inches above the leaves. Start out with the seedling flats elevated on a stand that can be gradually lowered as the plants grow taller. (A pile of books works nicely.) Or suspend the light fixture on chains that you can raise as the plants grow.

Watering from below allows you to evenly and thoroughly moisten the soil without dislodging seeds or tiny seedlings, as can happen with a stream of water from overhead. Set flats or pots in a container of water an inch or so deep until the soil surface feels moist, or use a specially made flat and wicking mat.

FEEDING SEEDLINGS

Since the soilless mixes for seed-starting contain almost no nutrients, you'll have to supply some as soon as seedlings develop their first true leaves (the second set they form). But don't go overboard; overfertilizing your seedlings can result in weak, floppy plants more prone to problems. Young seedlings can't handle full-strength fertilizer. Dilute liquid fertilizers to one-quarter the strength recommended on the label (or, if you use fish emulsion, half strength). Use the diluted fertilizer once a week for the first three or four weeks. After that, gradually work up to using a normal dilution.

If you've added compost to the seed-starting mix, you can probably wait to feed your seedlings until they are four or five weeks old. But check their color every day; at the first sign or yellowing or purpling, begin feeding once a week with a half-strength dilution of liquid fertilizer.

If you want to try growing seedlings without using artificial lighting, your best bet is a south window covered with sheer curtains (to keep the heat from becoming too intense) or a bright, unshaded east or west window. Turn the flats every day to keep the stems growing straight.

Water. Seeds and young seedlings need to be watered carefully so that the seeds aren't washed out of the soil and the delicate new roots aren't disturbed. The best approach is to water from below, setting the flats or pots in lukewarm water in a sink or special watering tray. Another technique is to mist the soil surface with a plant mister until the soil is thoroughly moistened.

Make sure your seedlings don't dry out; water stress can set back young plants permanently. But don't overwater either. Constantly soggy soil encourages root rot and damping-off. Water your seedlings when the soil is somewhat dry—early enough so that leaves can dry by dark.

Thinning and Transplanting Seedlings

When the seedlings develop their first true leaves—the second set of leaves to grow but the first that have the plant's characteristic shape—it's time to thin. You can thin by pulling up unwanted seedlings individually, snipping off the stems at soil level with nail scissors, or carefully lifting and transplanting the young plants to other containers.

Spacing for seedlings in flats or pots depends on the size of their leaves, but 3 inches is considered a good average spacing distance. Crowding seedlings together increases root competition, encourages the spread of damping-off and other diseases, and causes plants to shade each other, which makes them spindly. To avoid problems, keep seedlings far enough apart so their leaves don't touch. When the leaves threaten to touch each other, the plants are probably big enough to go into individual pots or, if weather conditions are appropriate, outdoors into the garden. (See "Transplanting Outdoors," below.)

If you've grown seedlings in an unsegmented flat, cut the soil into blocks a few days before transplanting. The cut roots will heal before the plants are transplanted.

Hardening Off

Seedlings started indoors need to adjust gradually to the harsher environment outdoors. Leaves, like skin that's been indoors all winter, can easily get sunburned. Before you move your indoor seedlings out to the garden, harden them off. Over a two-week period, cut back on watering slightly while also increasing their exposure to colder temperatures. Begin by setting seedlings outdoors in a sheltered spot for an hour or two; then bring them back inside. Move them outside for a longer time each day, eventually leaving them out overnight. By the end of the second week the plants should be ready to move into the garden. Plants can be hardened off in a cold frame if you open the lid a bit farther each day, removing it entirely for the last two or three days.

Transplanting Outdoors

Transplanting to the garden is largely governed by weather conditions. The best time to transplant is on a cloudy, calm day, ideally in mid- to late-afternoon. Bright sun and wind can dry out transplants.

Dig the planting hole before you remove a plant from its pot or flat, even on a cloudy, humid day. This advance preparation should protect the roots from drying out. Planting holes must be big enough to comfortably accommodate all the roots and deep enough to allow the plant to sit at the same depth as it did in its growing container. If the garden soil is dry, pour some water into the hole before planting. Set the plant in the hole, and fill in around its roots with soil. Firm the soil gently; don't compact it. Then water the plant thoroughly to help it settle in.

Protect your transplants from wind and bright light for the first few days. Floating row covers, made from lightweight spun polyester fabric, are convenient to use and effective for shading. Glass or plastic cloches, plastic gallon jugs with their bottoms cut out, and floating row covers all give wind protection.

Thin seedlings by snipping them off with scissors. Pulling them may disturb the roots of nearby seedlings.

Harden off seedlings in a cold frame by opening the lid for a gradually increasing length of time over several days, finally leaving it open all night.

Maintaining the Garden

Plant annuals among perennials to keep the garden colorful all summer. This gardener is planting petunias to carry on the show when the irises finish.

Garden maintenance will never be overwhelming if you keep up with it. Small weeds are easier to pull than big ones. A few pests are easier to eliminate than a full-blown infestation. Spending time in your garden on a regular basis enables you to spot and deal with problems before they get out of hand.

Conserving Moisture

Moisture needs vary from plant to plant, but unless you grow drought-tolerant plants or live in an extremely moist climate, you'll undoubtedly have to water your garden at least occasionally to supplement natural rainfall. With the threat of water shortages looming over us all occasionally, it's essential for gardeners to learn to water as efficiently as possible using modern irrigation systems and to conserve water as they can.

There are several ways to conserve water and still give your plants the moisture they require. First, water only when necessary. The old rule of giving the garden an inch a week doesn't hold true for all plants in all conditions. A garden in heavy soil in a cool, cloudy location needs less, while a seashore garden in hot sun needs more. Soils high in organic matter retain moisture well; add compost to reduce watering needs. Instead of blindly following rules or setting the timer on an automatic watering system and leaving it at the same setting all summer, water your plants when they need it.

Judging Water Needs. Check moisture levels frequently by poking a finger into the soil. When the ground feels dry more than an inch or two deep, it's time to water. Don't wait until your plants wilt or look limp; wilting indicates severe water stress. Some plants look a bit flaccid in mid afternoon on a hot, sunny day but perk up again later on, toward dusk. That doesn't necessarily mean they are suffering water stress. However, plants that look wilted in the morning or evening are in trouble. Water them immediately to avoid stunting and delayed development.

When plants need it, water deeply so that the moisture soaks far down into the soil. Deep watering increases drought tolerance by encouraging plants to send roots to lower levels where they'll be able to find more water during dry weather. In the long run, this strategy saves water because you'll need to irrigate less often. The plants will also be less dependent on you to supply all the moisture they need. On the other hand, if you water lightly and often—say, a quick sprinkling from the hose every day—the roots will stay near the soil surface where they will be more vulnerable to dry weather and hot sun.

Mulching is an easy way to conserve moisture. It reduces evaporation from the soil surface while also increasing the levels of organic matter and helping to eliminate weeding chores. (See page 197 for information on mulching.)

Conserve water by growing drought-tolerant plants if you live where summers are dry. Artemisias and other silver-leaved plants often tolerate dry conditions.

APPENDIX

Watering Efficiently

To use the least amount of water and avoid diseases caused by improper watering techniques, apply the water directly to the soil. Soaker hoses and drip irrigation systems are two ways to water at ground level.

Soaker Hose. Soaker hoses are made of a porous fiber, such as canvas, or recycled rubber. They allow water to trickle out slowly. The hoses connect to one another. Use a regular hose to connect the soaker hoses to the outdoor faucet and turn on the faucet only partway. Lay the hoses through the garden early in the season. If the hoses' appearance bothers you, cover them with mulch.

Drip Irrigation. Most drip systems use lengths of narrow plastic tubing with small perforations along the sides. The tubing is connected with couplings to header lines. The headers connect to the regular hose and that connects to the water faucet. If you want the system to operate automaticlly, hook up a timer to it. Remember to change the timer settings according to the weather and the needs of the plants.

Depending on the complexity of your landscape, you may want to install a system with different zones. Zoned systems allow you to water one or more areas more frequently or longer than you water others. They are particularly useful for yards that contain a number of gardens with different moisture requirements.

Drip irrigation systems are sometimes installed under the soil surface, but more frequently, they lie on top of it. You can also find drip systems that are appropriate for container gardens.

You can assemble a drip irrigation system from a kit or buy the components individually. If your system will be complex, you can usually get a free design service and detailed installation instructions from the supplier. All drip systems are costly, and some require a fair amount of labor to install. But once in place, drip irrigation is effective and convenient. And a big plus: it does not detract from the garden's appearance.

Watering Plants in Containers. Plants growing in containers need to be watered much more frequently than plants growing in the ground. That's because the volume of soil in a container—even a large tub—is so much smaller than even a minuscule garden in the ground and because water evaporates through the sides, bottom, and surface of pots. This is particularly true of containers kept outside. In hot weather, especially on windy days, you will need to water potted plants in all but large tubs and barrels daily—small pots perhaps twice a day. The smaller the container, the faster it will dry out. Plastic pots don't allow moisture to evaporate as quickly as porous clay pots. Grouping potted plants also helps to keep them moist. Many people add water-retentive polymers to potting mixes. Although this helps, you'll still need to water container plants often in summer. Check them every day—or twice a day—and water whenever the soil feels dry below the surface.

Soaker hoses allow water to trickle slowly out into the soil, minimizing waste from evaporation and efficiently delivering water right where plants can use it most—the root zone.

WATERING FROM ABOVE

While watering with a hose or sprinkler was once the preferred method, it is rarely recommended now. For one thing, overhead watering is wasteful because the water must filter down through the canopy of plant leaves. Before it reaches the ground, a great deal of it is lost to evaporation, especially on a hot day. Another drawback to overhead watering is its potential to promote fungal diseases. Plants are especially vulnerable if you water late in the day and the foliage remains wet at night.

Watering from above does offer the advantages of cleansing the foliage and helping to cool plants in hot weather. If you must use a hose or sprinkler, do it in the morning or late afternoon, avoiding the hottest part of the day when evaporation is greatest. But if you water late in the afternoon, be sure a few hours of daylight are left so that plant leaves will be dry by dark. If that's impossible, get a bubbler attachment for your hose, and move the hose around to water all the plants at ground level.

Mulching

If communing with nature on your knees is not your idea of a good time, you can virtually eliminate the need to weed by mulching. Quite simply, mulching involves covering the soil surface between and around plants with a choice of organic or inorganic materials. All mulches help to conserve moisture and keep down weeds. A dark-color mulch can help warm the soil in early spring, while deep loose mulches keep the ground frozen in winter so perennial roots aren't damaged by alternate freezing and thawing action. (See "Maintaining Perennials," page 78, for information about mulching for winter.)

Organic mulches are the most attractive. They also have the virtue of being the most beneficial to the soil because they add nutrient-filled organic matter as they decompose. Most organic materials make good mulches, but there are some exceptions. Pine needles are so acid that they are good mulches for acid-lovers such as azaleas, but poor mulches for most of the plants you grow. Hay often adds as many weed seeds to the soil as it is suppressing. And whole leaves can form water-repellant mats. However, if you shred them by running over them with a lawn mower, they make an excellent mulch for most ornamental plants. See the box at right for additional mulch materials.

When to Mulch. The best time to lay down a summer mulch is after the soil has thoroughly warmed in the spring and the plants are already several inches high. If you put down the mulch too early, it will actually keep the soil colder longer, delaying planting as well as retarding the growth of some tender plants. A 1- to 2-inch layer of fine-textured material is usually sufficient; coarser materials such as straw require more depth to provide good coverage. Mulch prevents light from reaching the soil between garden plants. The darkness prevents most weed seeds from germinating. Mulch also keeps the soil surface loose and crumbly because the sun can't bake it into a hard crust. Any weeds that do grow can be pulled out easily. All in all, a summer mulch is a tremendous work saver.

Mulch helps to keep down weeds, moderate soil temperatures, and conserve soil moisture. Pull aside the mulch to set out plants and then replace it.

MULCH MATERIALS

Material	Depth
Bark chips	3 inches
Shredded bark	2 inches
Cocoa bean hulls	2 inches
Compost	1 to 3 inches
Hay or straw	4 to 6 inches in summer, 8 to 12 inches in winter
Shredded leaves	2 to 3 inches in summer, 6 to 8 inches in winter
Lawn clippings	1 to 2 inches
Wood chips	2 to 3 inches

Shredded bark　　Cocoa hulls　　Wood chips　　Leaves

Sawdust　　Chipped leaves　　Straw　　Lawn clippings

APPENDIX

Controlling Pests and Diseases

The gardener's most important lines of defense against garden thugs are good garden practices: taking preventive measures, practicing good sanitation, maintaining the plants well, and intervening at the first sign of any problem.

Minimize disease problems by choosing resistant cultivars whenever possible. Zinnias are prone to powdery mildew, especially late in the season. However, 'Pulcino' and the Star hybrids are among the cultivars bred to be resistant to this disease.

Preventive Measures. Although you can't keep pests and diseases from invading your garden, you can do several things to make your garden less inviting to them. First and foremost, practice good sanitation. Simply keep the garden clean. Keep up with the weeding and pick up dead leaves, flowers, and other trash that falls to the ground. Plant debris provides excellent hiding places for pests to overwinter and lay their eggs, as well as sites for disease organisms to take hold.

You can spread disease organisms from one plant to another just by working in the garden, so be careful. Don't work in the garden when plants are wet; your hands, tools, or clothes could transfer harmful organisms that are in the water on the leaves. Don't smoke in the garden; if you smoke at all, wash your hands before working around your plants. (Tobacco carries plant viruses.) Keep infested plant materials out of the compost pile.

Avoid crowding plants together when planting. Plants need sufficient room to develop properly if they are to remain vigorous. Good air circulation helps to prevent fungal diseases and some pests that thrive in high-humidity conditions. Mixed plantings also have fewer problems than entire beds or large blocks of a single type of plant because they confuse insects that rely on odor or visual cues to find their hosts.

If your plants are attacked by the same pest and disease problems year after year, seek out plants that don't tend to get those problems, or plant varieties resistant to them. For example, if your zinnias always seem to get powdery mildew, look for varieties bred for resistance to it, such as 'Pulcino' or the Star hybrids. Growing pest- and disease-susceptible plants in a different part of the garden each year deprives pest and disease organisms of appropriate hosts. This simple straegy can prevent them from building high populations.

Monitor the garden. Keep a close watch on all your plants throughout the growing season, and take action whenever you notice the first signs of pests or a disease. Examine several representative plants of each type carefully, checking the leaf axils, undersides of leaves, growing tips, and flower buds for diseases or pest insects and their eggs. Remove diseased or severely pest-infested parts of plants as soon as you see them. To avoid spreading the problem, place the debris in a plastic bag and put it in the trash. These problems are easiest to solve in their early stages, before the pest population assumes major proportions or the disease spreads to several plants.

Learn to identify insect eggs—these will eventually hatch into larvae of one of the most useful insects in the garden, ladybugs.

Pest Control. The safest pest controls include traps, biological controls, and natural and plant-based materials that quickly break down into noninjurious substances after they are applied.

Sticky yellow traps suspended among plants are effective against aphids and especially whiteflies. These insects are attracted by the bright yellow color of the traps and stick to the adhesive coating. When the trap is covered with bugs, wipe it off and recoat it with commercially available Tanglefoot, or just discard it.

Blue and white sticky traps are also available. Thrips are attracted to blue traps, while tarnished plant bugs, or *Lygus* bugs, favor white ones. Again, the traps should be cleaned off and recoated or discarded when they lose their stickiness or run out of uncovered area.

Insecticidal soap is effective against aphids, whiteflies, flea beetles, and other small pests; it simply clogs their breathing holes. Plant-based insecticides include pyrethrum, neem, ryania, and sabadilla. These materials kill fairly selectively. (See the label.) However, because they can kill some benign or beneficial insects along with pests, use them with care. Rotenone, a botanical pesticide which is often recommended, kills so many insect species that it's best to use it only as the very last resort.

Biological controls are even more specific than botanical insecticides. *Bacillus thuringiensis* var. *kurstaki* (a bacterium sold as BTK or Dipel) is effective against all caterpillars. *Diatomaceous earth*, ground diatom skeletons, controls soft-bodied pests. If you use diatomaceous earth, buy a brand meant for horticultural use rather than the type sold for use in swimming pool filters.

Most organic insecticides and controls must be reapplied after it rains, but the extra effort seems a small price to pay for the peace of mind they afford.

It is a good idea, too, to familiarize yourself with the beneficial insects in your garden—the helpful predators and parasitoids of the pests. Learn to recognize ladybugs, praying mantids, green lacewings, and other allies. If you spot them in your garden, leave them alone and consider yourself lucky. You can also purchase beneficial insects by mail to release into your garden.

Fighting Disease. Early intervention is the best weapon against plant diseases. If you notice disease symptoms as you make your garden rounds, immediately remove the affected part of the plant. If more symptoms develop, pull up the entire plant and put it in the trash. Never put diseased plant material on the compost pile; even a hot pile doesn't get hot enough to destroy all types of pathogens. Sulfur and copper sprays can help control fungus and some bacterial problems before they really take hold and spread through the garden.

Read the labels on all fungicides before using them; some injure plants at certain temperatures. You'll also want to make certain that the product actually works on the disease you're trying to control and is safe for the plant you're treating.

Whiteflies and aphids will fly to sticky yellow traps suspended among the foliage of susceptible plants. Recoat or dispose of the traps when they're covered with bugs.

Lace wing: Both larvae and adults feed on aphids, mites, and other small, soft-bodied pests. Adults require nectar and pollen in order to reproduce.

smart tip

JAPANESE BEETLES

If Japanese beetles are a perennial problem for you and you live in Zones 6-10, sprinkle milky spore disease on the soil around affected plants. This disease kills the grubs that winter over in your lawn. In colder areas, apply predatory nematodes to the soil in the spring. (Both milky spore disease and beneficial nematodes are sold under several trade names and are available at most garden centers.) Pheromone traps can be helpful in controlling adult Japanese beetles, but they can actually lure more beetles to your garden if you place them too close to the area.

Glossary

Acid soil   A soil that tests lower than 7.0 on the pH scale.

Alkaline soil   A soil that tests higher than 7.0 on the pH scale.

Amendments   Organic or inorganic materials that improve soil structure, drainage, and nutrient-holding capacity. Some add nutrients.

Annual   A plant that completes its entire life cycle in one growing season.

Axil   The upper angle between a main stem and its branches or leaf petioles.

Basal plate   The flat structure at the bottom of a bulb from which the roots grow.

Biennial   A plant that completes its life cycle in two years. Most biennials form a rosette of leaves the first year and a flower stalk the second.

Bract   A modified leaf that sometimes looks like a flower petal.

Bud   An embryonic flower, leaf, or stem. Buds form on stems or plant crowns.

Bulb   A fleshy underground structure that stores nutrients during a plant's annual dormant period. A true bulb is a modified flower bud or shoot enclosed in scales, or enlarged overlapping modified leaves. Other types of underground storage structures—tubers, tuberous roots, corms, and rhizomes—are often referred to as bulbs.

Bulb pan   A wide, shallow pan or pot used for forcing spring bulbs.

Calyx   The protective modified leaves, or sepals, that surround the base of a flower.

Compound leaf   A leaf that is divided into two or more individual, distinct leaflets.

Corm   The underground swollen base of a stem from which new shoots and roots can grow. Crocuses grow from corms.

Corolla   The group of petals that form a flower.

Corona   The central cup- or tube-shaped part of a flower such as a daffodil.

Cotyledon   The first leaf or set of leaves that a plant grows; these are also called seed leaves.

Crown   The part of the plant where roots and stem meet, generally just below or at the soil line.

Cultivar   Short for cultivated variety. Rather than occurring naturally in the wild, cultivars are developed. Cultivar names are enclosed in single quotes.

Cutting   A piece of stem or root that is removed from a plant and used to propagate a new plant.

Deadheading   Removing flowers after they have faded. Some plants prolong their bloom time when deadheaded.

Disbudding   Removing some flower buds to promote larger flowers from remaining buds.

Disk flowers   The small flowers in the center of a composite flower head such as a sunflower or daisy.

Division   A propagation method that separates a plant into two or more pieces, each with at least one bud and some roots.

Foliar feeding   To spray a plant's leaves with a fertilizer containing immediately available nutrients.

Forcing   Causing a plant to flower indoors ahead of its natural blooming time.

Full shade   Refers to a site that receives no direct sunlight.

Full sun   Refers to a site that receives six or more hours a day of direct sunlight.

Genus (plural: genera)   A closely related group of species that share similar characteristics. Genus names are italicized and capitalized.

Harden off   To gradually acclimate a seedling that was started indoors to the harsher outdoor environment.

Hardiness   A plant's ability to survive the climate in an area without protection from winter cold or summer heat, often described in relation to official Hardiness Zones.

Hardy annual   An annual that can tolerate cool temperatures. Some hardy annuals tolerate freezing temperatures for short periods of time.

Herbaceous   Plants whose stems and leaves die back to the ground each winter.

Humus   Material derived from the almost completely decomposed remains of organic matter. Complex in makeup, humus buffers soil acidity and alkalinity, holds water and nutrients, improves soil structure, and contains compounds that enhance plant growth.

Hybrid A plant resulting from cross breeding parent plants that belong to different varieties or cultivars, species, or sometimes even genera. Hybrids can be indicated by a times sign (×) between the genus and species name or the designation F1 or F2.

Inflorescence Any sort of flower cluster on a common stem. Sometimes used to refer to a single flower.

Invasive A plant that spreads easily and thus "invades" adjacent areas.

Leaflet One of the divisions on a compound leaf.

Microclimate Conditions of sun, shade, exposure, wind, drainage, and other factors at a particular site.

Mulch A covering on the soil. Mulches can be inorganic, as in plastic films, or organic, as in straw, chipped leaves, or shredded bark.

Node The point along a stem from which a leaf or roots emerge.

Offset A new plant that forms vegetatively; it usually grows at the base of the parent plant.

Perennial A plant that normally lives for three or more years.

Pesticide An organic or inorganic substance that kills insect pests. The term is also used to describe other agricultural toxins, including fungicides and herbicides.

Petiole The stem of a leaf.

pH A measure of acidity or alkalinity. The pH scale runs from 0 to 14, in which 7 represents neutral; numbers higher than 7 represent alkalinity; and those lower than 7 represent acidity.

Plant habit The form a plant naturally takes as it grows, such as spreading, columnar, or rounded.

Propagate To create more plants. Plants also reproduce, or propagate, themselves.

Ray flowers The flowers surrounding the central disk in a composite flower.

Rhizome A creeping, often enlarged, stem that lies at or just under the soil surface. Both shoots and roots can form at nodes along the rhizome.

Rosette A low-growing, generally circular cluster of leaves that arises from a plant's crown.

Runner A low-growing stem that arises from the crown and runs along the ground. Runners can root at every node.

Seed leaf The first leaf or set of leaves produced by the embryo of a plant during its germination period. Also called a cotyledon.

Self-cleaning A term used to describe a plant that does not require deadheading. Spent flowers drop off by themselves, and the plant continues to make new blooms.

Species A group of plants that shares many characteristics and can interbreed freely. The species name follows the genus name, is italicized, and is not capitalized.

Succulent Fleshy, water-filled plant tissues. Plants with tissues like these are often referred to as a succulent.

Tender perennial A plant that is perennial in frost-free environments but dies when exposed to freezing temperatures.

True leaf The second and subsequent leaves or sets of leaves that a plant produces. The first leaf or set of leaves are seed leaves, or cotyledons. True leaves have the distinctive shape of the leaves of the mature plant.

Tuber A swollen stem that grows underground. Both roots and shoots grow from tubers.

Tuberous roots Enlarged roots that have growth buds at the crown (the area at which the plant's roots meet the stems).

Variegated Foliage that is marked, striped, or blotched with a color other than the basic green of the leaf.

Whorl Leaves or petals growing in a circular cluster around a stem.

Plant Index

Numbers in bold italic indicate pages with
photos or illustrations of the subject.

Subject Index

Note: Page numbers in italic type indicate photographs or illustrations.

Credits

KEY: R: Right, **L:** Left,
T: Top, **B:** Bottom, **C:** Center

p. 1: D. Cavagnaro *Decorah, IA* **p. 2: Charles Mann** *Santa Fe, NM* **p. 6: L, BR Jerry Pavia** *Bonner's Ferry, ID*; **TR** D. Cavagnaro **p. 7: TL John Glover** *Surrey, U.K.;* **TR, BL** D. Cavagnaro; **BR Derek Fell** *Pipersville, PA* **p. 8:** John Glover **p. 9: L** John Glover; **R** Jerry Pavia **p. 12:** Charles Mann **p. 13: T** Jerry Howard/ **Positive Images** *Haverhill, MA;* **B** John Glover **p. 14: L, C** D. Cavagnaro; **R** Jerry Pavia **p. 15: ALL** D. Cavagnaro **p. 16: ALL** D. Cavagnaro **p. 17: ALL** John Glover **p. 18: T BOX** Friedrich Strauss/ **The Garden Picture Library** *London, U.K.;* **B BOX** D. Cavagnaro **p. 19 ALL** D. Cavagnaro **p. 20: T Neil Soderstrom** *Wingdale, NY;* **B BOX** Janet Sorrel/ The Garden Picture Library **p. 21:** Jerry Howard/Positive Images **p. 22: BL** D. Cavagnaro; **BR** Neil Soderstrom **p. 23: T BOX** D. Cavagnaro; **B** Jerry Pavia **p. 24: TR** Neil Soderstrom; **BR** D. Cavagnaro; **BL** Neil Soderstrom **p. 25: TR** Lamontagne/ The Garden Picture Library; **BR, BL** D. Cavagnaro **p. 26: TL** Walter Chandoha; **TR** Neil Soderstrom; **BR** Jerry Pavia; **BL** D. Cavagnaro **p. 27: BL, TR** D. Cavagnaro; **C** Jerry Pavia; **BR** Michael Howes/ The Garden Picture Library **p. 28: ALL** D. Cavagnaro **p. 29: ALL** D. Cavagnaro **p. 30: ALL** D. Cavagnaro **p. 31: T** Brian Carter/ The Garden Picture Library; **C** Derek Fell; **B** Lamontagne/ The Garden Picture Library **p. 32: ALL** D. Cavagnaro **p. 33: BL, TR** D. Cavagnaro; **BR** Pam Spaulding/Positive Images **p. 34: T** Jane Legate/ The Garden Picture Library; **B ALL** D. Cavagnaro **p. 35: TL, BR** D. Cavagnaro; **B BOX** Neil Soderstrom **p. 36: T, B BOX** D. Cavagnaro; **BR** Charles Mann **p. 37: T** Densy Clyne/ The Garden Picture Library; **BL** D. Cavagnaro; **BR**

Charles Mann **p. 38: T Rob Cardillo** *Ambler, PA*; **C, B** D. Cavagnaro **p. 39: ALL** D. Cavagnaro **p. 40: T, BL** D. Cavagnaro; **BR** Ben Phillips/Positive Images **p. 41: T Liz Ball** *Springfield, PA;* **C** Geoff Bryant/ **Photo Researchers** *New York, NY;* **BL Karen Bussolini** *South Kent, CT;* **BR** Bob Gibbons/Holt Studios/Photo Researchers **p. 42: TR** Neil Soderstrom; **BR, BL** D. Cavagnaro **p. 43: ALL** D. Cavagnaro **p. 44: T** Rob Cardillo; **BL, BR** D. Cavagnaro **p. 45: T** Pam Spaulding/Positive Images; **BL, BR** D. Cavagnaro **p. 46: TL** John Glover; **TR BOX** D. Cavagnaro; **B** Derek Fell **p. 47: T** Bob Gibbons/Holt Studios/Photo Researchers; **B BOX** Neil Soderstrom; **BR** D. Cavagnaro **p. 48: ALL** D. Cavagnaro **p. 49: T BOX, BR** D. Cavagnaro; **BL** Derek Fell **p. 50: T** Jerry Pavia; **B BOX** D. Cavagnaro **p. 51: T** D. Cavagnaro; **BL** Karen Bussolini; **BR** Neil Soderstrom **p. 52: ALL** D. Cavagnaro **p. 53: ALL** D. Cavagnaro **p. 54: ALL** D. Cavagnaro **p. 55: TL** John Glover; **TR, BR, BL** D. Cavagnaro **p. 56: TR, BR** D. Cavagnaro; **BL** Derek Fell **p. 57: T** Neil Soderstrom; **B** D. Cavagnaro **p. 58: ALL** D. Cavagnaro **p. 59: L** Derek Fell; **C** Neil Soderstrom; **R** Jerry Pavia **p. 60: T, BL** D. Cavagnaro; **BR** Jerry Pavia **p. 61: ALL** D. Cavagnaro **p. 62: T** Karen Bussolini; **B** D. Cavagnaro **p. 63: ALL** D. Cavagnaro **p. 64: T, BL** D. Cavagnaro; **BR** Neil Soderstrom **p. 65: T, BR** D. Cavagnaro; **B BOX** Neil Soderstrom **p. 66: T, BL** Neil Soderstrom; **BR** D. Cavagnaro **p. 67: TL, BL, BR** D. Cavagnaro; **TR** Pam Spaulding/Positive Images **p. 68:** John Glover **p. 69: T** Charles Mann; **B Walter Chandoha** *Annandale, NJ* **p. 75:** Charles Mann **p. 76: L** Derek Fell; **R** D. Cavagnaro **p. 78: T** D. Cavagnaro; **B** Derek Fell **p. 80: T, BR** D. Cavagnaro; **BL Michael Thompson** *Eugene, OR* **p. 81: TL** Derek Fell; **TR** L. West/ **Bruce Coleman,** *New York, NY;* **BL**

Rick Mastelli *Montpelier, VT;* **BR** Neil Soderstrom **p. 82: T** Jerry Pavia; **BL** D. Cavagnaro; **BR** Derek Fell **p. 83: T, BL** John Glover; **BR** D. Cavagnaro **p. 84: TL, TR** John Glover; **B BOX** Neil Soderstrom **p. 85: ALL** D. Cavagnaro **p. 86: ALL** D. Cavagnaro **p. 87: T, BL** D. Cavagnaro; **BR Virginia Weinland** *Somers, NY* **p. 88: T** Derek Fell; **BL** Derek Fell; **BC** Liz Ball; **BR** D. Cavagnaro/Peter Arnold **p. 89: ALL** D. Cavagnaro **p. 90: ALL** D. Cavagnaro **p. 91: BL** Rob Cardillo; **BOX** Jerry Pavia **p. 92: T** D. Cavagnaro; **BL** Alan & Linda Detrick/Photo Researchers; **BR** Karen Bussolini **p. 93: ALL** D. Cavagnaro **p. 94: T, BR** John Glover; **BL** Jerry Pavia **p. 95: TL, BC** Ben Phillips/ Positive Images; **TR, BR, BL** John Glover **p. 96: T** Liz Ball; **BL** Constance Porter/Photo Researchers; **BR** Derek Fell **p. 97: ALL** D. Cavagnaro **p. 98: TL** John Glover; **TR** D. Cavagnaro; **BL BOX** D. Cavagnaro; **BR BOX** Jane Legate/The Garden Picture Library **p. 99: T** D. Cavagnaro; **BL** John Glover; **BR** Jane Legate/ The Garden Picture Library **p. 100: ALL** D. Cavagnaro **p. 101: T** Michael Thompson; **C, B BOX** D. Cavagnaro **p. 102: ALL** D. Cavagnaro **p. 103: ALL** D. Cavagnaro **p. 104: TL, BR** D. Cavagnaro; **TR** Neil Soderstrom **p. 105: TL, BR** D. Cavagnaro; **TR** John Glover; **BL** Sunniva Harte/ The Garden Picture Library **p. 106: TL** D. Cavagnaro; **TR, B** Neil Soderstrom **p. 107: T** D. Cavagnaro; **B** Charles Mann **p. 108: ALL** D. Cavagnaro **p. 109: ALL** D. Cavagnaro **p. 110: T, B BOX** D. Cavagnaro; **BL** John Glover **p. 111: TL, R** John Glover; **BL** D. Cavagnaro **p. 112: ALL** D. Cavagnaro **p. 113: T** Ben Phillips/Positive Images; **BL, B BOX** D. Cavagnaro **p. 114: L, TR** D. Cavagnaro; **BR** Lamontagne/ The Garden Picture Library **p. 115: T, BL** D. Cavagnaro; **BR** Howard Rice/ The Garden Picture Library **p. 116: ALL** D.

Have a home gardening, decorating, or improvement project?
Look for these and other fine Creative Homeowner books
wherever books are sold

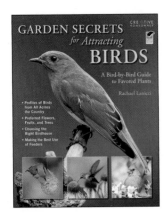

GARDEN SECRETS FOR ATTRACTING BIRDS
Provides information to turn your yard into a mecca for birds.

Over 250 photographs and illustrations.
160 pp.
8½" x 10⅝"
$14.95 (US)
$17.95 (CAN)
BOOK #: CH274561

SUCCESSFUL CONTAINER GARDENING
Information to grow your own flower, fruit, and vegetable "gardens."

Over 240 photographs.
160 pp.
8½" x 10⅞"
$14.95 (US)
$17.95 (CAN)
BOOK #: CH274857

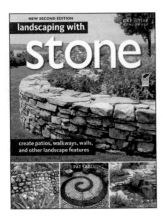

LANDSCAPING WITH STONE
Ideas for incorporating stone into the landscape.

Over 335 photographs.
224 pp.
8½" x 10⅞"
$19.95 (US)
$21.95 (CAN)
BOOK #: CH274179

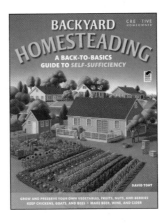

BACKYARD HOMESTEADING
How to turn your yard into a small farm.

Over 235 photographs.
256 pp.
8½" x 10⅞"
$16.95 (US)
$18.95 (CAN)
BOOK #: CH274800

DECORATING: THE SMART APPROACH TO DESIGN
A go-to how-to guide on decorating, explaining fundamental design principles, for real people.

Over 375 photographs.
288 pp.
8½" x 10⅞"
$21.95 (US)
$24.95 (CAN)
BOOK #: CH279680

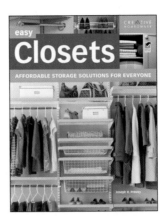

EASY CLOSETS
Introduces homeowners to the variety of closet types and closet systems available.

Over 275 photographs.
160 pp.
8½" x 10⅞"
$14.95 (US)
$16.95 (CAN)
BOOK #: CH277135

For more information and to order direct, go to **www.creativehomeowner.com**